NEW NARRATIVES

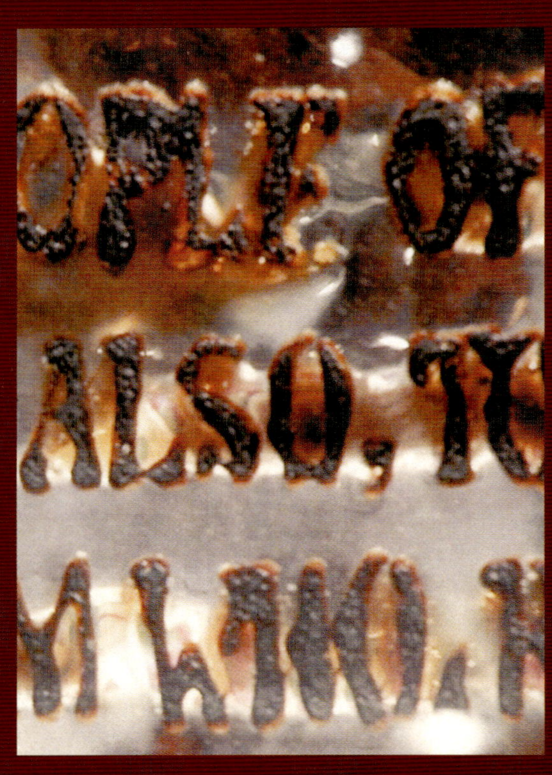

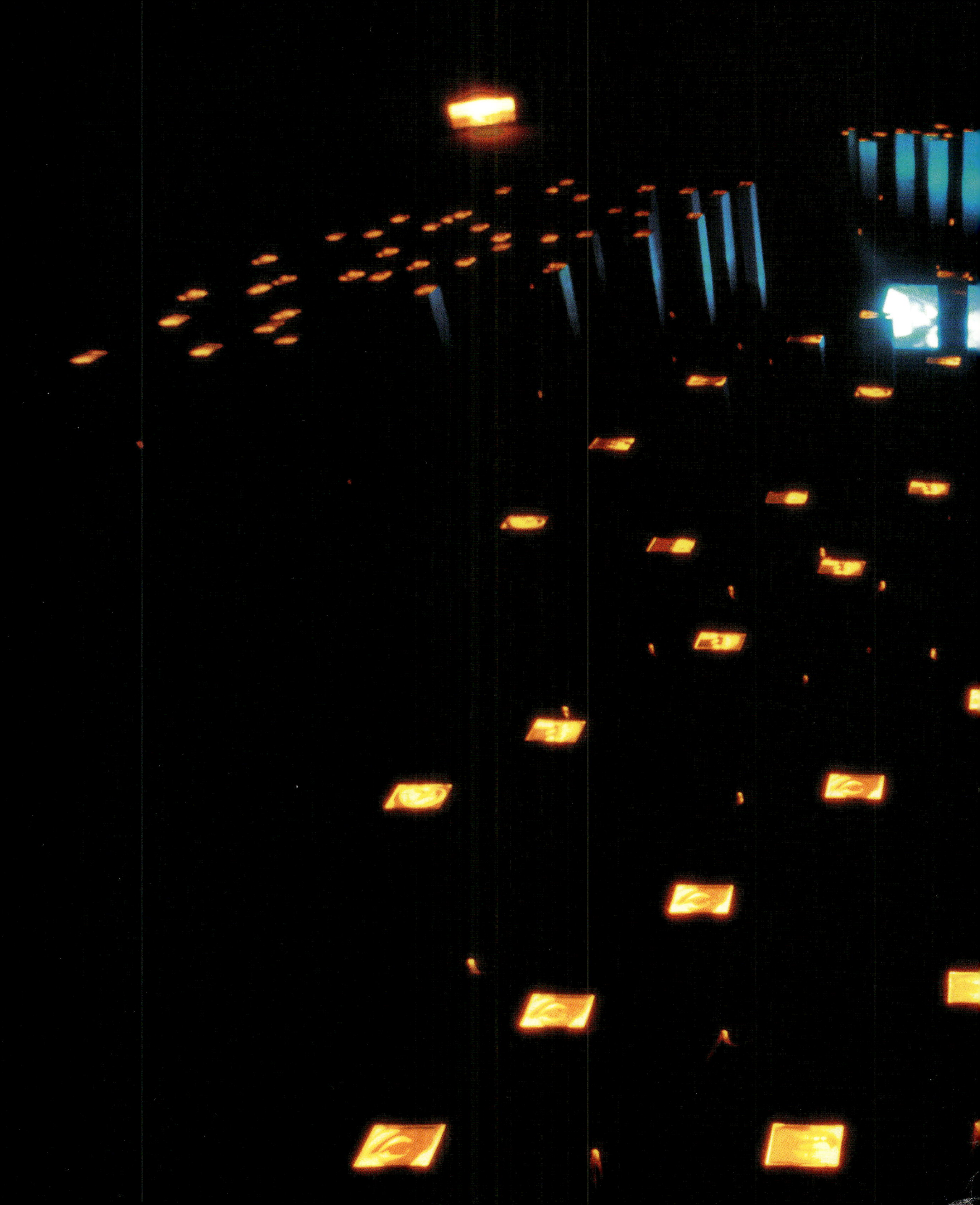

NEW NARRATIVES
Contemporary Art from India

Betty Seid

With contributions by Johan Pijnappel

Mapin Publishing

in association with

Chicago Cultural Center

First published in India in 2007 by
Mapin Publishing Pvt. Ltd.

In association with
City of Chicago
Chicago Cultural Center

This book is published in conjunction with the exhibition
'New Narratives' held at*:

Chicago Cultural Center, Illinois
July 21–September 23, 2007

Salina Art Center, Kansas
January 5–March 16, 2008

Jane Voorhees Zimmerli Art Museum
Rutgers, The State University of New Jersey,
New Brunswick
April 12–July 31, 2008
* at the time of publication

City of Chicago
Chicago Cultural Center
78 East Washington Street
Chicago, Illinois 60602
T: 312 744 6630
www.chicagoculturalcenter.org

Simultaneously published in the
United States of America in 2007 by
Grantha Corporation
77 Daniele Drive, Hidden Meadows
Ocean Township, NJ 07712
E: mapinpub@aol.com

Text © City of Chicago, Betty Seid and Johan Pijnappel
Illustrations © as listed

ISBN: 978-81-88204-82-3 (Mapin)
ISBN: 978-1-890206-08-6 (Grantha)
LCCN: 2006938645

Distributed in North America by
Antique Collectors' Club
East Works, 116 Pleasant Street, Suite 18
Easthampton, MA 01027
T: 1 800 252 5231 • F: 413 529 0862
E: info@antiquecc.com • www.antiquecollectorsclub.com

Distributed in the United Kingdom, Europe and the Middle East by
Art Books International Ltd.
Unit 200 (a), The Blackfriars Foundry, 156 Blackfriars Road
London, SE1 8EN UK
T: 44 207 953 7271 • F: 207 953 8547
E: sales@art-bks.com • www.art-bks.com

Distributed in Southeast Asia by
Paragon Asia Co. Ltd.
687 Taksin Road, Bukkalo, Thonburi
Bangkok 10600 Thailand
T 66 2877 7755 • F: 2468 9636
E rapeepan@paragonasia.com

Distributed in the rest of the world by
Mapin Publishing Pvt. Ltd.
1OB Vidyanagar Society Part I
Usmanpura, Ahmedabad 380 014 INDIA
T: 91 79 2754 5390 / 2754 5391 • F: 79 2754 5392
E mapin@mapinpub.com • www.mapinpub.com

Designed by Paulomi Shah / Mapin Design Studio
Edited by Diana Romany / Mapin Editorial
Processed by Reproscan, Mumbai
Printed in Singapore

Contents

Indian art and culture have been a somewhat regular offering at the Chicago Cultural Center over its nearly 30-year history. Both historical and recent photography from or about India have provided the subjects for two fascinating traveling exhibitions presented in 1984 and 1999. However, *New Narratives* represents a first outing for us to organize such a sizable and complex project of art coming out of India today. Building on our history and familiarity with things Indian, the Chicago Cultural Center is now in a privileged position to further explore the changing face of India, where the use of narrative composition has been and continues to be prominent. Rather than merely telling a story, though, many of today's artists working in India use the power of metaphor to comment on stories both personal and cultural, or to reflect on a specific aspect of the histories or religions of India.

Further, by enhancing this exhibition with a series of related educational and public programs, we will tap deeper into its international and local interest. Because the artworks may not all look "Indian" to many American viewers, this exhibition will also challenge stereotypes and preconceptions that may be associated with the art of the past century. We certainly hope that the visitors will leave the show with a new level of interest and insight into one of the world's oldest and still mysterious cultures. Rapidly changing, India has joined the global community of contemporary art by establishing a distinct place for itself between East and West. Indian artists now regularly show in Europe, the United States, Australia, and in East and Southeast Asia.

The timing of the exhibition in Chicago also coincides with the August 15 observance of 60 years since Indian Independence in 1947. As Delhi is a Sister City of Chicago, this seems to be a perfect opportunity for Chicago to launch this touring exhibition and to celebrate a new era in the Indian-American cultural exchange.

This exhibition presents the results of a major initiative of the Chicago Department of Cultural Affairs over the past several years. It was conceived and has been guest-curated by Betty Seid of Chicago, who has traveled in India extensively since her first visit there in 1996. Since then, Betty has specialized in historical Indian art and culture, which has informed her particular emphasis on Indian contemporary artists for this traveling exhibition. Its thesis on artists' continuing use of narrative in

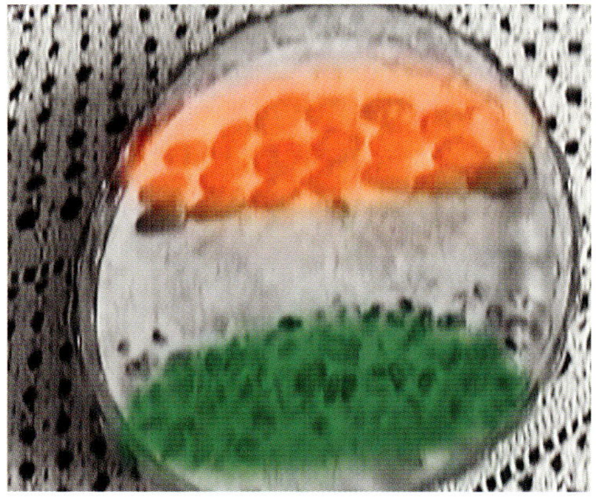
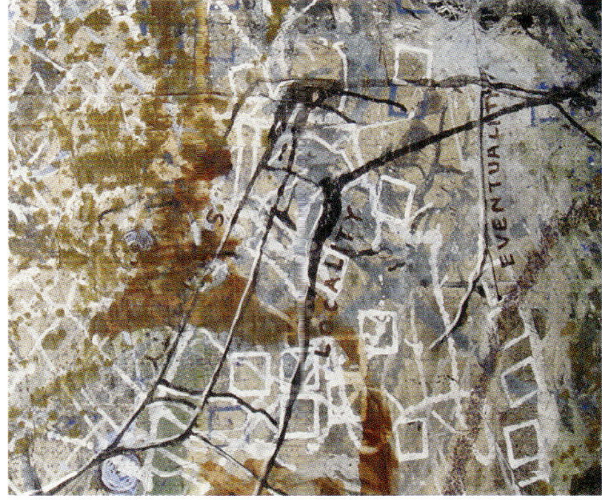
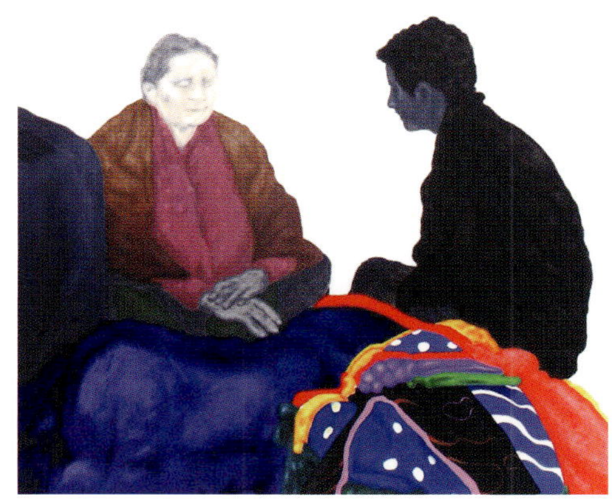

current art-making provides the basis for this project's bridging the narrative tradition with the contemporary impulse. In addition, Johan Pijnappel, a Dutch writer and critic living for several years now in Mumbai, has served as our consulting curator for new media in the exhibition, as well as being a contributing author to this publication.

This multi-year curatorial effort has involved extensive on-site research in India, as well as through galleries in Chicago, New York and Europe. It represents the first exhibition in the United States to feature new works of the twenty-first century in India, with many pieces coming straight from the artists' studios, in a number of cities on the subcontinent. Betty and Johan have selected more than 20 artists for this extensive exhibition of paintings, sculptures, installations, and works in video and new media. Some 60 pieces constitute this large-scale show, first presented in Chicago with several other American cities to follow.

I have had the pleasure to accompany Betty on two research trips to India—2004 and 2006—where we have had inspiring experiences in visiting the studios of talented and sharing artists to select new pieces for inclusion. Over and over again we heard about and personally witnessed exciting contemporary work being created there. Indian artists are now among the most sought-after internationally, with galleries and auction houses elsewhere boasting a booming market for the work of these talented artists. Galleries and private collectors throughout India have very kindly shown their support for this project by generously agreeing to lend significant works from their collections. Further, several of the artists have created new works or specific installation concepts for this show at the Chicago Cultural Center.

We wish to sincerely thank all the artists, lenders and our numerous other collaborators who have actively helped make this exhibition a reality. This special journey is an ongoing process, now only in mid-stream with its premiere in Chicago. As it continues to tour in the United States, and gains even broader recognition through this publication, we look forward to its cumulative contributions to a greater global recognition of these artists outside of India.

Gregory G. Knight

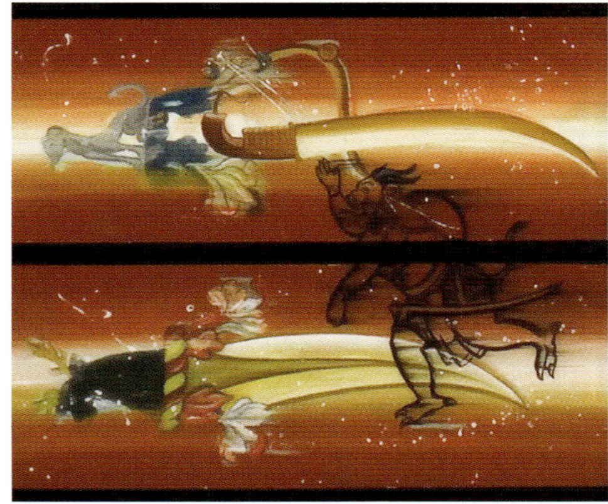
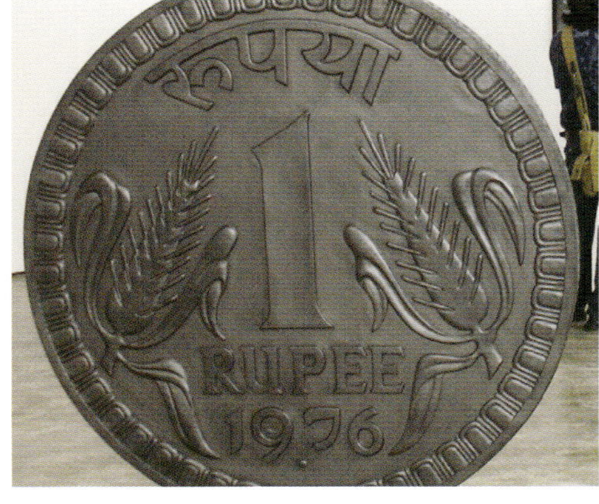
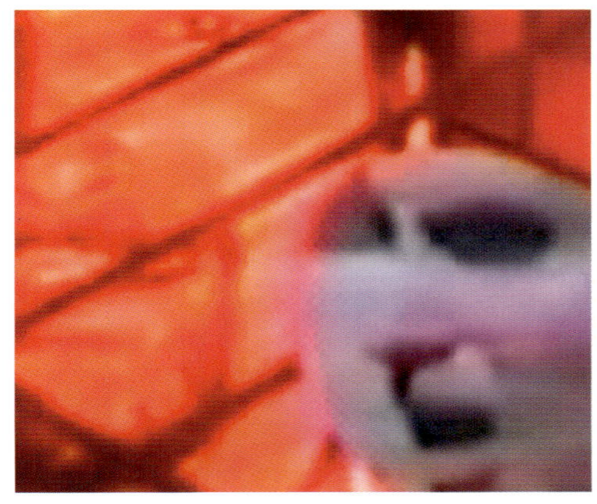

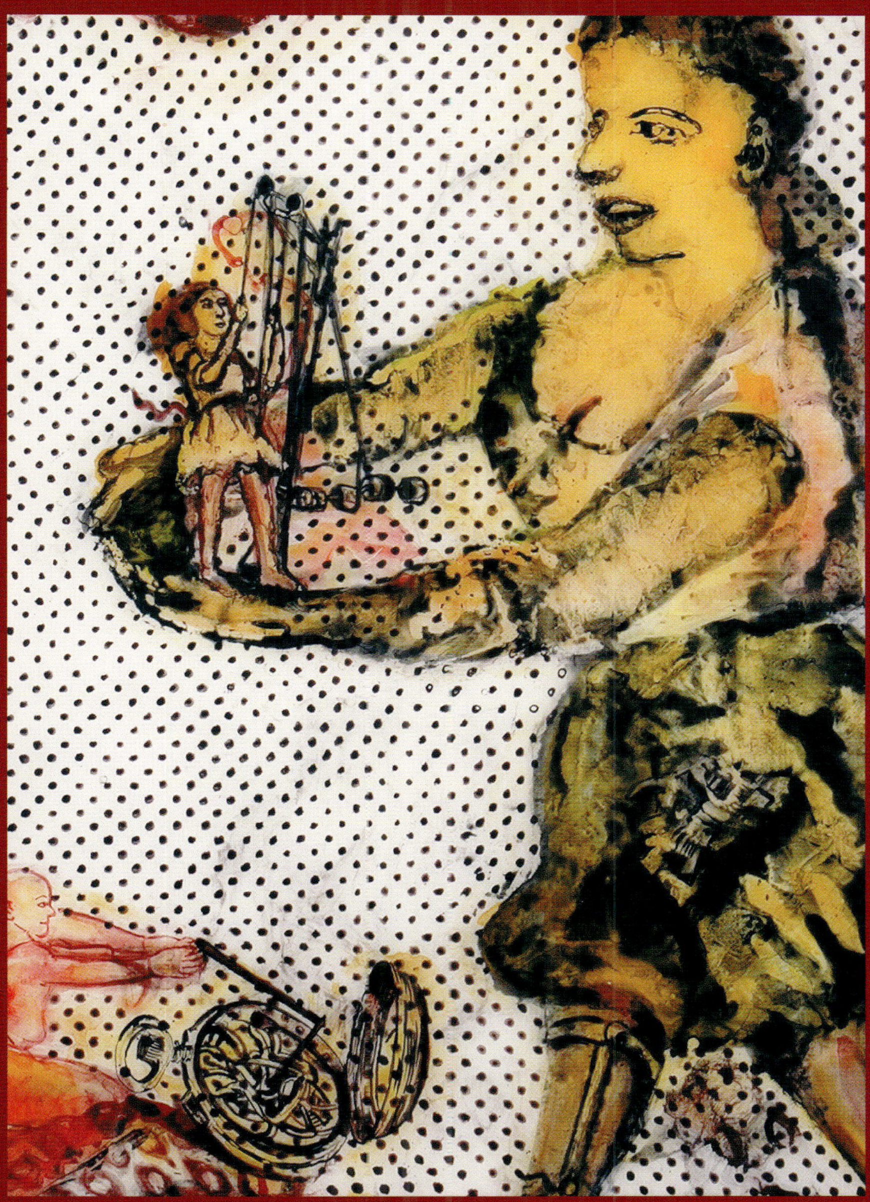

Nalini Malani. *Broken Alice I—Living in Alicetime*, 2005. Detail, see page 105.

Introduction

Betty Seid

Contemporary art in India reflects her world recognition as a major player in the new millennium. The journey from modern to contemporary art in India continues to be one from indigenous to global—intersecting with international art at increasingly frequent intervals as time progresses. By making "now" my curatorial priority, this book has a perspective that has been missing from most previous books and exhibitions of recent art from India. To celebrate only the "glorious" past was to miss the point of India's rising global presence, and how far she has come since her mid-century Independence. It is time to celebrate India's *artistic* independence.

Narration is the connective thread that binds contemporary artists to India's rich oral traditions. All narrative is ultimately personal, once the storyteller has chosen to tell his or her tale. But some narratives are more personal than others—investigations of the psyche through stream of consciousness, portrayal of dreams, exploration of family lineage, episodic self-portraiture. Others choose to make visual the milieu they exist in via observations of daily rituals, politics, and the general ironies of living in the twenty-first century. Literature draws other artists to go beyond illustration and to add, like sages of yore, a layer of commentary to existing tales.

Recent work by twenty-one artists has been selected to represent art-making in India today. This catalog is published in conjunction with an extensive exhibition of painting, photography, sculpture and installation art, along with works in video and new media that opens at the Chicago Cultural Center in July 2007. This endeavor has involved extensive on-site research in India, New York and elsewhere, to produce the first exhibition in the United States to feature works of only the twenty-first century, made in India, with several pieces being created solely for this exhibition.

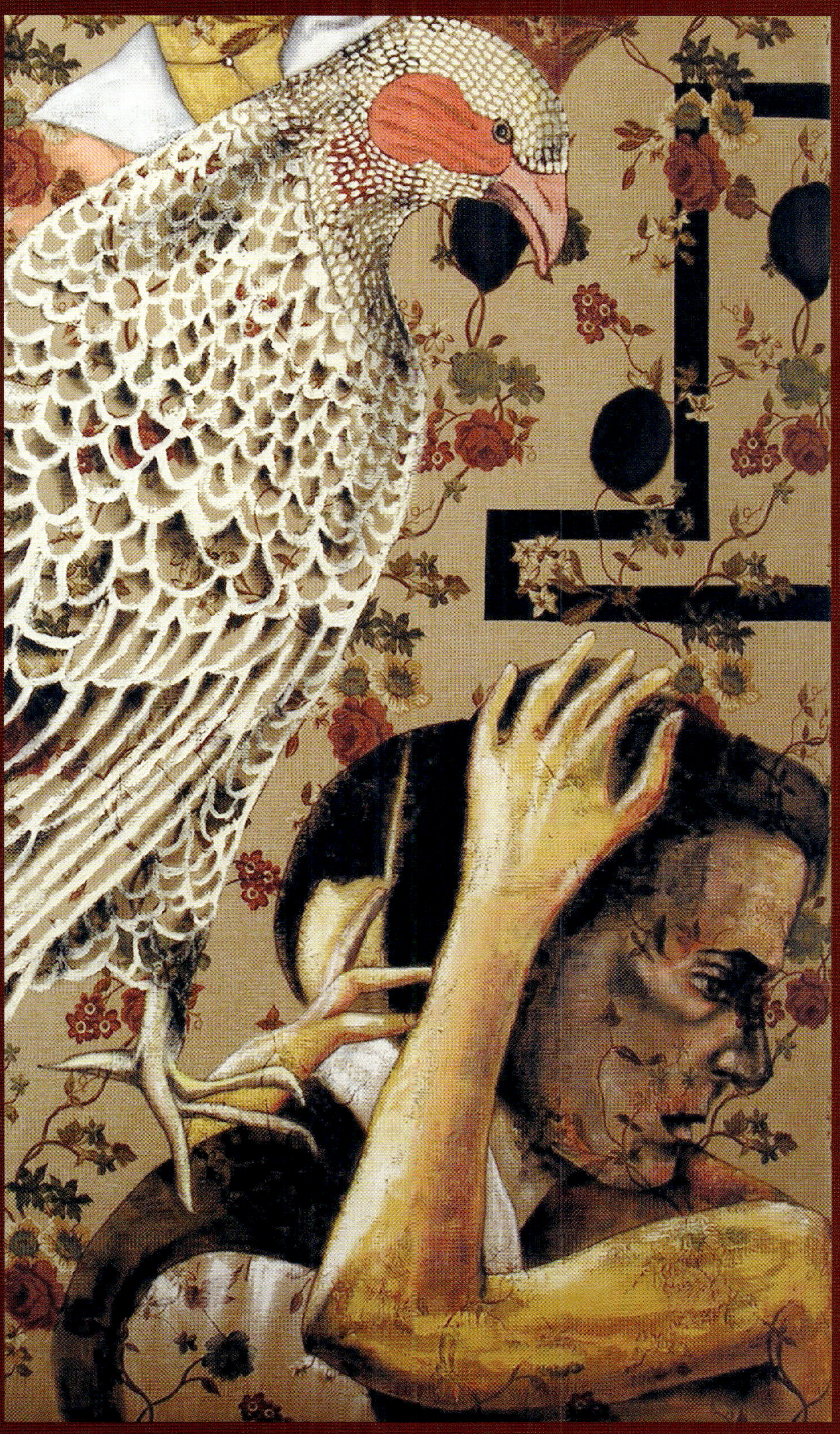

Anju Dodiya. *The Path of Berries,* 2005. Detail, see page 60.

New Narratives

Betty Seid

Narrative is a much-overworked word in contemporary academic discourse. It has come to mean "meaning," "definition" or "purpose" rather than plotted storytelling. Whether with an Aristotelian beginning, middle and end, or by suggestions that ask the viewer to fill in the blanks, all of the works in this exhibition have a story to tell. Fact, fiction or something in between, they are stories. Contemporary artists from India have stepped back from the Modernist rejection of plot and returned to picture-making with *New Narratives*. There are new stories to tell and new ways to tell them.

In his essay, "Reading for the Plot," Peter Brooks discusses how narrative is the means we use to order and give meaning to our lives, in effect to overcome and control the chaos that is human existence.

> Our lives are ceaselessly intertwined with narrative, with the stories that we tell and hear told, those we dream or imagine or would like to tell, all of which are reworked in that story of our own lives that we narrate to ourselves in an episodic, sometimes semi-conscious, but virtually uninterrupted monologue. We live immersed in narrative.[1]

All the artists in this exhibition have a narrative agenda. Through the making of art, they command an audience. The purpose of each of them varies; for some, the depiction of their story is equivalent to being on a psychoanalyst's couch. For others, it is the occasion to speak out politically. Or it is an opportunity to clarify and make public their identity. Again, by manipulating the data, perception is controlled.

Some of these narrators choose to tell their stories through personal means—investigations of the psyche through the stream of consciousness, portrayal of dreams, exploration of family lineage, episodic self-portraiture. Others choose to make visual the moment in which they exist via observations of daily rituals, political extremities. and the general ironies of existence. Still others go beyond illustration, like sages of yore, adding a layer of commentary to an existing tale. "True" narrative, like any oft-told tale, changes with the telling.

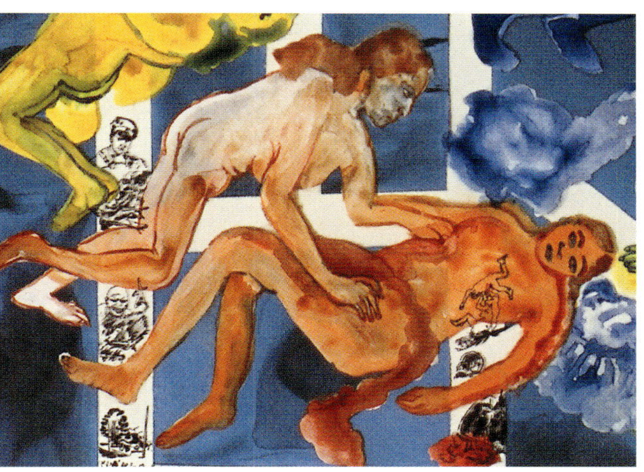

Nalini Malani. *Ecstasy of Radha*, 2004. Detail, see page 100.

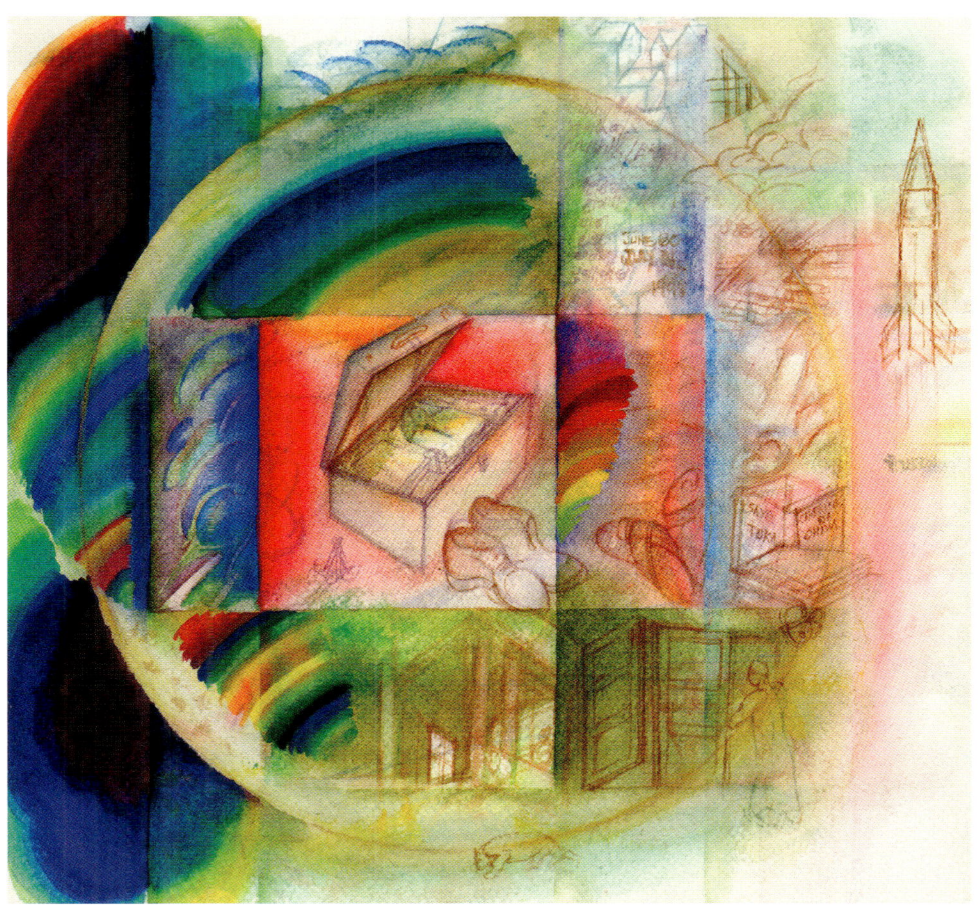

Gulammohammed Sheikh. *Book of Journeys*, 1996 onwards. Detail, see page 38.

What, then, is narrative and why are stories told? Obviously, there is the impulse to entertain. At the same time, that entertainment may be used to inculcate cultural values through the teaching of myths and traditions. Narrative is about culture; in storytelling, the narrator manufactures a cultural identity on a macro-level and an individual identity on a micro-level. Stories impress, particularly if they are told well. Ultimately, in the telling, there is the impulse to order the chaos of life.

Aristotle grandly philosophized about what was necessary for a story to be a story. His essentials are those famous "W" queries that journalists have codified and today widely employ: Who? What? Where? When? and Why?—Character, Event, Setting, Time and Meaning. *Character* drives the plot, suggesting the "what," that is the narrative *event*. Often the protagonist is the artist. The *setting* may vary, and is a potent visual device for locating the narrative, both physically and psychologically. *Time*, as we shall see, is not always an Aristotelian linear progression. And "why"—the impact of *meaning*—is always determined by a tacit agreement between artist and viewer.

Searching for meaning in myths or symbols requires that there be a known story. Symbols mandate a mind for interpretation. Historically, a patron

determined much of the impact of meaning. A historic work of art, sponsored by
church or court, has a significantly different content from that created by an
autonomous artist. And, oh the difference in context! Propaganda is essential, but the
impetus has shifted from patron to artist. Today's patron is the art-buying, museum-
going public, but he no longer dictates what the art will be simply because he has
underwritten it. The arena for an artist expounding a point of view is enormous, and
the opportunity for that point of view to be personal, rather than determined by a
patron, is paramount. Historically, as in the West, art in India has been also supported
by church (temple) or state (princely court)—e.g., magnificent Chola bronzes or exquisite
Mughal or Rajput album paintings. It is now the lay collector who buys art. The new
narratives of contemporary art are directed to this educated, elite audience.

For the curator, a triangular relationship exists between artist, public
and museum. Until recently, American museums have avoided collecting and/or
exhibiting contemporary art from India.[2] The connoisseurship of Indian contemporary
art has been stuck in an ethnocentric mode of self-comparison. Western curators
haven't had the training or vocabulary (beyond "hybrid," "syncretism" or "influence") to
locate culturally what has been happening in India. Often, no distinction is made
between modern and contemporary art, and the word "derivative" has been bandied
about. Contemporary art from India has, for the most part, been ignored by Western
art museums. Currently that is changing. Western curators of contemporary art are
beginning to catch on about India. Layering is universal; identities, people and cultures
have always overlapped. Although some specificity remains, we need not continue to
exoticize the international conversation about art from India.

What makes these narratives *new*? Does it matter that these works
are by Indian artists? Are the stories Indian, but the art global, or vice versa?
Perceptions of Indian art have long been mired in Orientalist theory. The West has
wanted art from India to "look Indian," but most contemporary Indian artists have
come to realize that "Indianness" is not in itself an artistic pursuit. They have broken
away from that expectation. In a sense, they are saying, "Know me! Know my
ancestors, my fears, what I read, what I see, what I hear. Let go of your Orientalist
stereotypes of me and who I should be." Contemporary artists from India are *of the
world* but happen to be living and working in India.

None of these artists is working in the modes that long have
identified art from India: the miniature or the folk/tribal painting. They have
ontologically progressed beyond the initial appeal of Modernism and the attendant
desire to use acknowledged Western idioms. More than anything else (and possibly
more than any*where* else), they respond to politics and work to impact social justice.
They are doing this—and here is where tradition enters—*via narrative*. They tell,
expound, dramatize and regale us with stories. Storytelling is an important element of
India's traditional character and the narrative impulse continues to be a motivating
muse for contemporary artists. What is *new* about these narratives is that the tales
have moved from local to global, women have a stronger voice, and the technology
for telling them has expanded into new media.

Since the earliest days of the twentieth century, an artistic struggle
has existed between being Indian and being Modern. That push-pull "between a rock

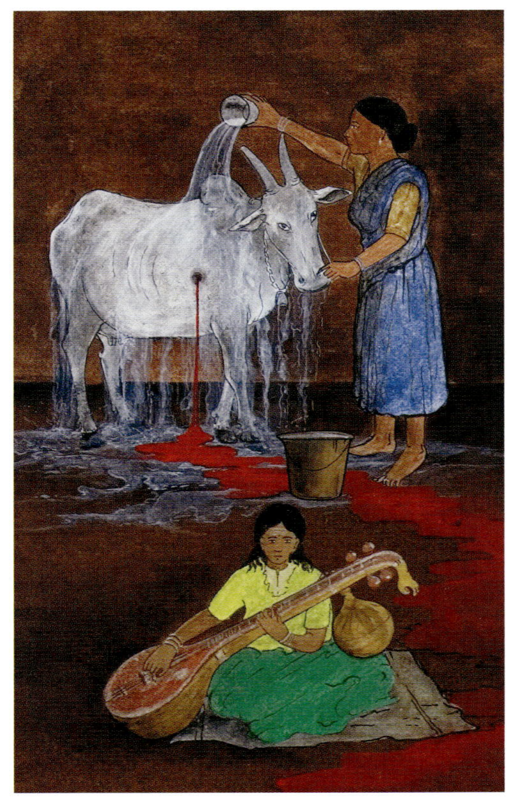

N. S. Harsha. *On my way to museum*, 2006.
Detail, see page 74.

Vasudha Thozhur. *Sanctum*, 2006.
Detail, see page 57.

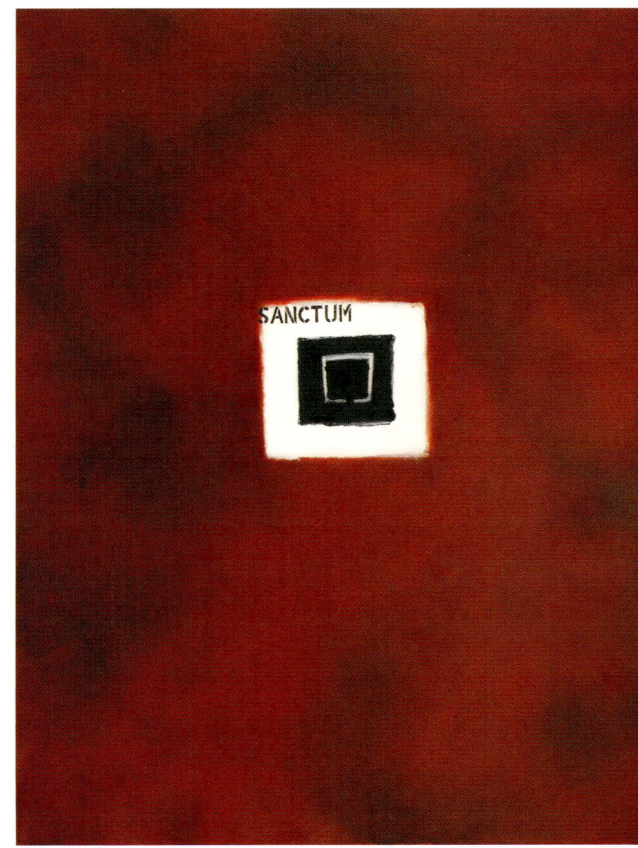

and a hard place" began in the early 1900s, with the Swadeshi Movement, which urged the creation of a national identity, separate from the Orientalist vision the British assumed. For some Indian artists, having a national identity meant looking back with an eye toward indigenism. But although *modern* may have signified "foreign," *indigenous* could appear "archaic." Global modernity and national specificity continued to vie for artistic supremacy in India throughout the twentieth century. However, by mid-century, modern artists aspired to discover an "Indianness" within the modern idiom. By then, aesthetic concerns were surpassing the need to create a national identity but not without social commentary.

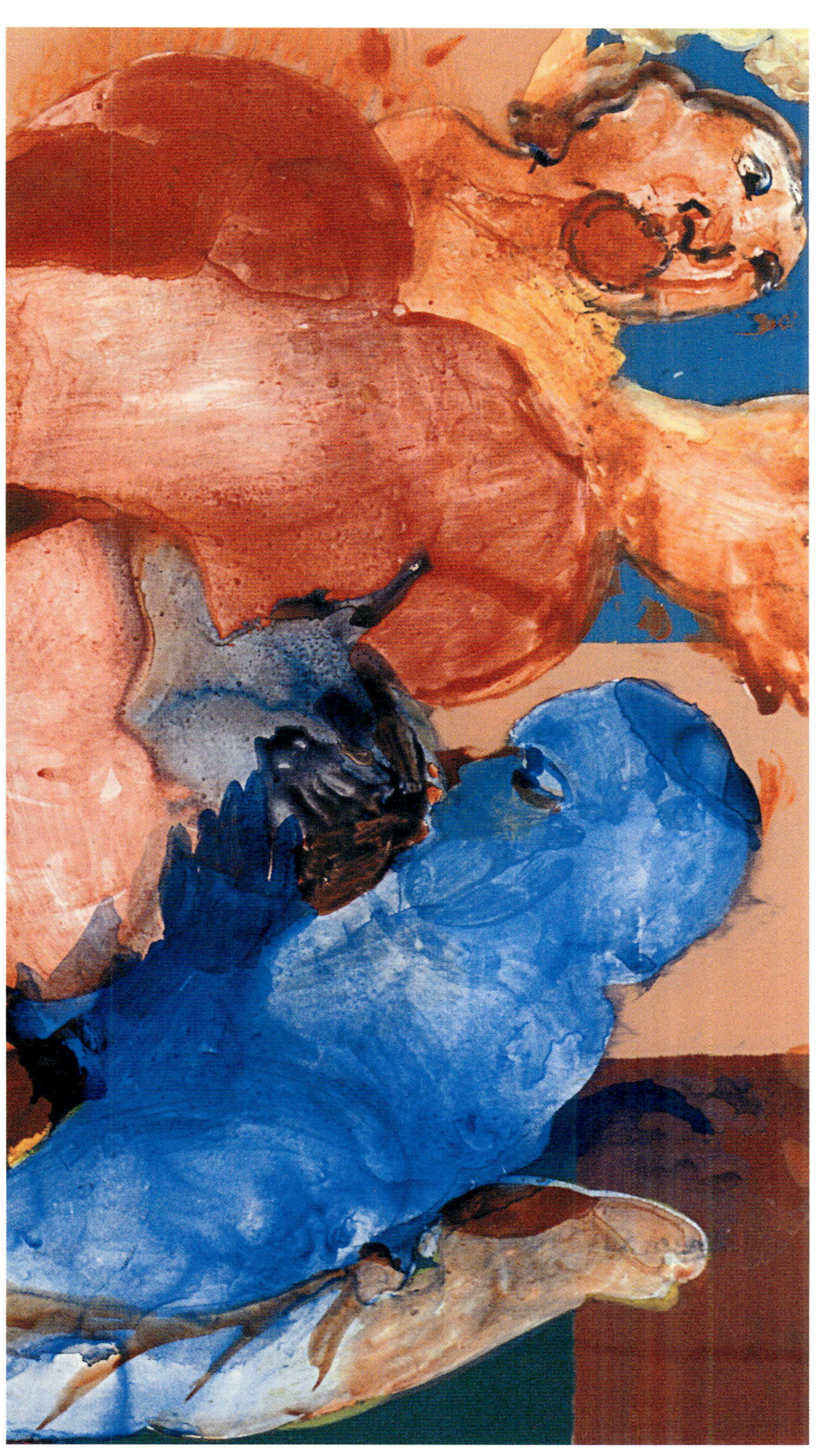

Nalini Malani. *Stories Retold—Putana*, 2002. Detail, see page 100.

Artists may not be canaries in a coal mine—harbingers of impending disaster. However, they are often "first responders" to crises—translating with personal narratives the distressing experiences of violence, social injustice and environmental crimes. Contemporary Indian artists in particular face national—and increasingly global—issues head-on, refusing, even unable, to excise art from their body politic. Nalini Malani has said, "I strongly believe in a partisan space . . . I do believe if you are neutral you cannot be passionate . . . my endeavor is to make visible that which is invisible."[3]

The feminist art movement of the 1970s was quite self-revelatory. Those who had been marginalized wanted their essence revealed. Women bared themselves. The human body, particularly the female body, has long been an allegorical device in painting. But nakedness is vulnerable. By stripping, contemporary women artists expose not only their vulnerability, but also their willingness to *be* vulnerable, to take risks—physical, psychological, artistic. Using their own female bodies as stand-ins for outrages against colonization, violence to women and violence to the earth itself, they respond with focused narratives. This is particularly evident in Malani's *Stories Retold*, in which she reinterprets traditional female monsters as victims of abuse. Putana has been deceived, Medea dispossessed. Both have been tricked into allowing their bodies to be misused by domineering men. The stories of these heroines are easily understood allegories for the rape of a nation, politically or ecologically. As Malani has said, "After the caste system, one of the biggest scourges in Indian society is the lowly status of women. In the latter case there is a paradox, as she can be swung up to become a goddess, made into a metaphor for the Motherland or flung down to be the dirt beneath the male foot."[4]

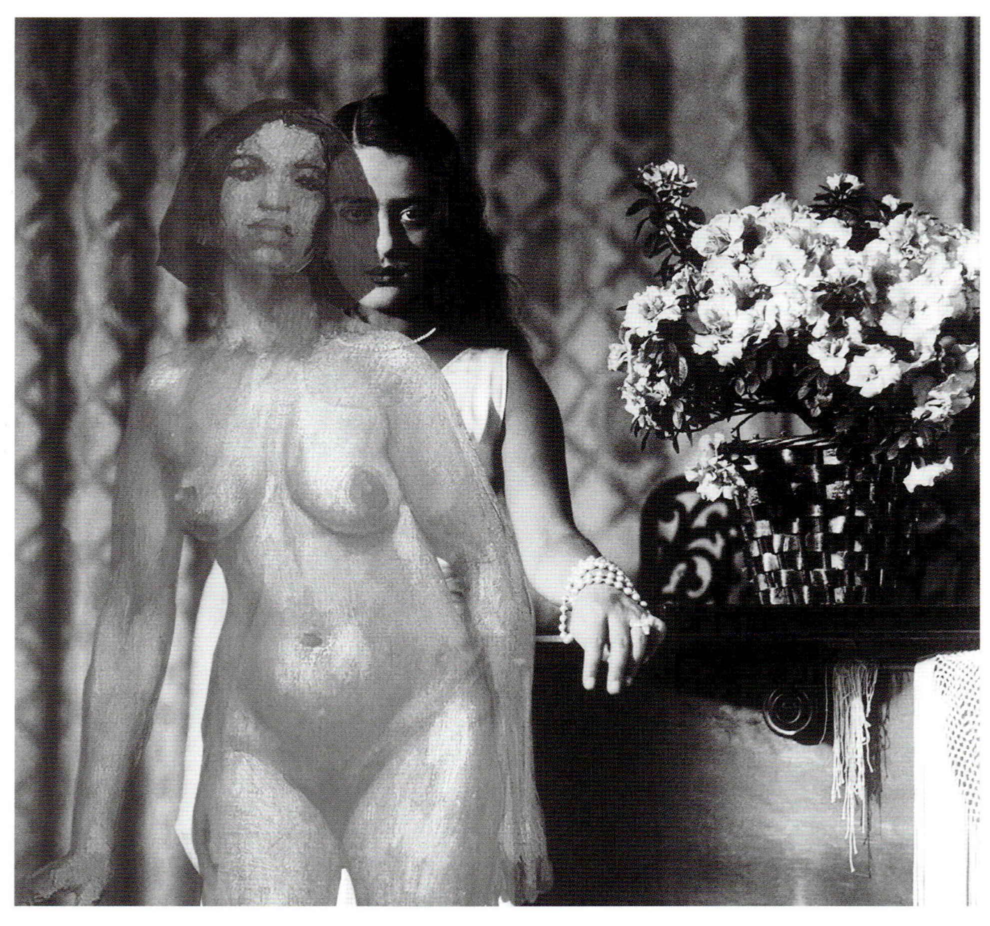

Vivan Sundaram. *Black Nude*, 2001.
Detail, see page 55.

Like Modernism, feminist art came to India later than to the West. With the exception of Amrita Sher-Gil (1913–41), women artists did not participate in the early stages of Modernism in India. Men fought those earlier battles of national identity. Women artists were much less concerned with the large concept of "Indianness." They sought modes of individual expression. And, like the Modernists before them, they tried to juggle issues of identity—not the indigenous/modernist discourse, but rather a balancing act that teetered between traditional representations of women and representations of the self. The "self" was becoming more and more a proxy for larger communal issues.

In a recent dialog, Arpita Singh was asked by her colleague Nilima Sheikh, "[Is it that] not having staked our ideologies in the making of polar art movements [groups of male artists in the forties and fifties . . . negotiating their space in the east versus west/modern versus traditional debates] we are not so committed to their exclusive grammar?" Singh replied, "[Being] unmindful of them gives us our freedom."[5] That freedom is embodied in Singh's use of formal patterning and textile motifs (traditional feminine arts) to expose her own psyche. Over the years, the bodies of the women in Singh's paintings have matured, as has her own. Her earlier fear of aggression against young women has morphed into fear of larger aggression—against society in general. Her current ogres are the holders of power, "men in suits."

The feminist agenda only acknowledges the political nature of all human relationships. What might be read as a mere record of an event, a daily occurrence or a ritual, becomes political narration because the artist recognizes that living a contemporary life is political. A broader political vision focuses on social issues and social injustice. Religious fundamentalism and its attendant violence cause urban chaos.

Reena Saini Kallat. *Blueprint: Birthmarks and Tattoos*, 2005. Detail, see page 66.

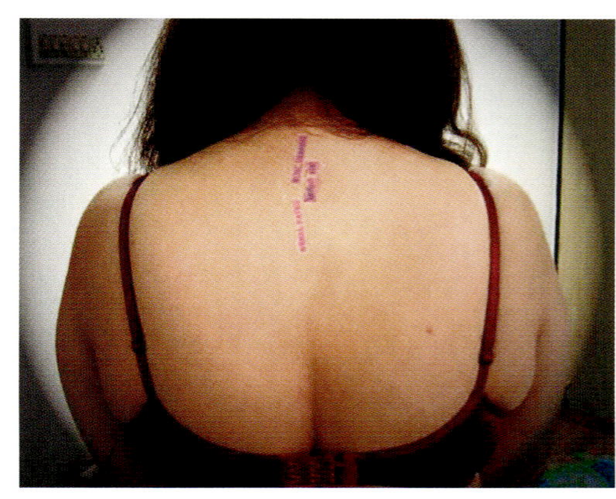

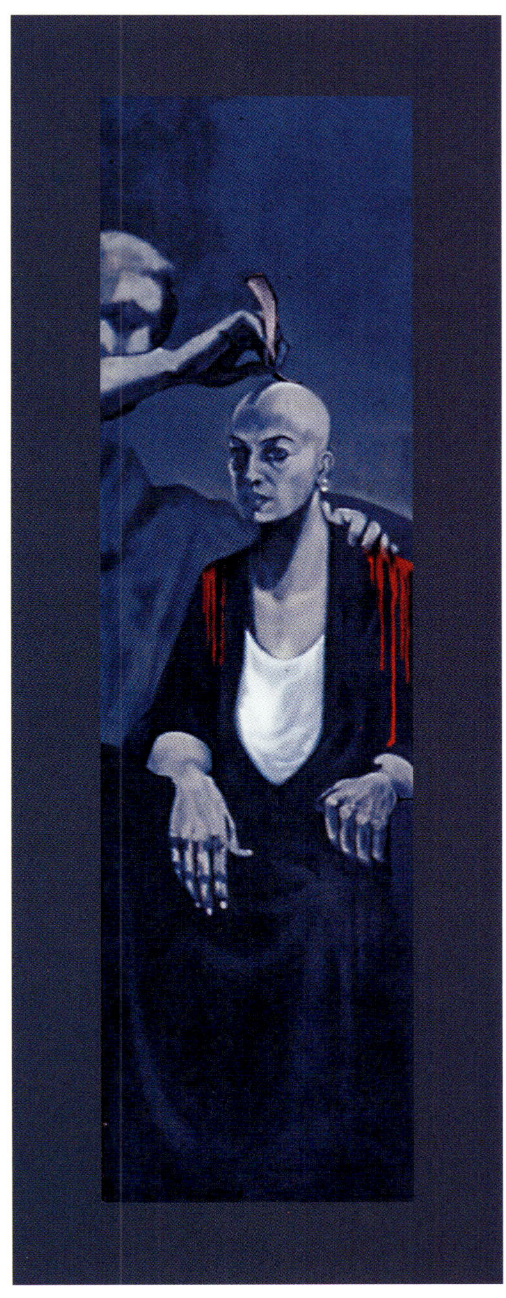

Vasudha Thozhur. *Untouchable*, 2002–3.
Detail, see page 56.

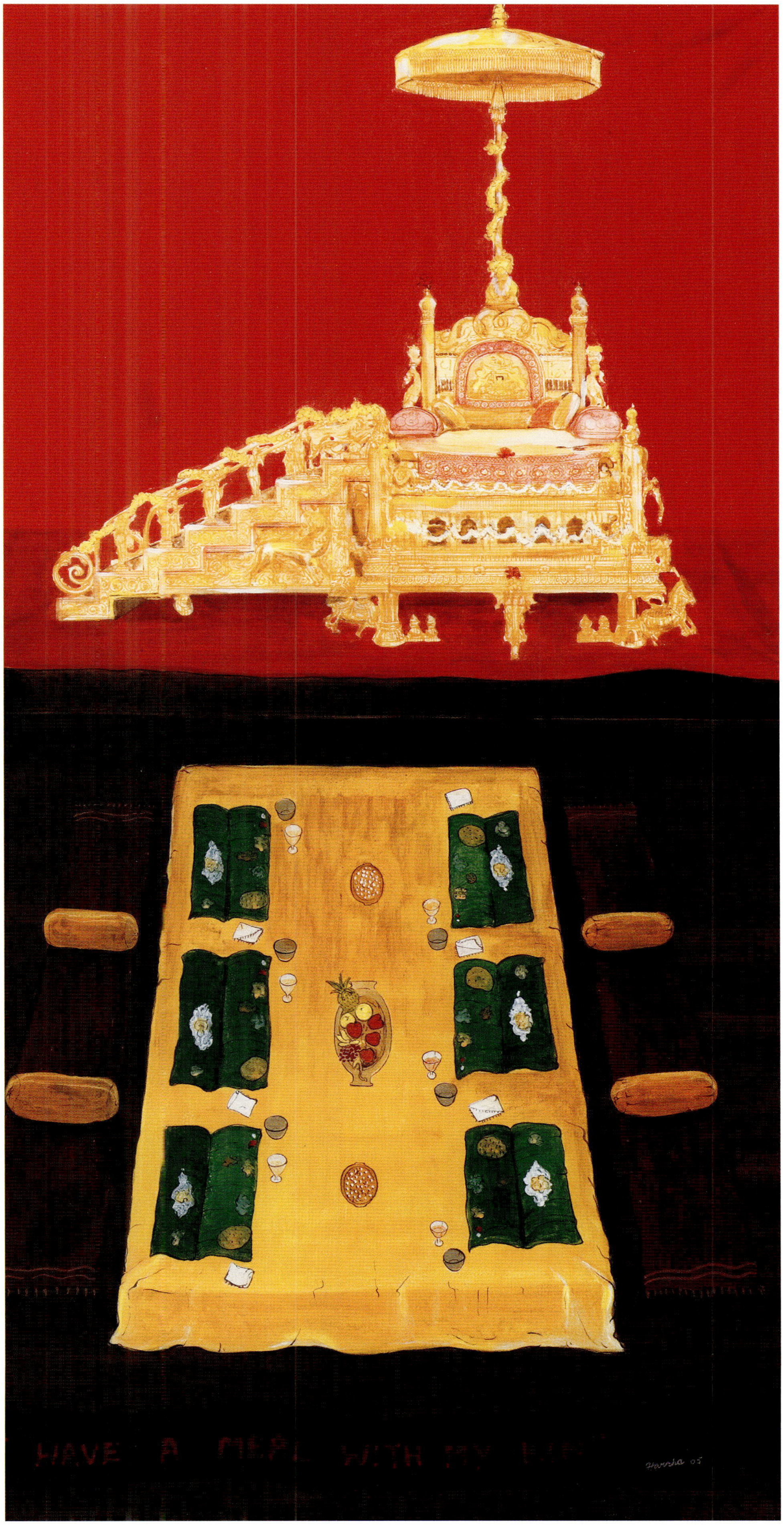

N. S. Harsha. *Come have a meal with my king,*
2005. Detail, see page 72.

Inequalities cause homelessness, poverty and hunger. These inequities inspire politically narrative art. Jitish Kallat and N. S. Harsha understand that ironic narratives characterize contemporary life. Kallat juxtaposes the disparate value of a single rupee between rich and poor. Harsha straightforwardly paints parables of the frustrations of the "have-nots" in a world of "haves." Sheba Chhachhi has constructed a city in toxic decline as a cosmic diagram (mandala), challenging the much-revered central deity to rescue us from our own defilement.

Technology has been a major player in the global impact of twenty-first century artists from India. The Bangalore "Silicon Valley," the beneficiary of multi-national outsourcing, has literally put India on everyone's "radar screen." Interestingly, none of the artists in this exhibition has made that a subject of his/her narrative. Rather, they have used electronic technology to broaden their own media options, using edgy techno means to enhance their visual storytelling. Ranbir Kaleka has used video projections perfectly synchronized to his paintings to demonstrate the vagaries of boundaries. Shilpa Gupta engages her viewers to believe they have cyber-power to control global terrorism. (See essay and entries by Johan Pijnappel.)

Ranbir Kaleka. *Crossings*, 2005.
Detail, see page 84.

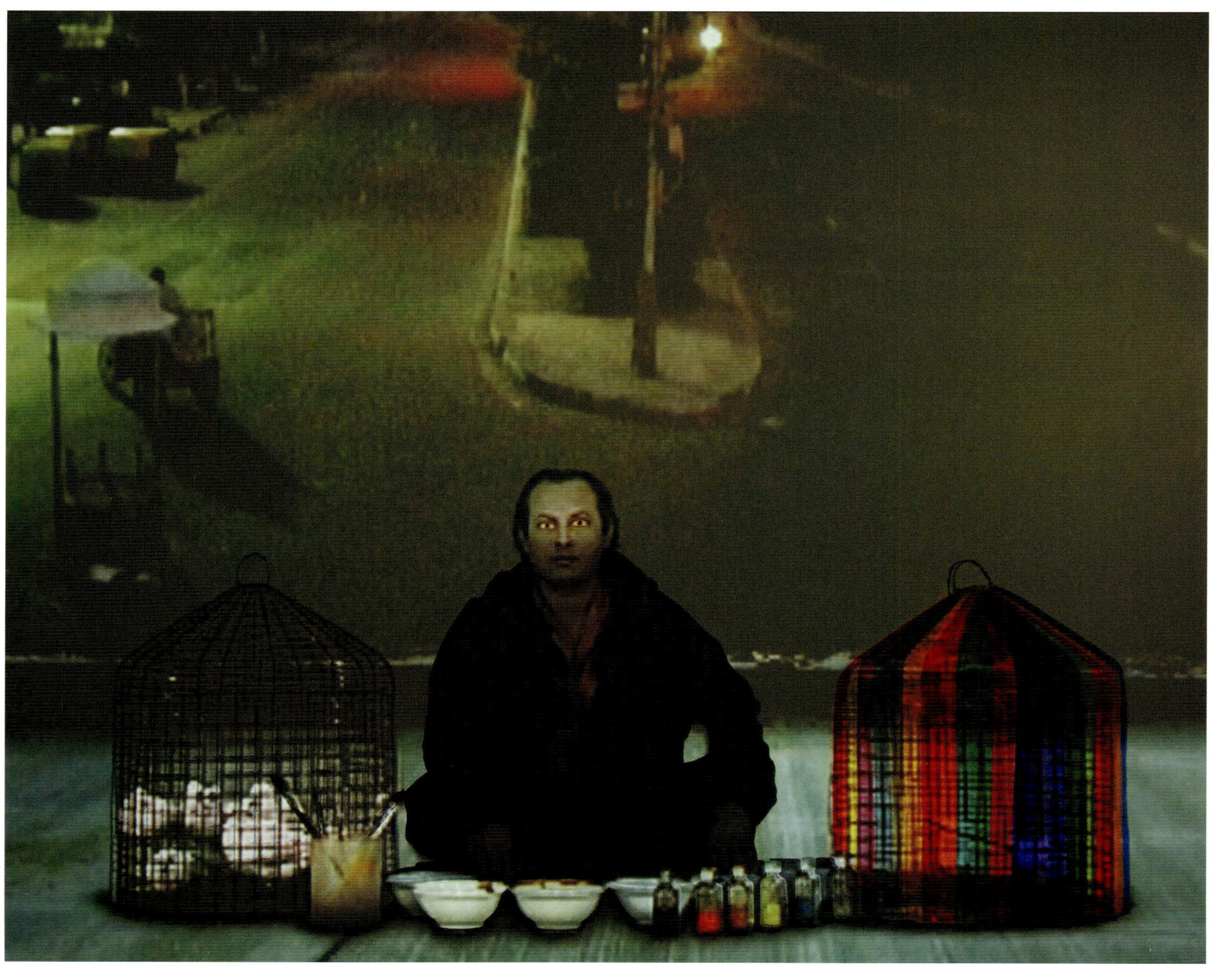

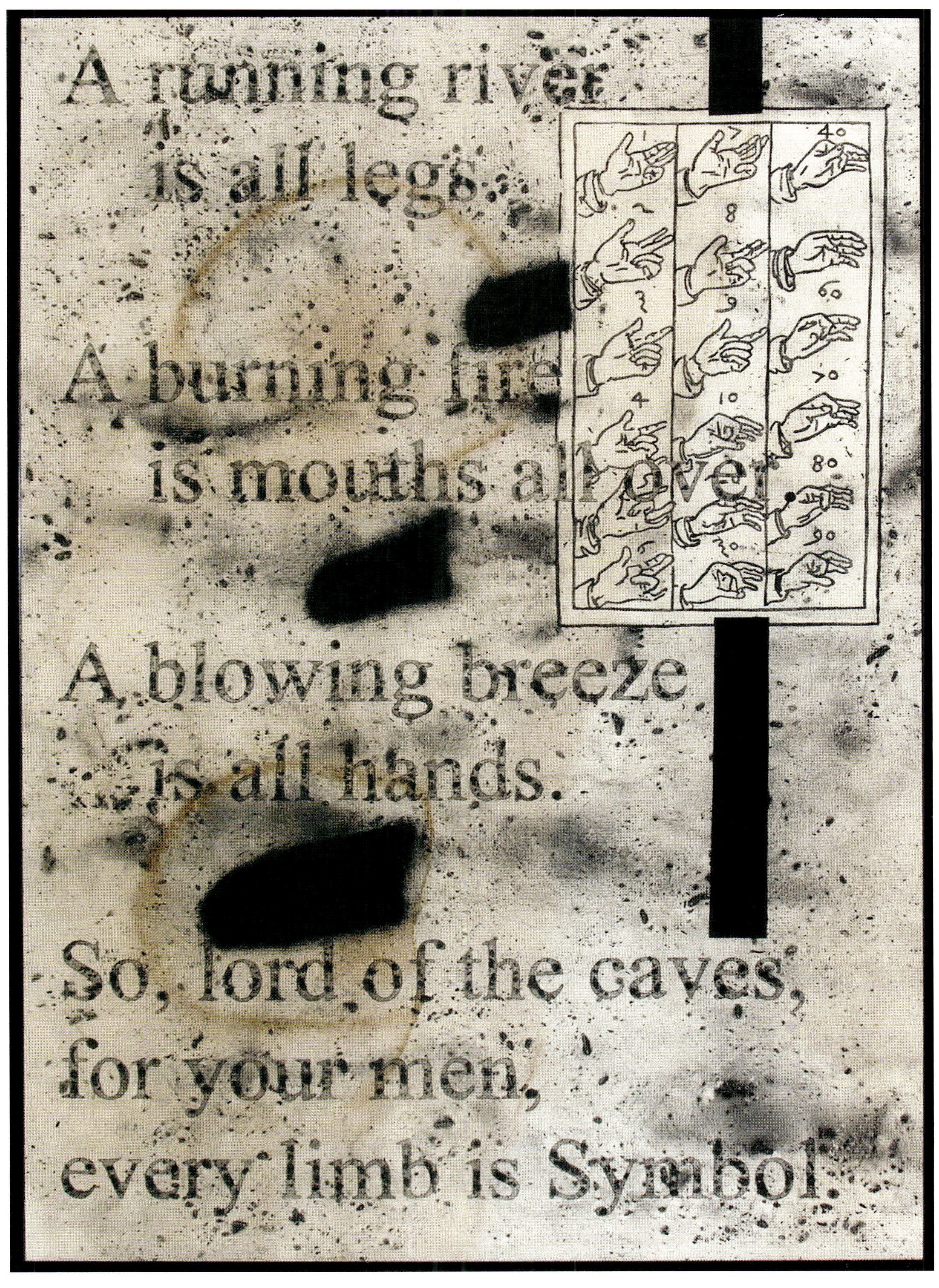

A running river
is all legs.

A burning fire
is mouths all over.

A blowing breeze
is all hands.

So, lord of the caves,
for your men,
every limb is Symbol.

The communication capabilities of our electronic age have provided global cognition of the art-making world that was unavailable to many mid-twentieth-century artists of India. Before Independence in 1947, Western modern art was virtually unknown in India. Indian artists had not been exposed to the gradual evolution of modern art history. Rather, they were bombarded with the entirety of it, with exhibitions in India and newly available opportunities to travel and study abroad. A more recent generation of artists has not been shocked the way their modernist predecessors were by the sudden awareness of Western avant-garde art. They are beyond the "influenced by" or "is derivative of" dismissive commentary that characterized so much of what little attention the West paid to Indian art in the past.

India's twenty-first-century artists now enjoy the luxury of being personal, even self-involved. Vasudha Thozhur is a self-portraitist, both representational and symbolic. Jayashree Chakravarty maps her personal peregrinations on mountainous paper scrolls. Anju Dodiya, also a representational self-portraitist, exposes her dreams by painting them on mattresses. Hema Hirani Upadhyay connects with her maternal lineage by literally planting a message in the earth of South India. Vivan Sundaram manipulates photographically the lineage of his esteemed artistic family.

How do we recognize narrative in a work of art? Whether by coherent text or merely bits of writing, narrative is insinuated by the use of alphabets. The mere use of text cues the viewer to read. Arpita Singh employs alphabets to imply a narrative —one that further unfolds through visual symbols. Hema Hirani Upadhyay uses the format and text of a personal missive. Jitish Kallat painstakingly revives Swami Vivekananda's historical speech by searing it, letter by letter, on a triptych of mirrors. Atul Dodiya reconfigures the meaning of Allama Prabhu's tenth-century altruistic poetry by installing it next to potent symbols of inhumanity. Valay Shende superimposes the text of a contemporary ethnic battle on the mythic warfare between the jealous

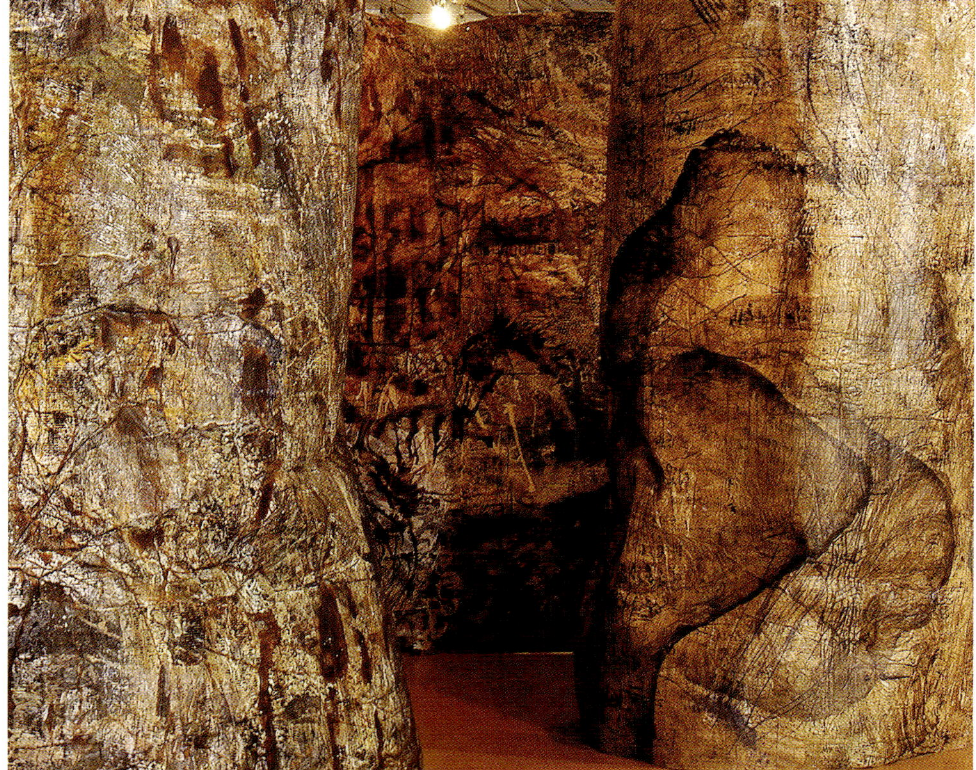

Jayashree Chakravarty. *Personal Space*, 2003. Detail, see page 58.

Opposite page:
Atul Dodiya. *Devoured Darkness V*, 2006. Detail. Steel, fiberglass, mirror; watercolor and charcoal on paper; 114x60x36 in (overall installation dimensions).
Collection of Anurag Bhargava, New York.
Photography: Courtesy of the artist.

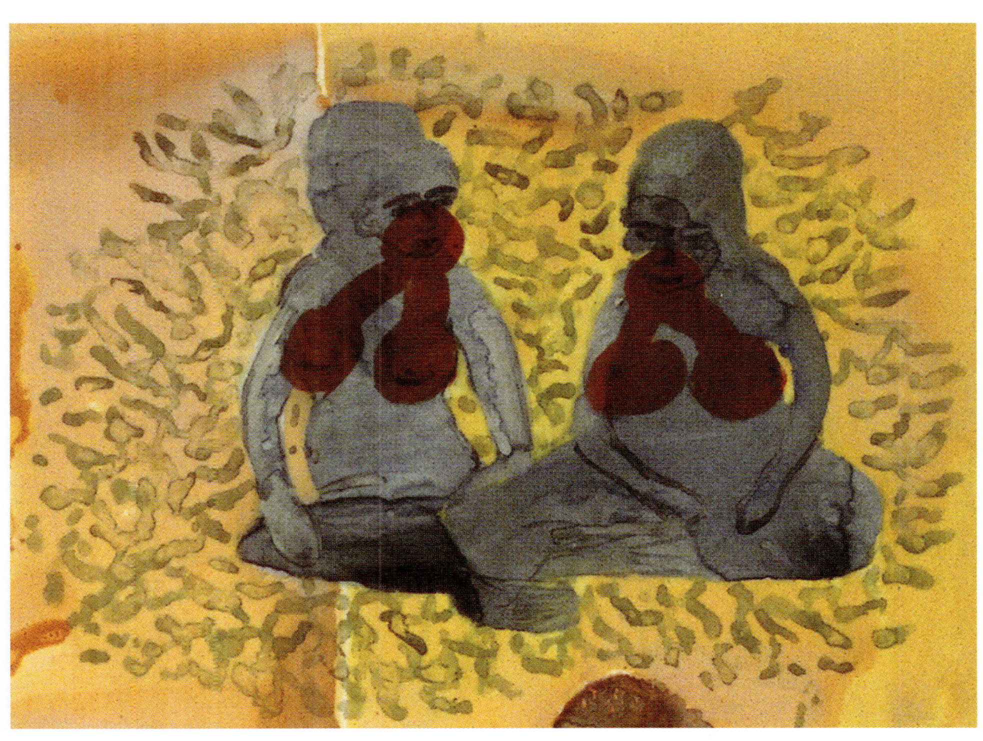

Nalini Malani. *Sita/Medea 2*, 2004.
Detail, see page 102.

cousins of the *Mahabharata*. N. S. Harsha creates ironic political tableaux, flamboyantly titled on *trompe l'œil* banners. Shilpa Gupta applies a cyber-text menu to engage the viewer in a war game on terror. And Gulammohammed Sheikh underscores his narrative purpose utilizing a book format to illuminate his life's journey.

Dreams—both waking and sleeping—are another source of fantastic personal narratives. Oneiric time does not have to be linear and events do not have to be ordered. Interpretation is left to the viewer or the dreamer/artist. As Ursula Le Guin said in her 1980 essay, "Some Thoughts on Narrative:"

> Dream narrative differs from conscious narrative in using sensory symbols more than language. In dream the sense of the directionality of time is often replaced by spatial metaphor, or may be lowered, or reversed, or vanish. The connections dream makes between events are most often unsatisfactory to the rational intellect and the aesthetic mind. Dreams tend to flout Aristotle's rules of plausibility and muddle up his instructions concerning plot. Yet they are undeniably narrative: they connect events, fit things together in an order or a pattern that makes, to some portion of our mind, sense.[6]

What then is dream narration? With the artist as author and protagonist, it is a segment of probing self-examination, set in dreamtime. Anju Dodiya invokes dream narratives by staging them on mattresses. The events in her head are displayed on the bed. These are dreams of the nighttime variety—Jungian in their symbolic imagery. Jayashree Chakravarty's deep daydreams are subconscious treks on arduous paths. Her mammoth scrolls display signposts that guide, but also might mislead with too many choices. Again, quoting Ursula Le Guin:

> In the telling of a story, reason is only a support system . . . Only the imagination can get us out of the bind of the eternal present, inventing or hypothesizing or pretending or discovering a way that reason can then follow

Anju Dodiya. *Island of Greed*, 2005.
Detail, see page 62.

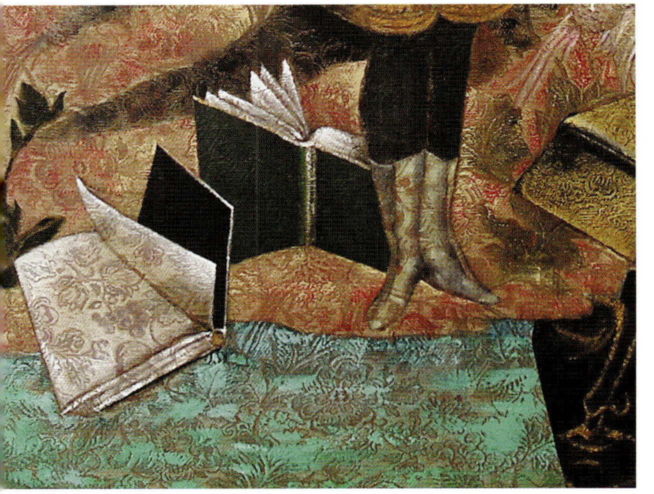

into the infinity of options, a clue through the labyrinths of choice, a golden
string, the story, leading us to the freedom that is properly human, the
freedom open to those whose minds can accept unreality.[7]

An awake mind is required to decipher the stream of a daydream or the sometimes
oddly juxtaposed images of sleep.

Much has been said about the historic fluidity of culture via
adventurous travel and trade. Think of the ubiquitous references to the mythic Silk
Road as the cultural conduit of its time. Those who journeyed on this legendary path
transported not only precious goods, but also tales that continue to keep tradition alive in
the diverse societies along its route. Time too has transported the narratives that identify
a culture—from ancient roots to contemporary interpretations. And just as in ancient
times, stories continue to inspire the making of art. Whether revealing dreams,
commenting on current events or re-imagining the great epics, contemporary artists in
India are inspired by narration. It is the connective thread that binds today's Indian artists
to their rich tradition of storytelling; stories from foreign cultures are a source of narrative
inspiration. It is in the *re*telling that the artist appropriates them. Anju Dodiya mines
diverse literary traditions to enhance her autobiographical tales. From Penelope, heroine
of the *Odyssey*, to the "beauties" of Edo-period Japan, Dodiya shows us the breadth of her
literary curiosity. Nalini Malani finds parallels in the human condition in European and
Indian classics. In her series *Stories Retold*, she fuses the tragic heroines Sita and Medea
in sisterly pain. In *Living in Alicetime*, Lewis Carroll's Alice finds herself lost and needing to
renegotiate her physical and psychological world in Malani's topsy-turvy India.

Narrative is what we use to describe events that occur in Time.
Whether linear or cyclical, Time is the great equalizer. Although some of the narratives in
this exhibition are linear, few of the artists are concerned with an Aristotelian beginning-
middle-end. Much of the Indian narrative tradition is best understood if one comprehends
that Time is cyclical, not linear. It is measured in unfathomable rotating eons in which
events recur infinitely. Every myth repeats (and repeats and repeats itself), mocking the

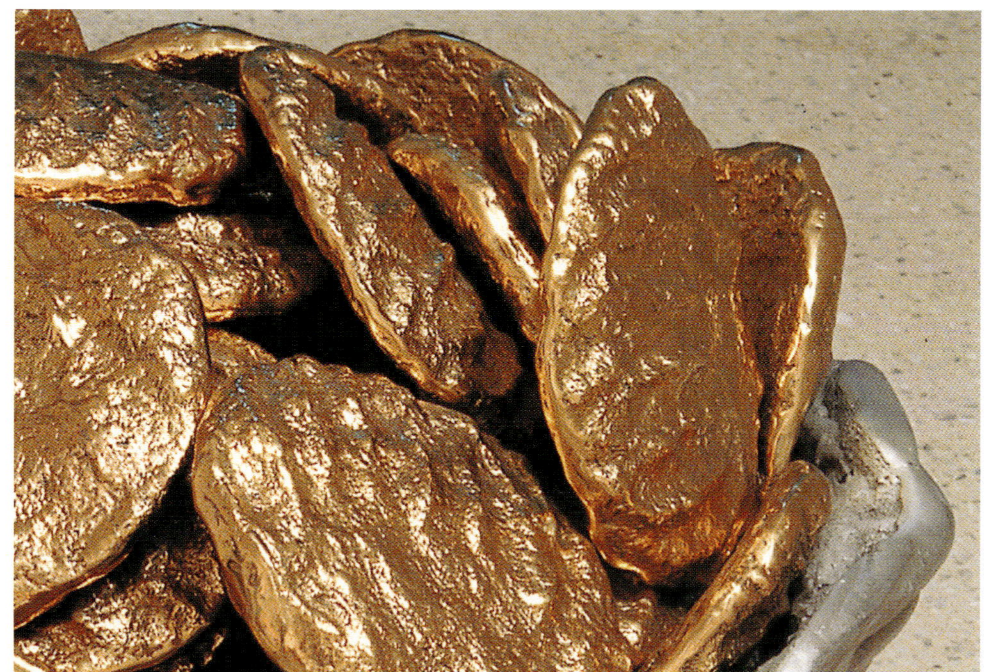

Subodh Gupta. *Every Day Is Less*, 2003.
Detail, see page 69.

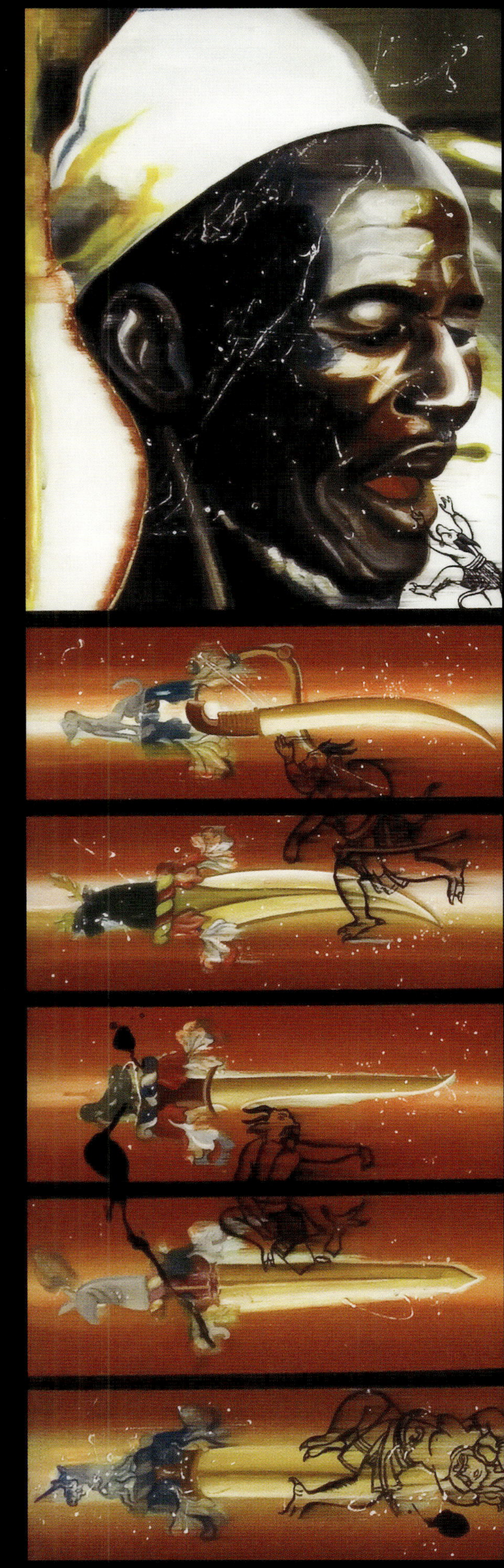

Reena Saini Kallat. *Sword Swallower, No. 2,* 2004.
See page 94.

transience of time with the permanence of repetition. Nature mimics the regenerating great eons with revolving seasons—never more evident than with the coming and going of monsoons. On a smaller, more immediate scale, nature fluidly cycles through biological creatures, particularly the symbolic cow. With his invocation of that most ubiquitous of Indian symbols, the Holy Cow—and particularly the fluids associated with it—Subodh Gupta has incorporated the concept of cyclical flow into his artistic output.

The unfolding of epic stories gets a particular spin with each generation of retelling, further exemplifying how ideas spiral through time. Although myths and symbolic events in traditional Indian narratives recur infinitely in great cycles of time, the concept of direct lineage—family, caste, society—remains an important factor in the development of each artist's personal aesthetic narrative.

In her series of *Sword Swallowers*, Reena Saini Kallat demonstrates the historical Indian belief that divinity resides in every person. She situates mythological narratives in horizontal panels where the bodies of her people-on-the-street should be. Gulammohammed Sheikh's *Book of Journeys* is an autobiographical trip that returns again and again to the idea of home. Hema Hirani Upadhyay collaborates with her mother to represent symbolically the threads that connect their bloodline. *Mum-my* combines Bina Hirani's crocheted tablecloth with her daughter's paintings in a cozy room-like installation. Vivan Sundaram maneuvers his venerated relatives along a timeline of his own devising, imaginatively reconfiguring their relationships to each other and to himself.

Just as the text gives authority to the author of the written narrative, these visually driven narratives are imbued with the authority of the artists who created them. The telling of one's own story gives it power. Whether a known narrative or one newly revealed, the artist owns it. What you see (or do not see) is managed by the artist who determines what you will know. All narrative is ultimately personal, once the storyteller has chosen to tell a story. We all carry bits of our personal history in our memories. Whether short stories or tomes, favorite passages get memorized, rites of passage form the chapter headings, life-changing moments stand out in bold face. The opportunity for artists to move memories from mind to canvas (or paper or film) is one of the privileges of artistic narration.

1   Peter Brooks, *Reading for the Plot: Design and Intention in Narrative* (New York: Vintage Books, 1985), 3.

2   In 2003, the Peabody Essex Museum in Salem, Massachusetts opened the Chester and Davida Herwitz Gallery of Contemporary Indian Art to accommodate the gift of Chester and Davida Herwitz's extensive private collection. It is the first gallery dedicated to India's modern and contemporary art in an American museum.

3   Nalini Malani, quoted in "Phantasmagoria and the Lanternist: The Video/Shadow Plays of Nalini Malani," Rhana Devenport, *Nalini Malani: Stories Retold* (New York: Bose Pacia, 2004).

4   Nalini Malani, quoted in Peter Nagy and Johan Pijnappel, "Nalini Malani: Interview by Johan Pijnappel," *Icon: India Contemporary* (Montalvo, CA: Lucas Artists Programs, 2005), 40.

5   Arpita Singh quoted by Nilima Sheikh, "Of target-flowers, spinal cords, and (un)veilings," Nilima Sheikh, Peter Nagy, and Deepak Amanth, *Arpita Singh: Memory Jars* (New York: Bose Pacia Modern, 2003).

6   Ursula K. Le Guin, *Dancing at the Edge of the World: Thoughts on Words, Women, Places* (New York: Grove Press, 1989), 41–42.

7   Le Guin, 45.

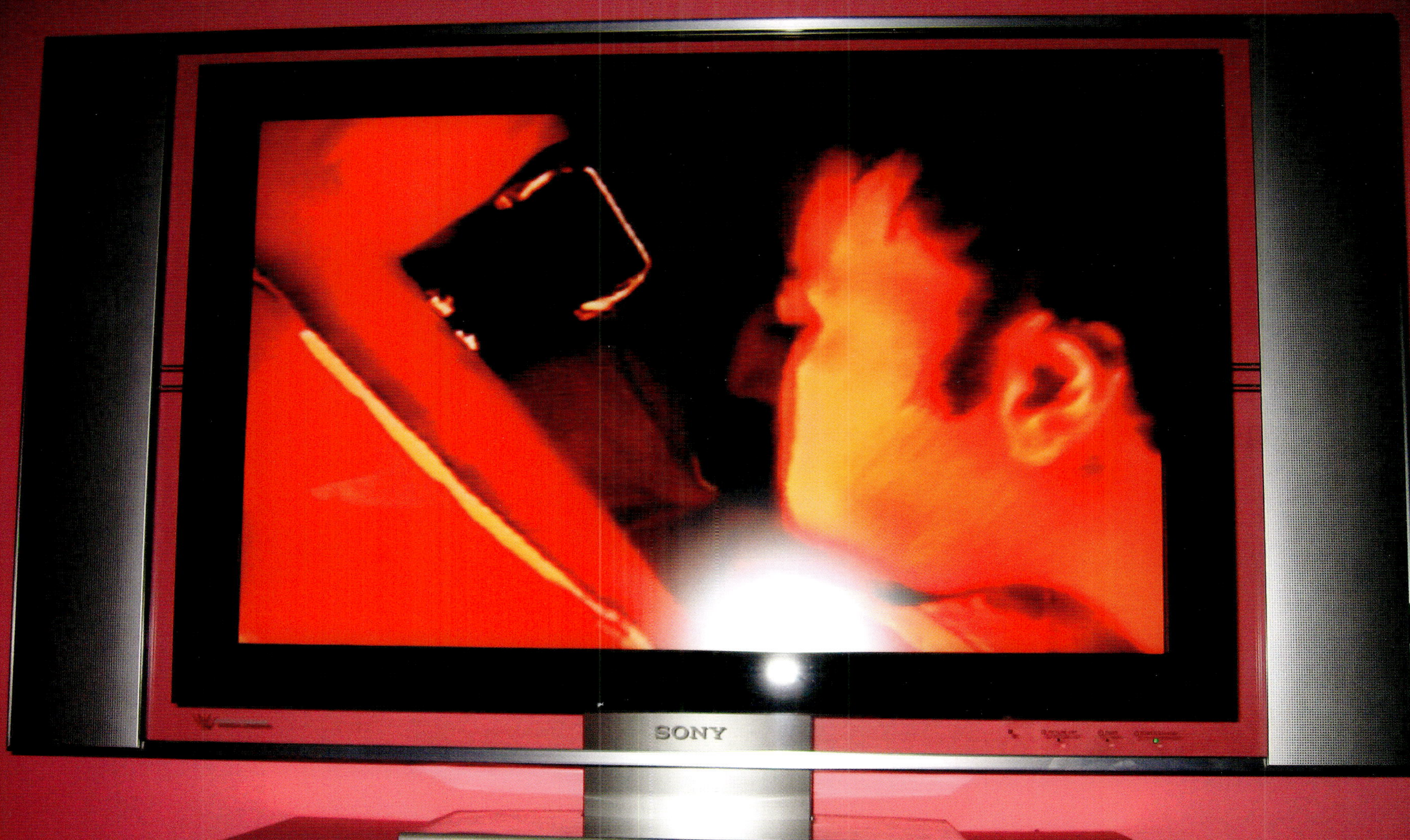

Tejal Shah. *Chingari Chumma/Stinging Kiss*, 2000.
Single-channel video, sound, 8 minutes.
Collection of Lekha and Anupam Poddar, New Delhi.
Photography: Courtesy of Johan Pijnappel.

Indian Video Art
and
the New Narrative Matrix

Johan Pijnappel

Place for People

India is known for its culture that spans over 5000 years. Narrative has always been a dominant force in variations as diverse as the Ajanta paintings that picture the Buddha in his previous births in the allegorical *Jataka* tales, going back to the second century BCE, the *Hamzanama* paintings made for entertaining the court of the Mughal emperor Akbar, in the sixteenth century, or the *patwa* storytellers of Bengal who are still prevalent today.

The development of a kind of Modernism after Independence—largely in Mumbai—in the field of contemporary visual arts that excluded narrative structures, can be seen as a minor interruption. This continued for a few decades until 1980, and then a change occurred with the historical exhibition "Place for People." The art historian Chaitanya Sambrani wrote about this show: "'Place for People' took a stand that was informed by a concern with the local, intimate, the personal, the autobiographical, even the confessional . . . it retained what in retrospect was surely a reaffirmation of faith in the humanity of its figures and a conviction in progressive social action that included a place for the artist in the body politic even as it made place for members of that body in the work of the artists."[1]

Place for Video

Interestingly enough, this change of content is exactly what developed ten years later within the visual arts, with the inception of video art in India. Around 1990, Nalini Malani (Karachi, 1946) and Vivan Sundaram (Simla, 1943)—both members of "Place for People"—and other artists such as Navjot Altaf (Meerut, 1949) and Rummana Hussain (Lucknow, 1952) broke out of the painting frame and started to present their ideas through the medium of installations with all kinds of materials including video, photographs, ordinary building construction materials, ephemeral wall drawings, and more. Over time, video matured into the preferred medium, but in contrast with "Place for People," which comprised five male and only one female artist, what followed was a more female-oriented direction.[2] In recent videos, narration plays an important role. As India's first video artist, Malani explains: "The story has complex functions. The stakes one incorporates in the human image include the skill to map out social destinies through the art of narration. For me history, fantasy, ritual remembrance, dream life, memory, transformation can all be melded in the crucible of the narrative."

Video art developed in India at the same moment that a second dramatic change in favor of video took place in the Western art world. After a period of decline in the eighties, when the West focused on painting and regionalism, the nineties brought—to many people's bewilderment—a whole new generation of artists who used video to tell their stories. This movement that has proven not to be a temporary whim, has extended and expanded in the twenty-first century into a whole new narrative matrix which is that of multi-screen digital storytelling.[3]

The New Silver Screen

A large part of Indian video art consists of single screen works which, when exhibited, might look like a derivation from the movies or television. However, from its inception it became clear that this video art, in its more experimental mode, would not follow the narrative style found in cinema. It shunned Bollywood's conservative content, continuity editing and single narrative plots.[4] Also, it seldom made links to experimental film and favored socially-engaged documentary work, such as that made by the well-known filmmakers Anant Patwardhan and Madhushree Dutta.[5] *Stinging Kiss* (2000) by Tejal Shah (Bhilai, 1979) is one of the rare video works that does relate to the Bollywood dream industry, in which she ironically overturns the oversimplified role models of man and woman with a provocative reverse-gender mini-drama.

Nor does Indian video art follow the narrative structure that is provided by the TV soap opera. In contrast to the first years of video art in the West in the late sixties and early seventies, video art reacts in only a few cases to the popular time-based medium that took India by storm after the single national channel, Doordarshan, was extended to multi-cable television. Exceptions are when the artist actually connects with popular TV iconography, as in *Scrolls* (2002) by Valay Shende (Nagpur, 1980) where he appropriates extracts from the *Mahabharata* (TV) serial by B. R. Chopra. In Shende's reaction to the Gujarat violence in 2002, he overlays/superimposes a "breaking news" scroll, sending appeals for Muslims and Hindus who are lost or wounded in hospitals. Another exception is when Anita Dube (Lucknow, 1959)

makes a typical TV confessional-style work, *Kissa-e-Noor Mohammed* (*Garam Hawa*) (2004), in which an ordinary Muslim citizen achieves his moment of fame à la Andy Warhol, when he is given fifteen minutes to speak.

The majority of single-channel works use a type of narration that is more like a personal, fragmented, poetic observation. The sets are not elaborate, the editing is done with a poverty of means, for obvious financial reasons and the camera is, instead, focused on the artists themselves, as for instance, in Subba Ghosh's work *Remains of a Breath* (2001). But even with these circumstances, and no special editing

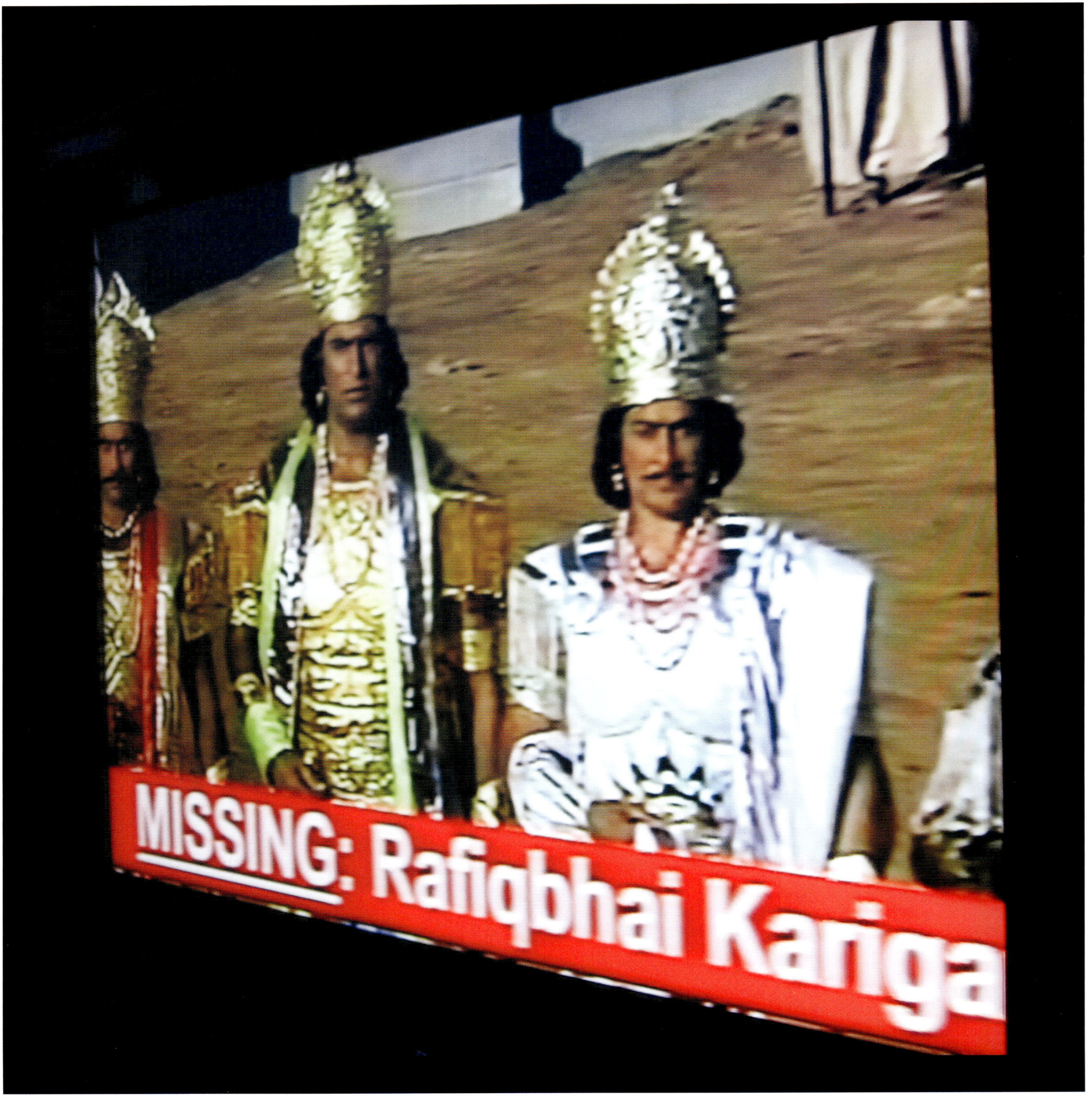

Valay Shende. *Scrolls*, 2002.
Single-channel video, sound, 17 minutes.
Collection of the artist, Mumbai.
Photography: Courtesy of Johan Pijnappel.

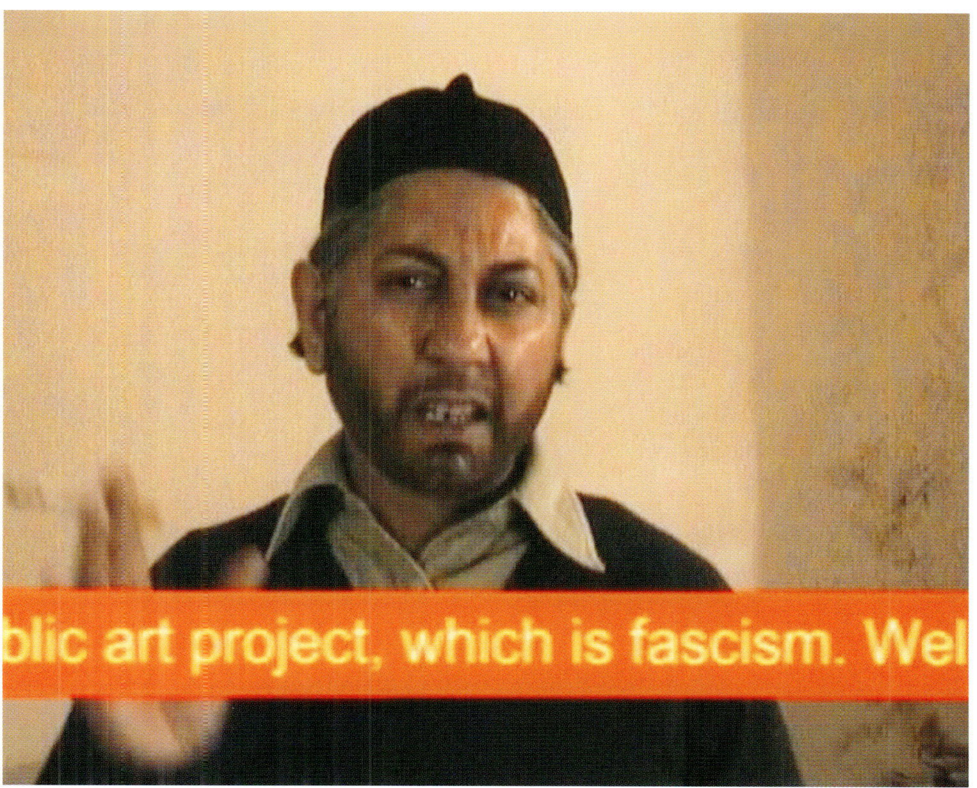

Anita Dube. *Kissa-e-Noor Mohammed (Garam Hawa)*, 2004.
Single-channel video, sound, 15 minutes.
Collection of the artist, New Delhi.
Photography: Courtesy of Anita Dube.

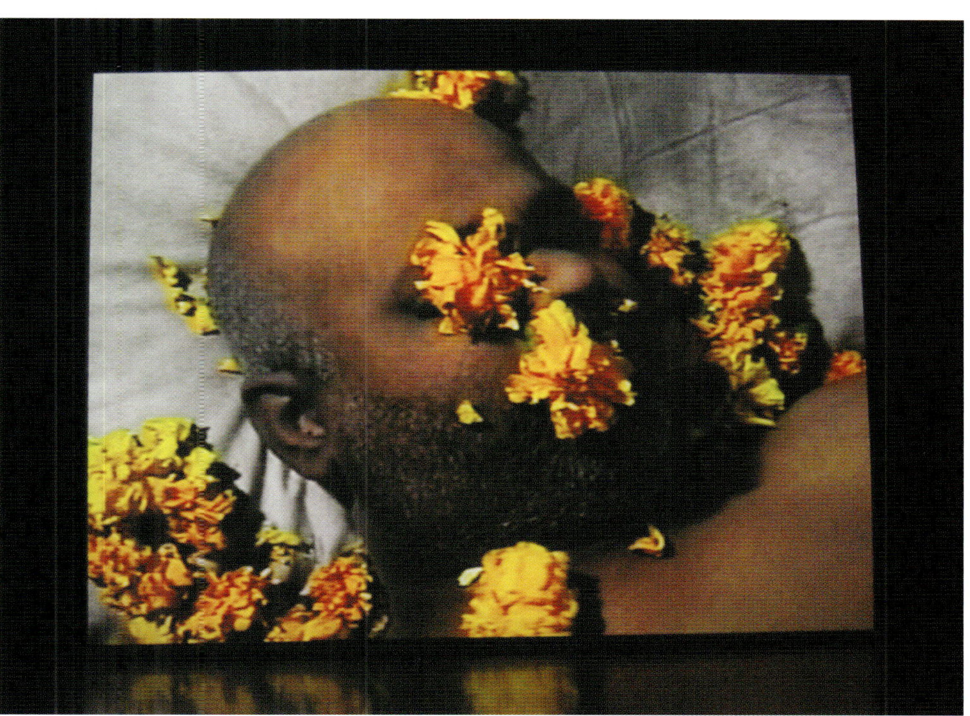

Subba Ghosh. *Remains of a Breath*, 2001.
Single-channel installation, sound, 12 minutes.
Collection of the artist, New Delhi.
Photography: Courtesy of Johan Pijnappel.

software, single channel can be highly original. One wonders how the artist was able to turn around the linear time structure in *Pure* (2000) by Subodh Gupta (Khagoul, 1964) or even convincingly create an omnipresence in *Between Myth and History* (2001) by Umesh Maddanahalli (Bangalore, 1967).[6]

Sometimes these works, in their contents and visual approach, are of such provocative nature that they would never be officially allowed a public presentation. In India, it is mandatory for films to get a censorship certificate—a signed permission for public screening from the Central Board of Film Certification. And that

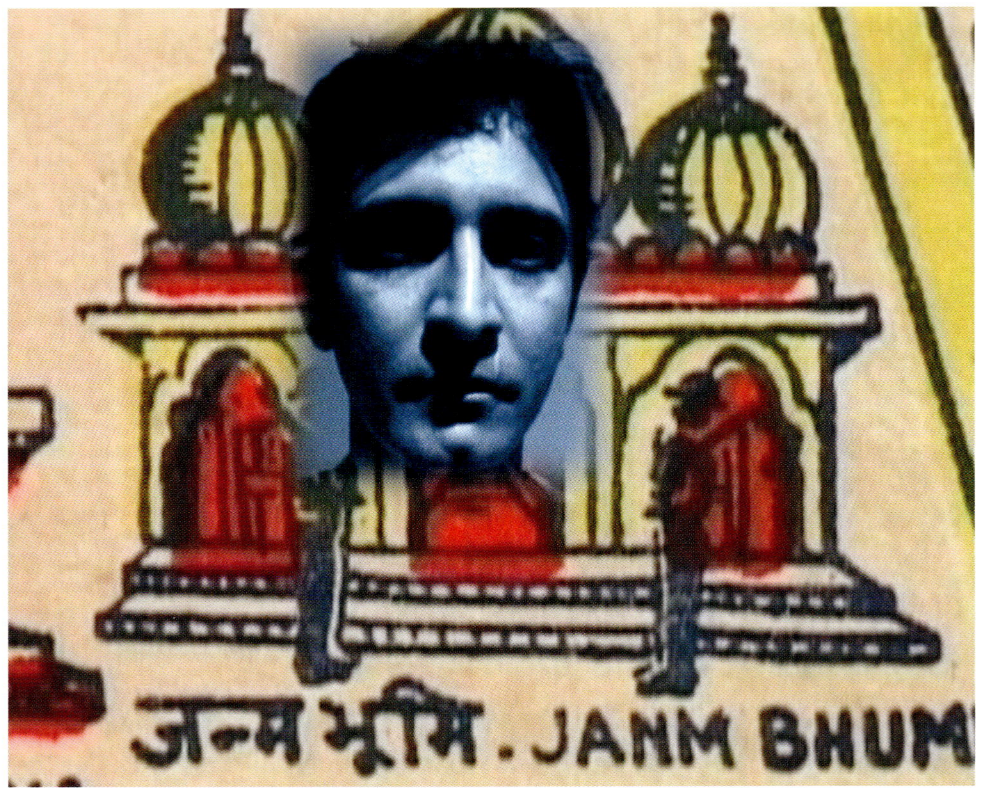

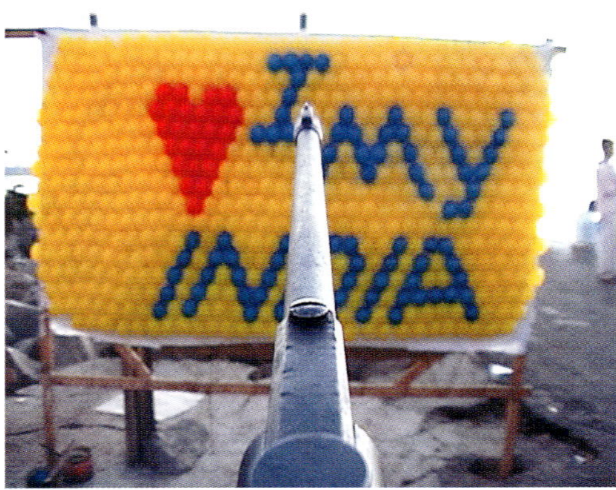

Tejal Shah. *I Love My India*, 2003.
Single-channel video, sound, 10 minutes.
Collection of Centre Pompidou, Paris/Lekha and
Anupam Poddar, New Delhi.
Photography: Courtesy of Tejal Shah.

Tushar Joag. *Phantoms*, 2002.
Single-channel video, sound, 4 minutes.
Collection of Lekha and Anupam Poddar,
New Delhi.
Photography: Courtesy of Tushar Joag.

counts for all films—even advertisements that are meant for public exhibition,
irrespective of their length. We find examples of this especially in videos made by
women artists using a confessional style in which they talk through the camera with
candid freedom. In such a soliloquy, *A Scarlet Letter* (1999) by Eleena Banik (Calcutta,
1971)—"whether she will lose her creativity if she ceases to menstruate"—the lens is
constantly focused on a mundane pot of tomato purée boiling on the stove. Tejal Shah
goes even a step further in her work *Untitled* (1999) when she and her colleague, a
female dancer, sensuously discover each other's naked bodies, risking the wrath of
Hindu conservatives. The latter had, after all, stormed and shut down the Eros Cinema
on December 2nd, 1998 in Mumbai, when the film titled *Fire* by Deepa Mehta was
screened, even though the film only implied same sex relationships and had no
explicit visuals whatsoever.

The other provocative issues that single channel has focused on are
in the vein of progressive social action. Video art in India began in a period of political
turmoil, when artists such as Nalini Malani and Navjot Altaf came to the conclusion
that classical art mediums like painting no longer had the vitality to make socially
engaged statements. The 1992/93 Mumbai riots accelerated the exigency for moving
out of the "frame." A decade later, the younger generation (who had already become
familiar with video through studying abroad) found themselves in a similar quandary
at the time of the devastating Gujarat violence of 2002. So imperative was the need to
speak out that a plethora of single-channel videos surfaced at that time. The artists—
even first timers—no longer focused the video camera on themselves, but on the
horrific world outside, while trying to make sense of the insane situation. Highly
original narratives that did not resort to using the obvious footage showing arson and
murder delivered by television were produced. They did not seek to shock, but instead,
to further enter the process of trying to make sense in these times of turbulence and
brutal violence. *A Story* (2002) by Sharmila Samant (Mumbai, 1967), in which she

makes an animation tell children a metaphoric tale from this black page in India's history, is worth noting. Or Tushar Joag (Mumbai, 1966) in *Phantoms* (2002), who is searching desperately for clues and signs through time past—his own and the nation's—in order to find answers. Or *I Love My India* (2003) by Tejal Shah, a video art "documentary" in which she questions people about Gujarat at a Sunday fair on Chowpatty Beach in Mumbai, while they shoot at colored balloons forming the words of the title.

The New Narrative Matrix

At its inception, the new narrative matrix grew when experimentation in multi-channel modes was utilized. This happened in India initially with multi-monitor works as, for instance, by Vivan Sundaram in works like *House/Boat* (1994) or *Indira's Piano* (2002). The latter has two monitors standing in front of a piano. Each tells separate stories about his grandmother, Marie Antoinette, and his mother, Indira. The monitors stand in for the actual protagonists, while parts of their history overlap. Sonia Khurana (Saharanpur, 1968) is probably the only one among the younger artists who has really explored the possibilities of two-monitor works. In one of them, titled *Lone Women Don't Lie* (1999), one monitor sits on top of the other showing the artist smiling and blowing kisses to herself.

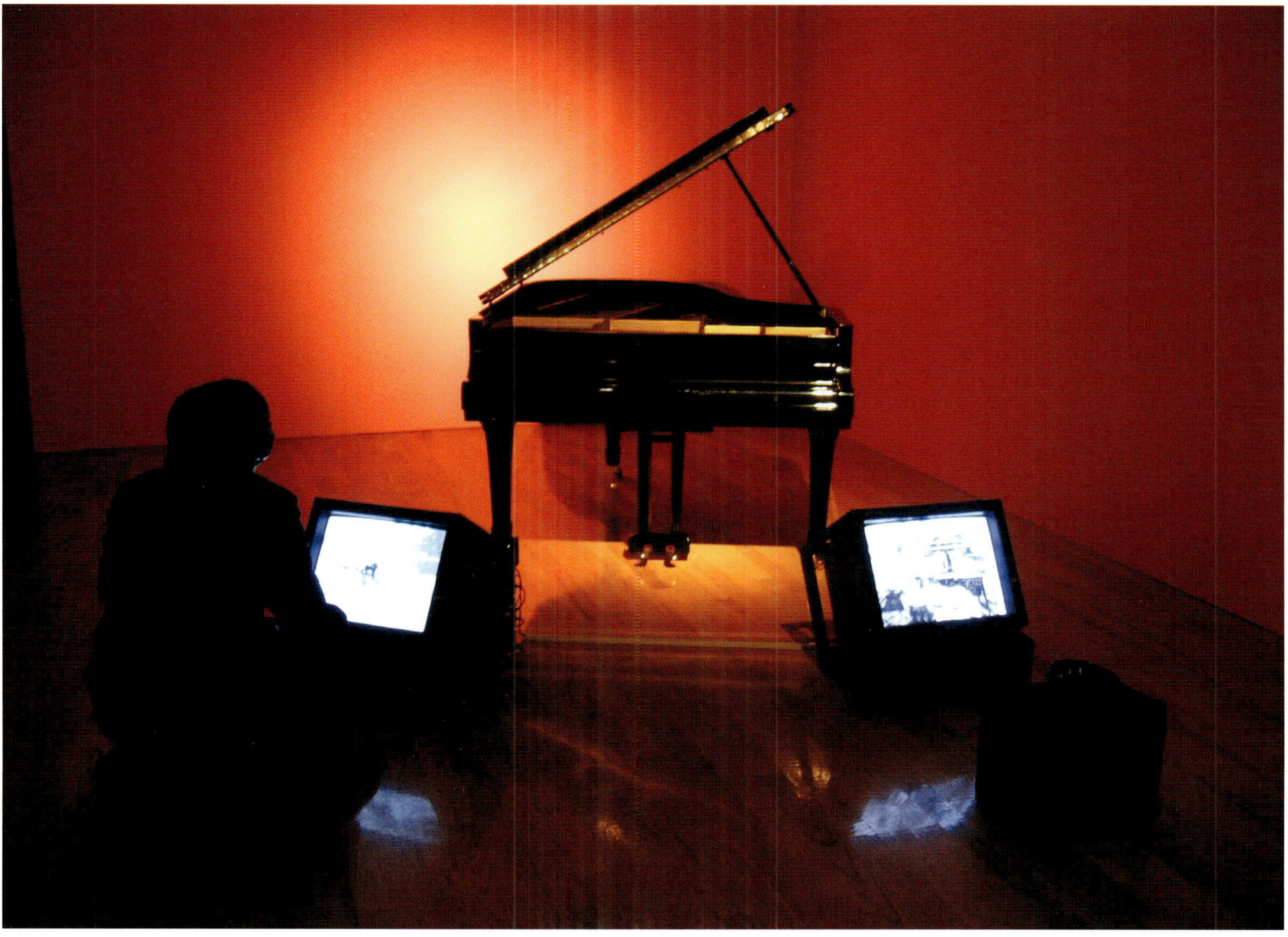

Vivan Sundaram. *Indira's Piano*, 2002.
Two monitor video installation, headphones and piano, sound, 8 minutes.
Collection of the artist, New Delhi.
Photography: Courtesy of Johan Pijnappel.

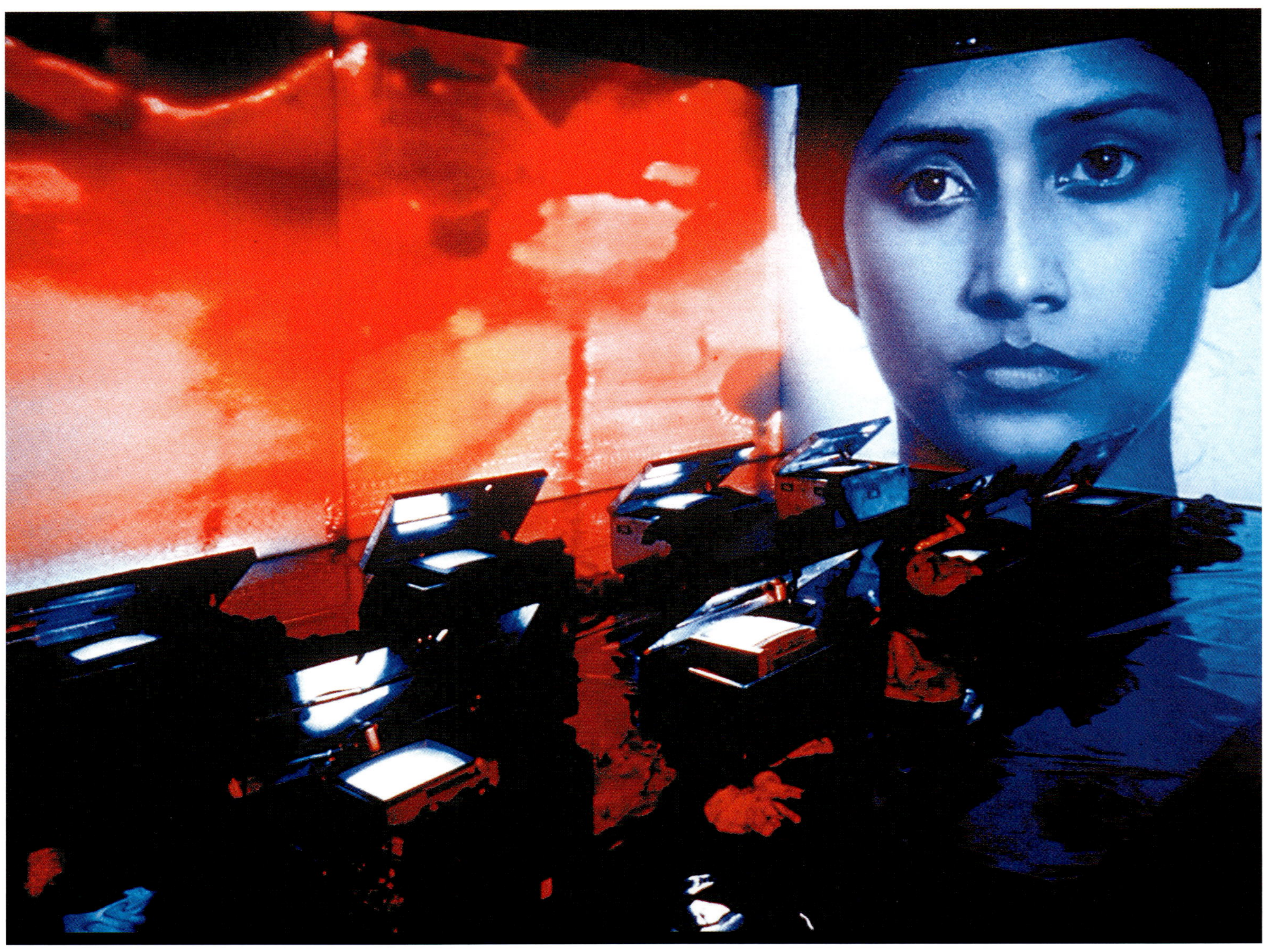

However, the full implementation of the new narrative matrix came about with multi-projection configurations. This made it possible to go beyond single linear narration and monitor-shaped format when a new type of video projector came on the retail market and prices became somewhat reasonable. India's first contribution was the installation *Remembering Toba Tek Singh* (1998) by Nalini Malani, that addresses the nuclear threat and the history of violence. To tell her story, she shapes an all-encompassing digital surround, with four projectors and twelve monitors, to come to a multilayered, and multi-angled narrative environment. On approaching the installation, one sees light flickering from the half-open trunks. On a closer view, a series of Pandora's boxes open, throwing up victims of the atom bombs of 1945 and burning bodies on the streets of Mumbai in 1993. Moving around in the installation, the spectator/participant's phenomenological presence becomes part of the narration for other viewers. Inside the installation, the participant, who ceases to be only an observer, is haunted by her/his own image captured through the mirroring effects of the reflective floor. Willy-nilly s/he is inducted at once as observer, actor and narrator. *Remembering Toba Tek Singh* addresses the history of violence over national borders with a multitude of new images colliding with documentary images coming from countries as diverse as Japan, USA, India, Pakistan, the Netherlands and those in the Balkans. With this, Nalini Malani develops not a multicultural but rather an intercultural

Nalini Malani. *Remembering Toba Tek Singh*, 1998. Installation of four projections on three walls, with twelve monitors in tin trunks surrounded with mirror reflecting material, sound, 20 minutes.
Collections of Queensland Art Gallery, Brisbane/Lekha and Anupam Poddar, New Delhi.
Courtesy of the World Wide Video Festival, Amsterdam.
Photography: Gert Jan van Rooij.

approach, wherein the melding of a new form of understanding grows.[7] Just a few years later, Malani creates yet another dimension to the possibilities of video installation art, with the four-channel work *Hamletmachine* (2000). With a Japanese digital actor and excerpts from the acclaimed and controversial German playwright Heiner Mueller, Malani turns the video installation about Indian political climate into a hybrid that she calls a "video/theatre play."

At the beginning of the twenty-first century, other artists also started to use multi-screen projection configurations. An important figure in this is Navjot Altaf, with titles like *Between Memory and History* (2001), on the history of sectarian violence in India, *Lacuna in Testimony* (2003) and *Mumbai Meri Jaan* (2004). Other works in a multi-screen format are for instance *Reduced Spaces* (2000) by Shakuntala Kulkarni, *Meat* (2002) by Sonia Khurana, *Tracking* (2003) by Vivan Sundaram, *Cleanse* (2004) by Sharmila Samant, *Crossings* (2005) by Ranbir Kaleka and *A Measure of Anacoustic Reason* (2005) by Raqs Media Collective. All these socio-politically motivated works provide the viewer with a surrounding where s/he is confronted with a collage of digitally reconstructed stories.[8] Each of them proves how suitable the new narrative matrix is in its attempt to reveal in an engaging way the fast growing complexity of the Indian cosmopolitan society.

An important extension to the new narrative matrix is the addition of interactivity. It was Shilpa Gupta who was the first Indian artist to develop this into a creative device, with website-based monitor installations such as *diamondandyou.com* (2000) and *blessed-bandwith.net* (2003). She made her first projection-based interactive installation in *Untitled* (2004) for the third Media City Seoul Biennial. While we see

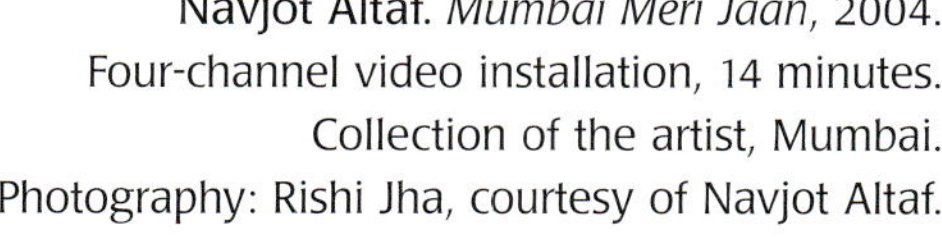

Navjot Altaf. *Mumbai Meri Jaan*, 2004.
Four-channel video installation, 14 minutes.
Collection of the artist, Mumbai.
Photography: Rishi Jha, courtesy of Navjot Altaf.

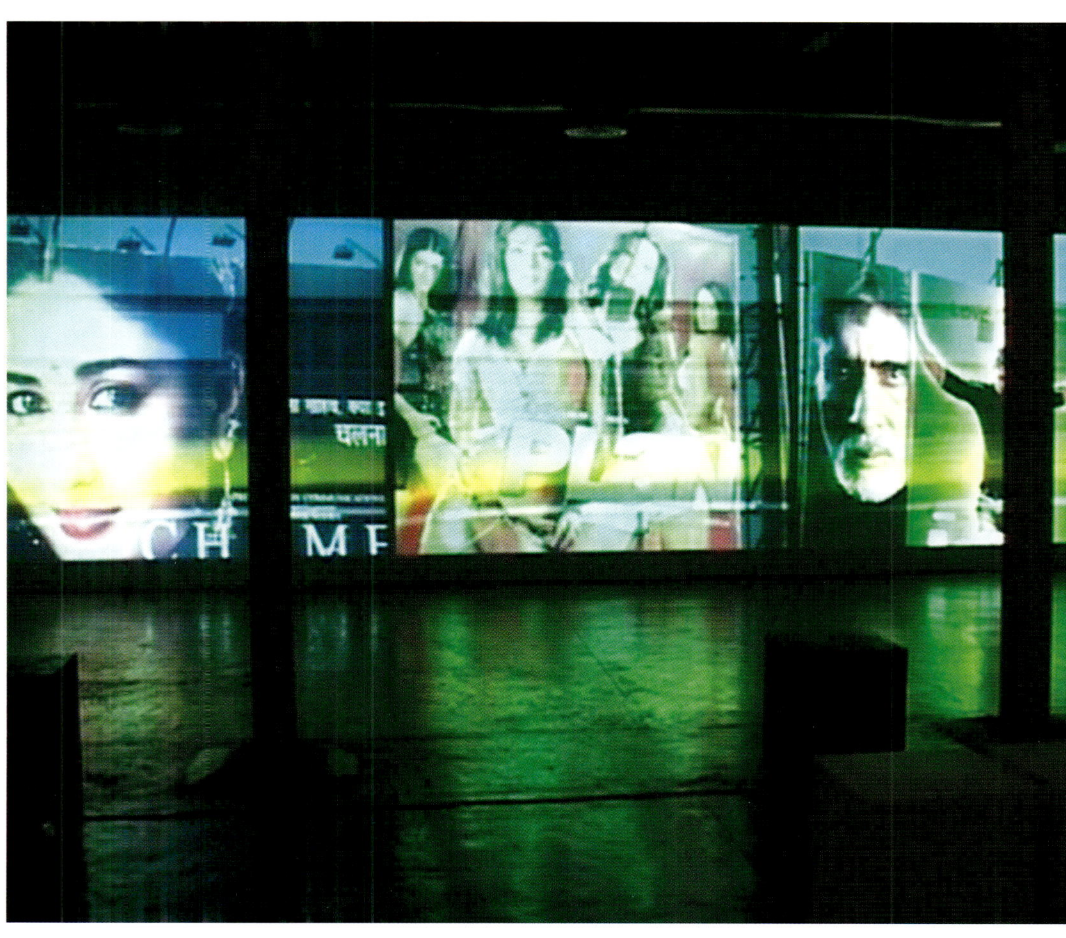

seven young girls gaily exercising on the floor, a running text line reveals an ongoing drill of "war on terror." The viewer/participant controls and changes the mode of the different exercises by means of the computer mouse. What initially seems random, actually follows a premeditated construct by the artist. Narration is locked without the viewer's participation. In Gupta's latest interactive, multi-channel projection work called *Untitled* (2006), the public cannot even escape from participating. Wherever you walk in front of the white screens, you automatically create a shadow that is plagued by shadowy characters, the projection of which keep finding you and leaping on your head.

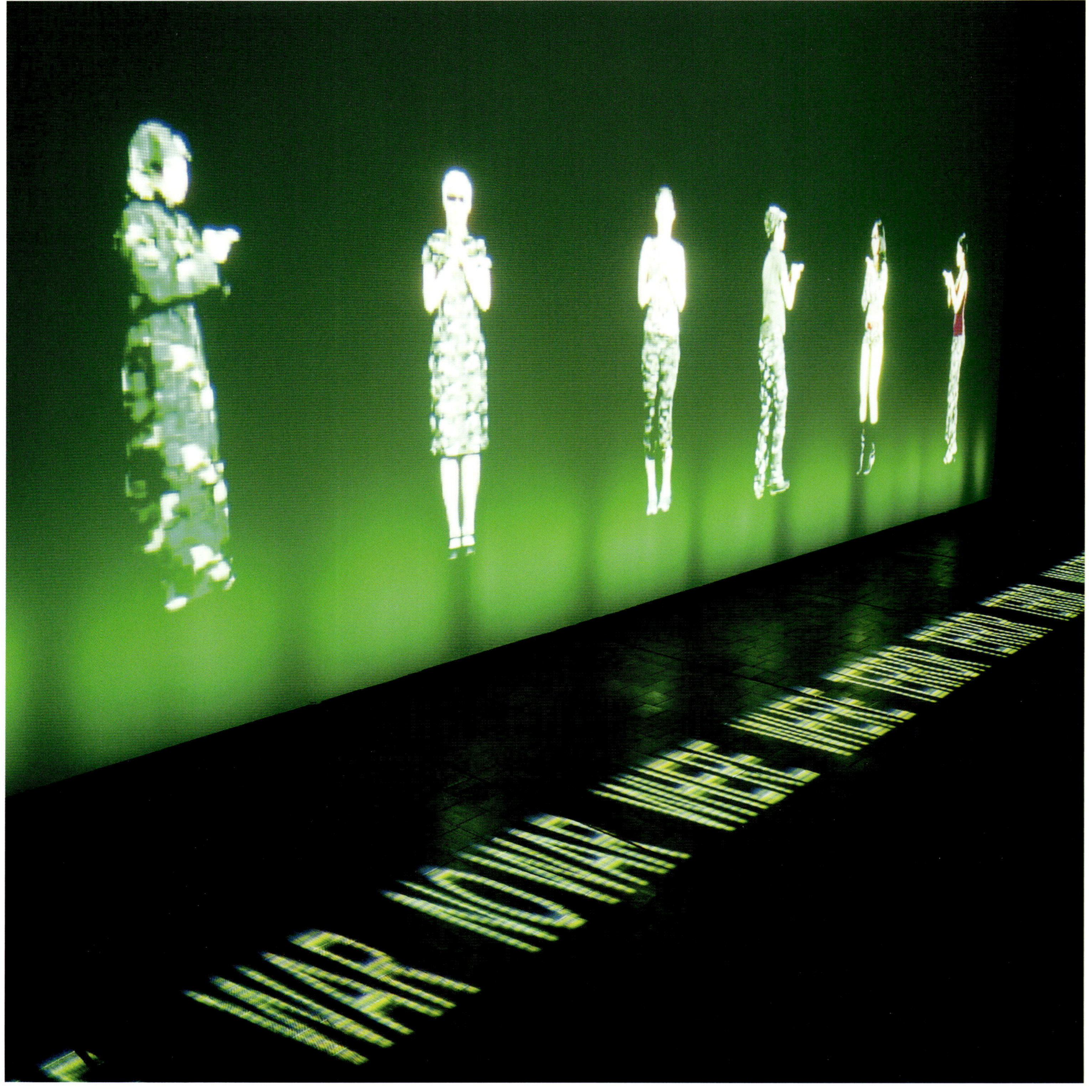

Shilpa Gupta. *Untitled*, 2004.
Interactive single wide angle projection installation, sound.
Collection of Fukuoka Asian Art Museum and Daimler Chrysler, Stuttgart.
Photography: Courtesy of Hyung Min Moon, Seoul.

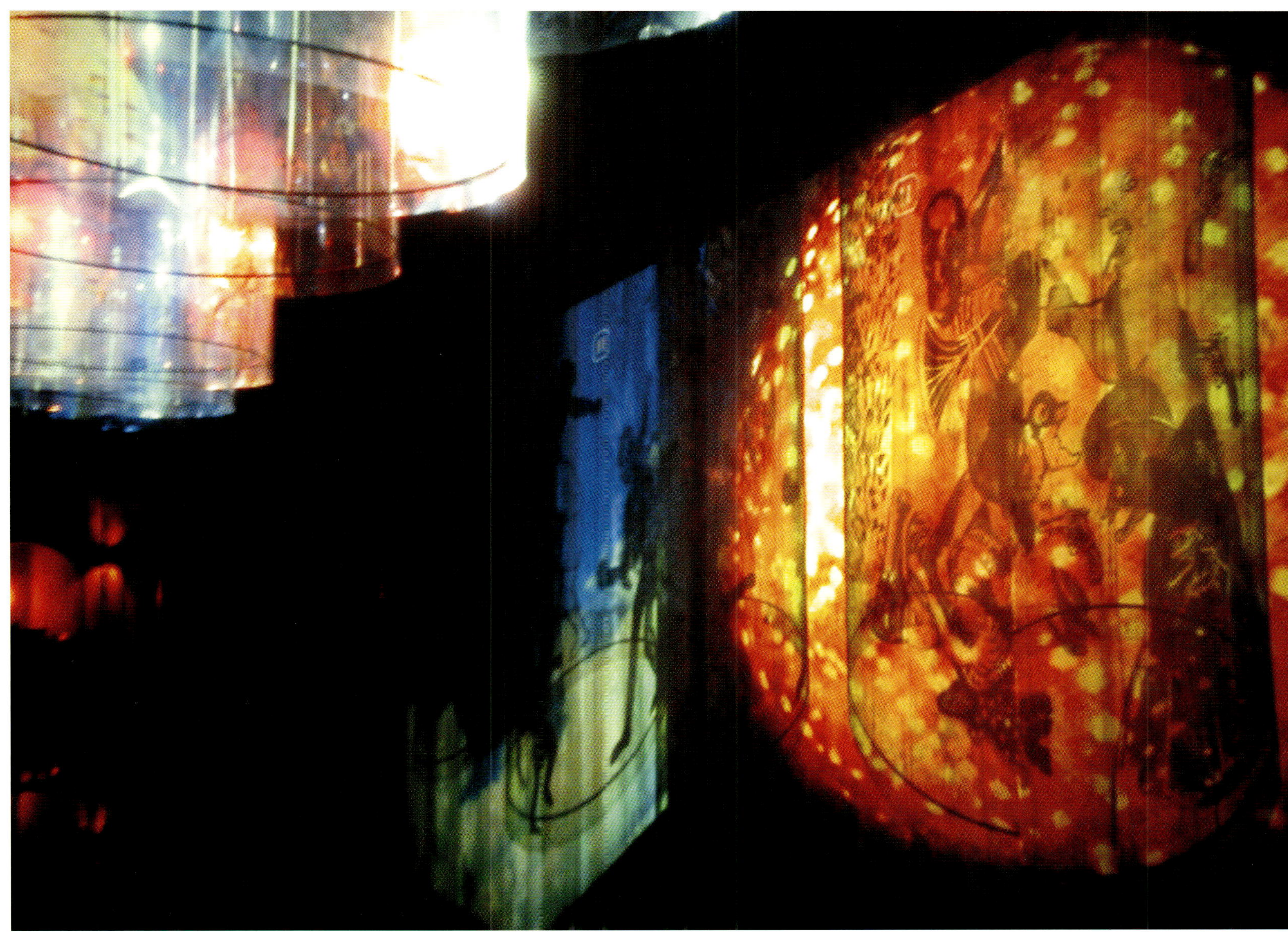

Nalini Malani. *Gamepieces*, 2004.
Installation, shadow/video play of four
connecting wall projections and six rotating
reverse painted Mylar cylinders, sound,
4 minutes.
Collection of the artist, Mumbai.
Photography: Courtesy of Johan Pijnappel.

Looking at these examples of the new narrative matrix, one might assume that the further development of it just follows the line of art embracing digital technology and the use of a multitude of screens. However, one could be wrong. For instance, in 2002, Malani surprised the art world with a whole new form of installation that she called "video/shadow plays" by combining the contemporary (video) with the past (paintings). In these mysterious *Gamepieces*—an indictment against the testing of nuclear devices—videos are projected through painted figures on rotating Mylar cylinders. Together there are five registers of narration—the painted story, the continuous moving shadow play, the images in the videos, the melding of the video and the shadow images, and the sound piece. As a result, different combinations of stories come together and dissolve in a seemingly endless mingling. Interestingly, it is here that Malani, unknowingly, makes a contemporary version of probably India's first experiments with art and technology, the magic lamps done by Mahadeorano Patwardhan in 1884, with what he called *Shambarik Khadolika* (Lamp of the Prankster by Nightfall). Here Patwardhan used prepared painted slides in multi-colors with three movable lanterns to start a new way of storytelling that somehow got lost in history and would only be picked up again 100 years later in the experimental art.[9]

Digital "Homo Fabulans"

For the near future it seems to be clear that whatever form it is expressed in, narrative continues to play a major cultural role in India, to present and re-present experiences.[10] In that light, it is noteworthy to recall that one of the most impressive philosophers of the twentieth century, Paul Ricoeur, defined human beings as "homo fabulans" (species that tell stories and interpret narratives).

As for the Indian digital new narrative matrix, one can only look forward to the day when a generation of experimental artists receives proper support and finds opportunity to combine their critical creativity with the booming Indian software industries. Some day multi-users, cyberspace-linked exhibition platforms/ shopping malls in Mumbai, Bangalore (now Bengalooru), Pune etc. will be the beginning of a new age and a different place for people's interaction/experiences. What the narration will look like and what its contents will be at that time, one can only guess. As Martin Rieser and Andrea Zapp analyze our future: "We are entering an age of narrative chaos, where traditional frameworks are being overthrown by emerging experimental and radical attempts to re-master the art of storytelling in developing technologies."[11]

For more information on this subject, visit www.videoartindia.com

1   Chaitanya Sambrani, "Of Places and of Departures," in *Watercolours A Broader Spectrum–III* (Mumbai: Gallery Chemould, 1996), 1.

2   Johan Pijnappel, *Video Art in India* (New Delhi: Apeejay Press, 2002), 26.

3   Martin Rieser and Andrea Zapp (ed.), *New Screen Media–Cinema/Art/Narrative* (London: British Film Institute, 2002).

4   M. Madhava Prasad, *Ideology of the Hindi Film–A Historical Construction* (New Delhi: Oxford University Press, 1998).

5   Brad Butler and Karen Mirza (ed.), *Cinema of Prayoga–Indian Experimental Film & Video 1913–2006* (London: no.w.here, 2006).

6   The first exhibition of these video artists who pointed the camera literally on themselves was done in "SELF," at the Institute of Modern Art, Brisbane, 2002.

7   We see this new approach taking place in the film world as well, where a new wave of transnational cinema addresses the narrative and aesthetic dynamics that are related to more than one national or cultural community. See Elizabeth Ezra and Terry Rowden (ed.), *Transnational Cinema–The Film Reader* (London: Routledge, 2006). It adds a new chapter to important questions on culture and identity that James Clifford raised in works like *The Predicament of Culture–20th Century Ethnography, Literature and Art* (Cambridge: Harvard University Press, 1988).

8   During the last decade, my curatorial attempt in India was also to make exhibition modes of video art in the line of the new narrative matrix. It began in 1999 by showing *Remembering Toba Tek Singh* outside "the white cube" culture of the modern art world in the ancient Indian sculpture section of the Prince of Wales Museum. In 2002, this was explored further at the Apeejay Media Gallery in New Delhi, for their inaugural video exhibition, by leaving the "black box" and spreading the installations all over their empty office complex under the dark evening sky. In 2004, in the exhibition *CC: Crossing Currents–Video Art and Cultural Identity* at the Lalit Kala Galleries in New Delhi, it took on another dimension. Here, 17 video installations were juxtaposed in an open-ended, three-storey architectural setting which created multi-faceted trajectories for the viewers. The "black box" culture was eschewed and the artists were invited to choose a color pertinent to their piece.

9   Gautam Kaul, *Cinema and the Indian Freedom Struggle* (New Delhi: Sterling Publishers, 1998), 9.

10 Graham Coulter-Smith (ed.), *The Visual-Narrative Matrix* (Southampton: Fine Art Research Centre, 2000).

11 Martin Rieser and Andrea Zapp (ed.), *New Screen Media–Cinema/Art/Narrative* (London: British Film Institute, 2002), xxv.

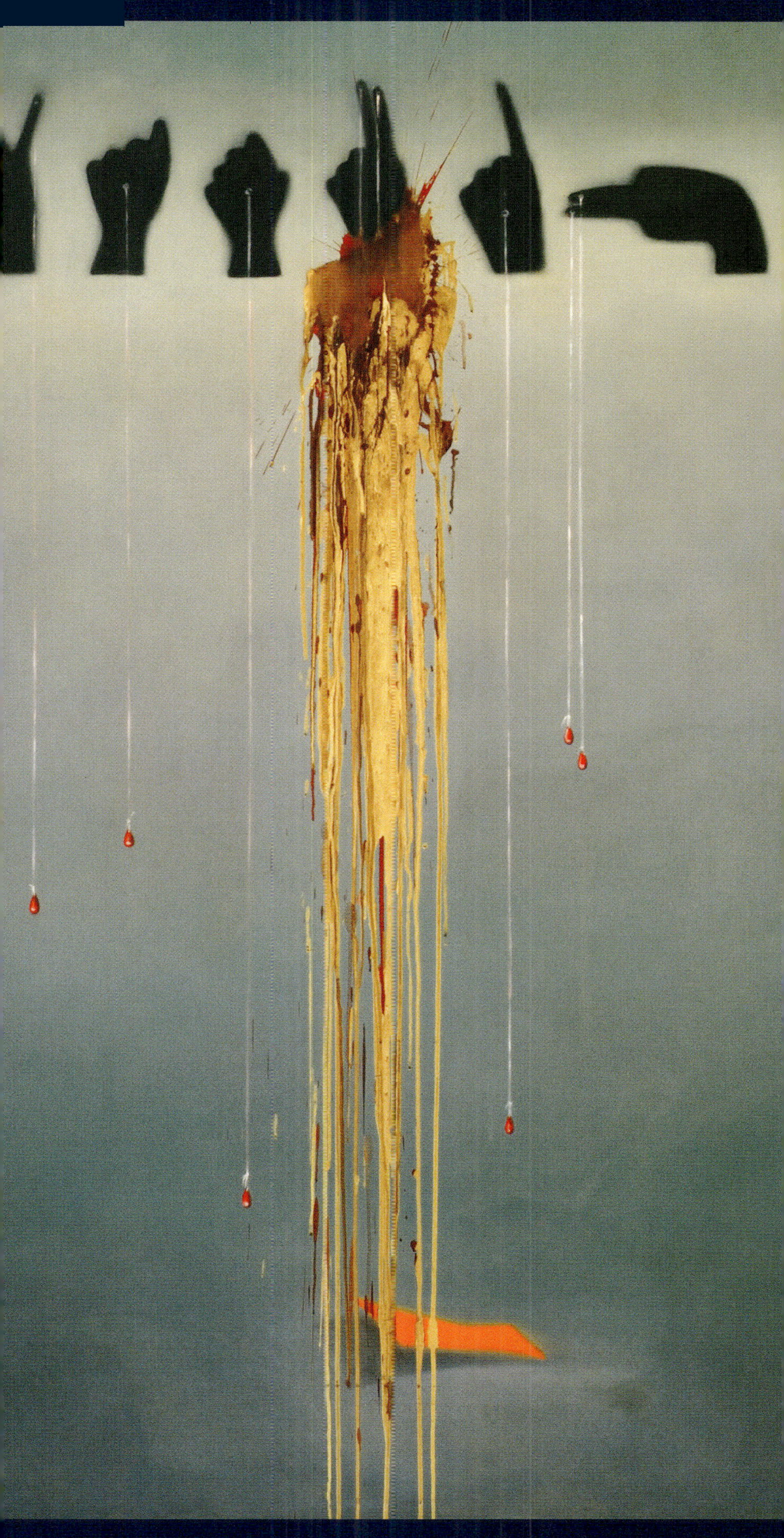

Vasudha Thozhur. *Sanctum*, 2006. Detail, see page 57.

LOOKING INWARD
Narratives of the Self

Gulammohammed Sheikh

•

Arpita Singh

•

Hema Hirani Upadhyay

•

Vivan Sundaram

•

Vasudha Thozhur

•

Jayashree Chakravarty

•

Anju Dodiya

GULAMMOHAMMED SHEIKH

Gulammohammed Sheikh's *Book of Journeys* is itself a journey, one that remains in progress. Progress through time, by its very nature, is narrative. Although episodes may be recorded, progress through one's life is never as linear or orderly—or complete—as one might wish. After all, the autobiographical artist can never illustrate the end of his own life story.

Sheikh was inspired by publications of *The Tale of Genji* and by Chinese scrolls that had been produced in accordion book format. He wanted to explore accordion construction for its potential to allow images to be linked in a continuum that could also be read in multiple (and non-linear) combinations. His idea was that connections between the images would emerge in the process of painting. His stories-within-stories eventually gave way to maps and places-within-places, locating himself using Google Earth for closer and closer magnifications of his home in Vadodara. *Book of Journeys* proceeds with references to momentous times and places important for the artist. Indeed, the book provides Sheikh with the possibility of using different painterly modes to work out different images and ideas. These include an image of the poet Kabir spreading a shroud in front of an approaching angel, an allusion to mountain retreats in Ladakh and maps of the cities of Vadodara and Ahmedabad after the traumatic ethnic genocide in 2002. When India exploded its nuclear device in 1998, Sheikh responded with an image of escape—the packing of a suitcase. Following the invasion of Iraq in 2003, Sheikh appropriated the image of a charging demon from a fifteenth-century folio painting by Turkish artist Siyeh Qalem.

Google Earth may be the artist's cyber tool, but in a sense, Sheikh has used the making of this book as a non-cyber blog (what once would have been

Pages 38–41:
Gulammohammed Sheikh. *Book of Journeys*, 1996 onwards.
Digitally reproduced 36-page bound book in accordion format; inkjet facsimile images on Arches 300 GSM watercolor paper (printing supervised by the artist;) 9.76x10.55 in (when fully extended.)
Collection of the artist, Vadodara.
Scanned from original and printed by Sukhdev Rathod.

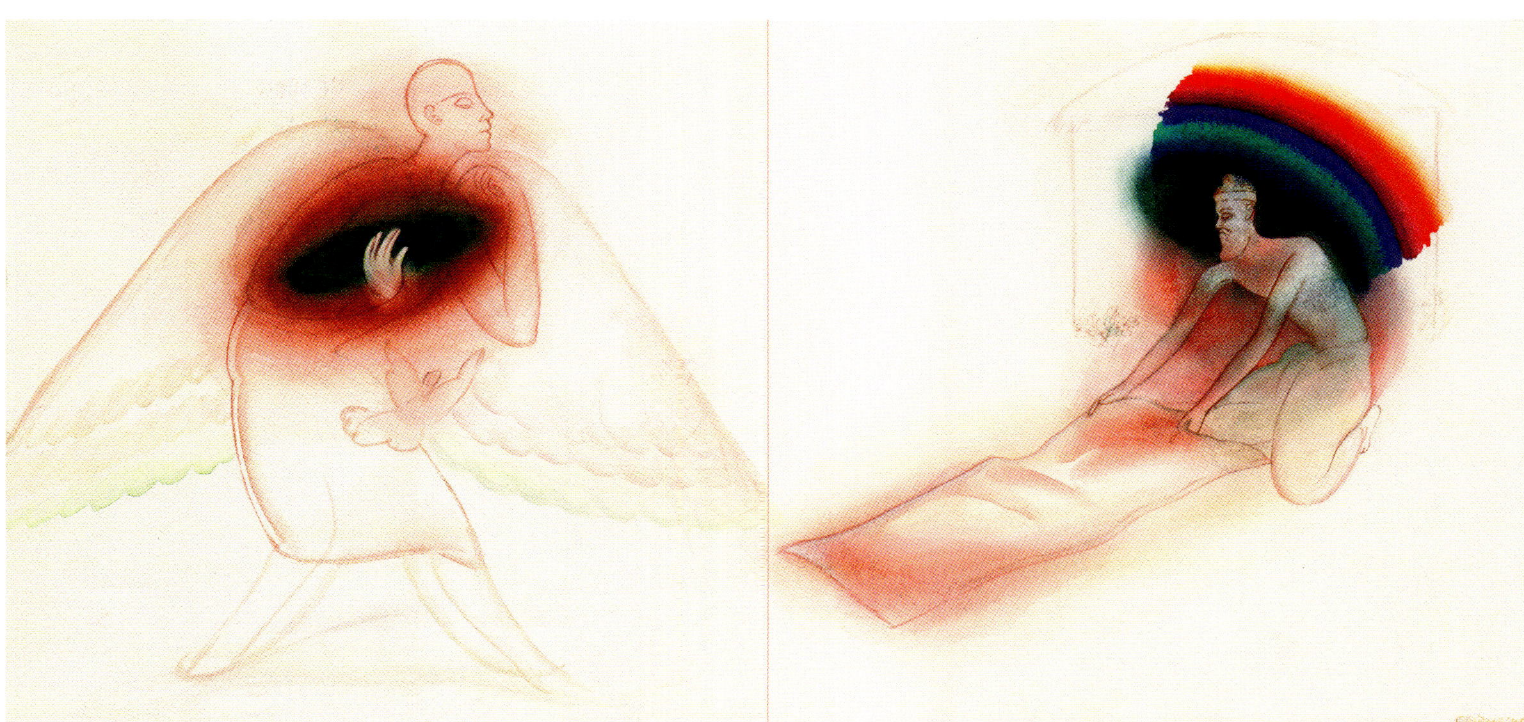

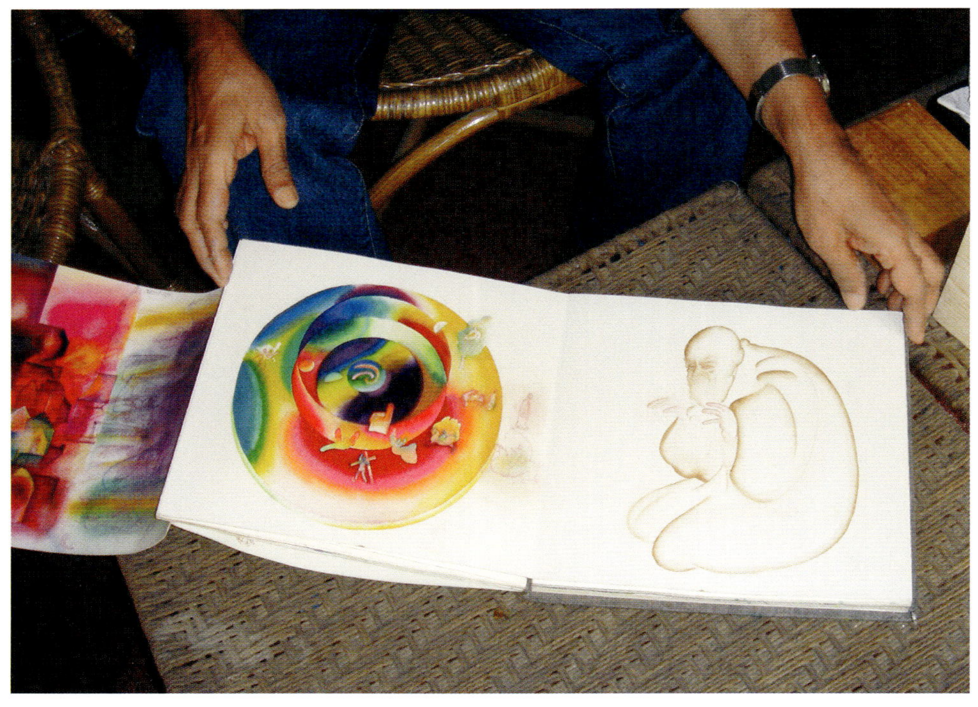

The artist showing *Book of Journeys* to the
author, October 2004.
Photography: Betty Seid.

called a diary). Resonant occurrences, public and political or private and personal, have
influenced the form and content of Sheikh's images, often necessitating changes on
already painted pages. The resilient paper has withstood repeated erasures and re-
painting. He has returned to the first page, uncertain and unresolved from the outset,
to paint a small town reminiscent of his childhood home in a Gujarati village. For
Sheikh, the theme of the multiple journeys of a life, in some way, deals with the idea
of being away, but then returning again and again to the refuge of home.[1]

[Author's note: Because of its being unfinished, Sheikh was reluctant
to release *Book of Journeys* for publication and exhibition. Ultimately, we compromised
and he created a facsimile version using high quality color on heavy watercolor paper.
I believe that *Book of Journeys* is a keystone for thinking about contemporary art from
India, not only for its aesthetic and narrative qualities, but also because it is
Gulammohammed Sheikh's. He has played a vital role in the development of
contemporary art in India, both as artist and teacher. An important chapter (to continue
the book metaphor) begins with him.]

BS

---

1   Gulammohammed Sheikh, "Note on *Book of
     Journeys*" (Vadodara: correspondence with the
     author, 20 October 2006).

ARPITA SINGH

The relationship of Arpita Singh's paintings to textiles, imitating with paint the textile crafts—weaving, stitchery, embroidery, tapestry—fosters a deceptive sense of comfort. In her early years as a designer for the Weavers' Service Centre (Gandhi's mandate that sent designers into villages to keep indigenous textile arts alive), she developed an instinct for repeating forms on her canvases, along with an appreciation for the beauty of ornamentation. Her paintings could be designs for colorful block-printed fabrics that have been tufted into cozy quilts, with animated personal touches embroidered onto the borders. But the rhythm of the repeated elements in Singh's paintings—alphabets, bones, motorcycles, teapots—while adding the lyricism of modern poetry or music (think Gertrude Stein or Philip Glass), might also function as a sort of visible mantra, a means of transporting the artist—and perhaps the viewer—to another level of consciousness.

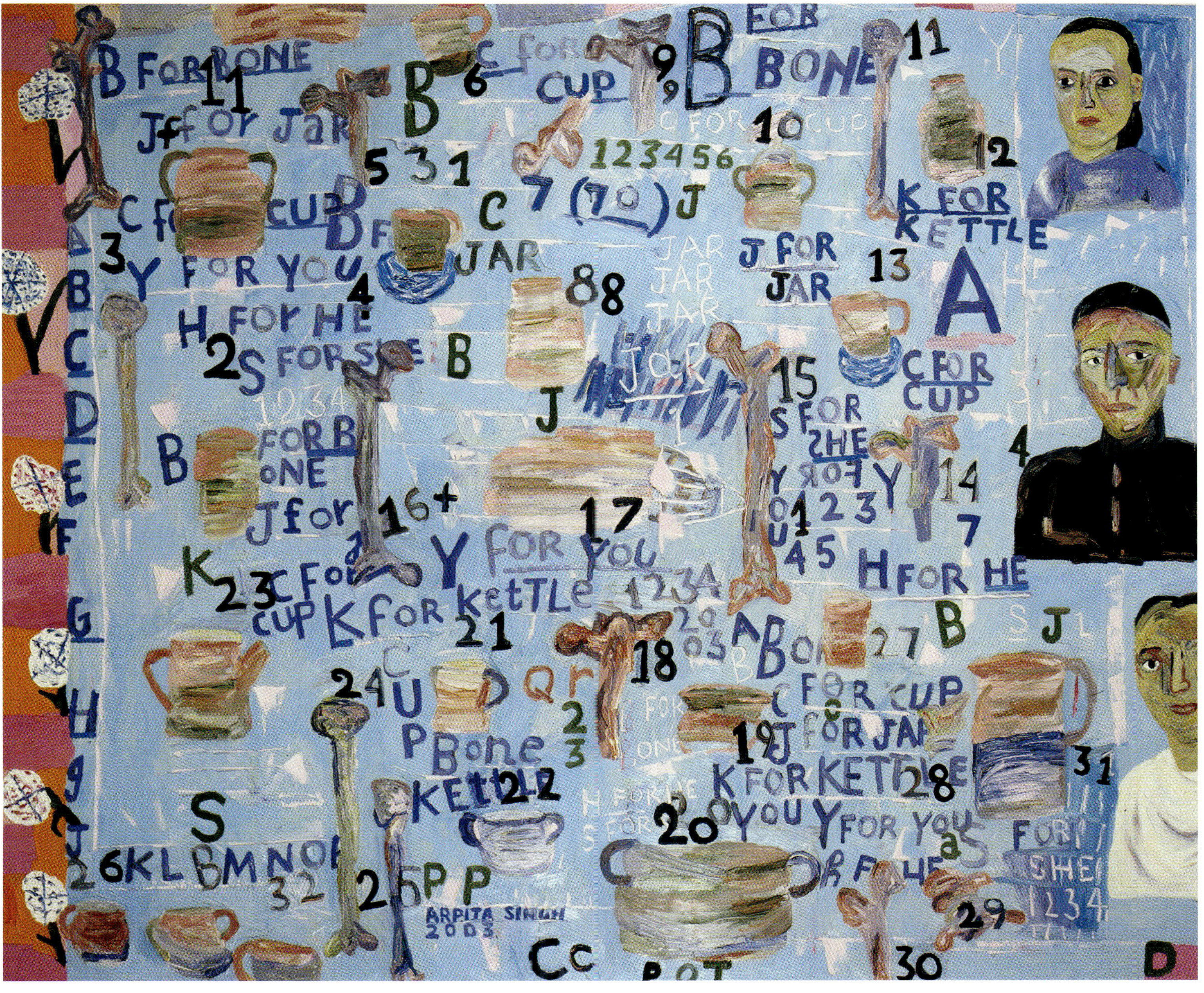

Arpita Singh. *Alphabets*, 2003.
Oil on canvas; 48x60 in.
Collection of Radhika and Rajan Anandan, Bangalore.
Photography: Courtesy of Bose Pacia Gallery and the artist.

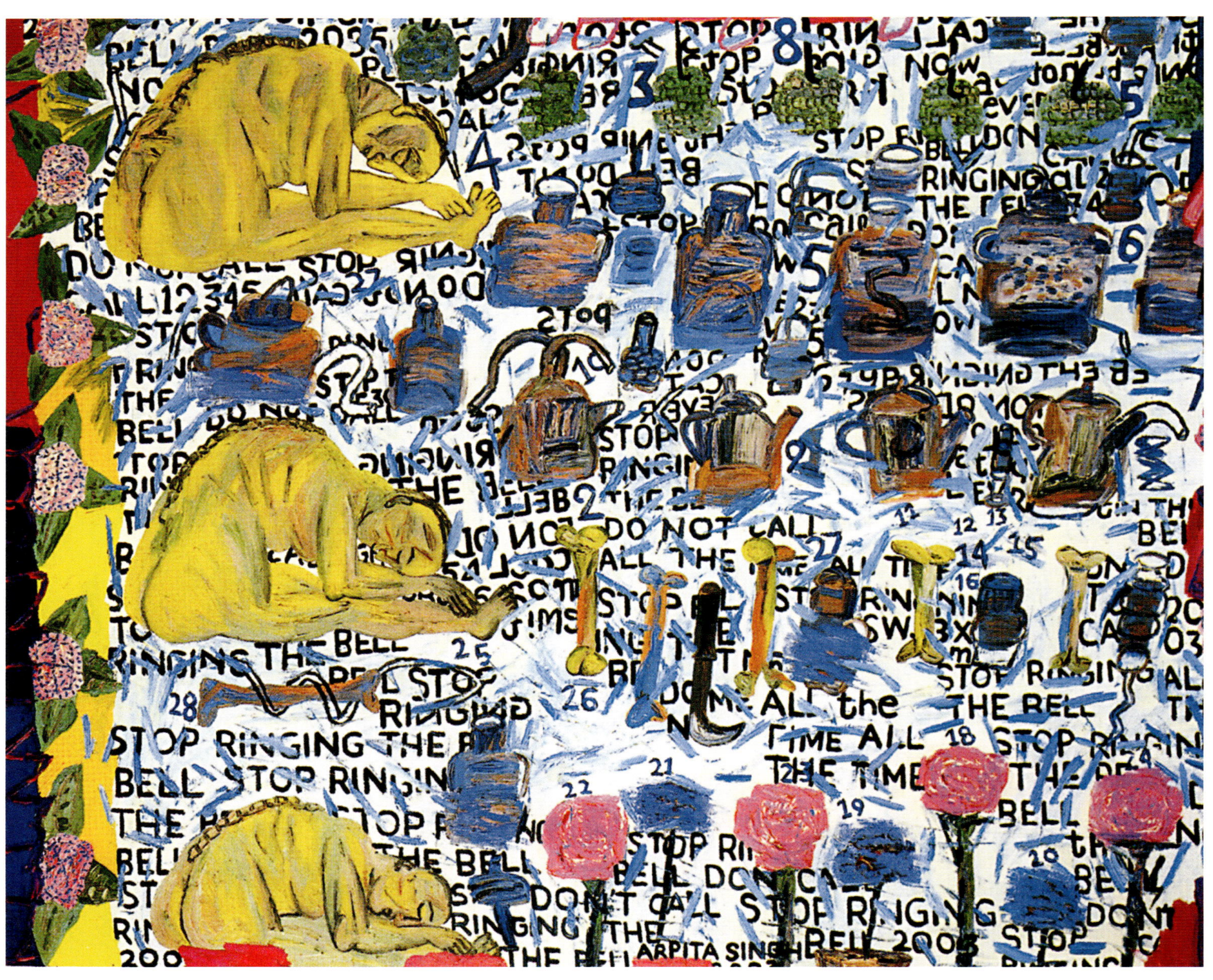

Arpita Singh. *Stop Ringing the Bell,* 2003.
Oil on canvas; 48x60 in.
Private collection.
Photography: Courtesy of Bose Pacia Gallery and
the artist.

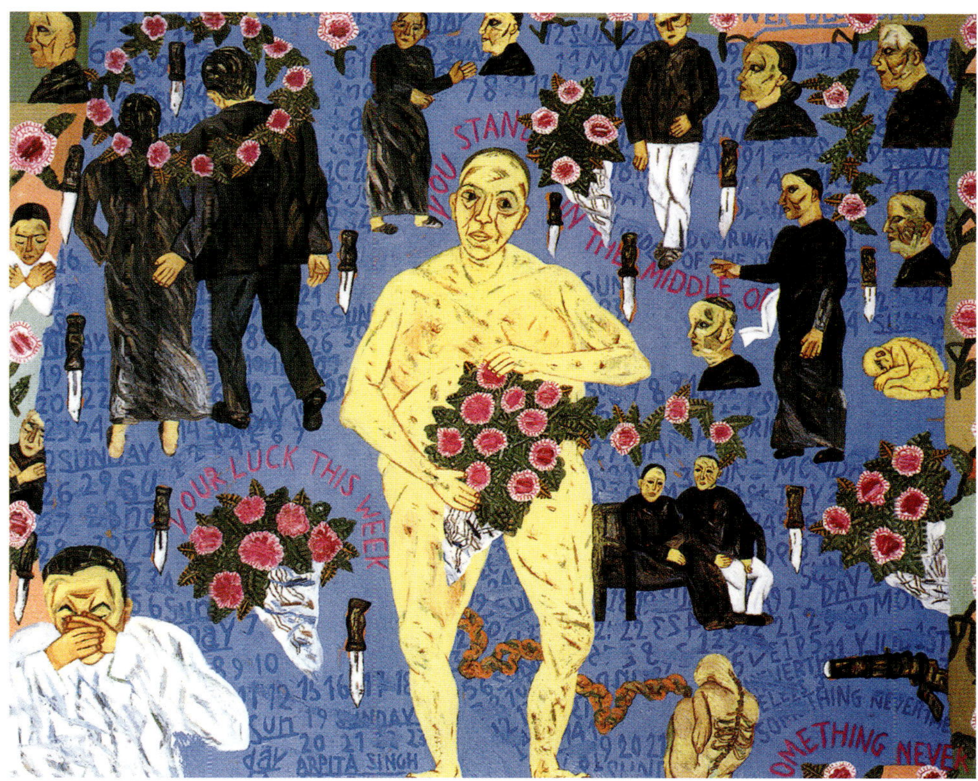

Arpita Singh. *Summer Months*, 2003.
Oil on canvas; 48x60 in.
Private collection.
Photography: Courtesy of Bose Pacia Gallery
and the artist.

To continue the quilt metaphor, the borders of Singh's paintings often contain ancillary forms, like the hem of a quilt where new colors or designs—and perhaps a bit of gold thread—are added. They function narratively like the footnotes in a Nabokov novel, telling a parallel story. Singh has stuffed her paintings with personal information, and like an over-stuffed quilt, the inside sometimes comes spilling out of the edges.

The surface of *Alphabets* resembles a schoolgirl's slate, inscribed with elementary lessons for a future woman, alongside her ABCs and 123s—S for She, H for He, K for Kettle, B for Bone, J for Jar, C for Cup, Y for You. On the right side, three generations of women are depicted, like individually embroidered patches on a *phulkari* (a trousseau textile), suggesting an emotional mother-daughter legacy of knowledge. The left border bears a repeated image of a hot pink and gold landscape in late afternoon light—perhaps a sunset reflected on the hills, seen from a schoolroom window or the dreamy place of escape from the prosaic drudgery of housework. We learn by reading. A narrative is suggested by simply using alphabets and bits of text. A story emerges by picking out keywords.

Summer Months is also filled with a background of words and numbers that suggest, like a calendar, that cycles of weeks and months can frame the narrative of a life. An aureole of text, "you stand in the middle," crowns the older nude woman who covers her belly with a floral bouquet. Her vulnerable body dominates the painting. No longer the blood-red icon of fecundity of Singh's earlier paintings, her flesh is yellow and withering with age. Though she no longer monitors her youthful fertility on a monthly calendar, she reminds us that even an aging woman is subject, like the tides of oceans, to the erotic pull of the moon. [The repeated text reads, "once every month a flower blooms," "your luck this week" and "something never the less."]

Opposite page:
Arpita Singh. *Memory Jars*, 2003.
Oil on canvas; 60x48 in.
Shumita and Arani Bose Collection, New York.
Photography: Courtesy of Bose Pacia Gallery and
the artist.

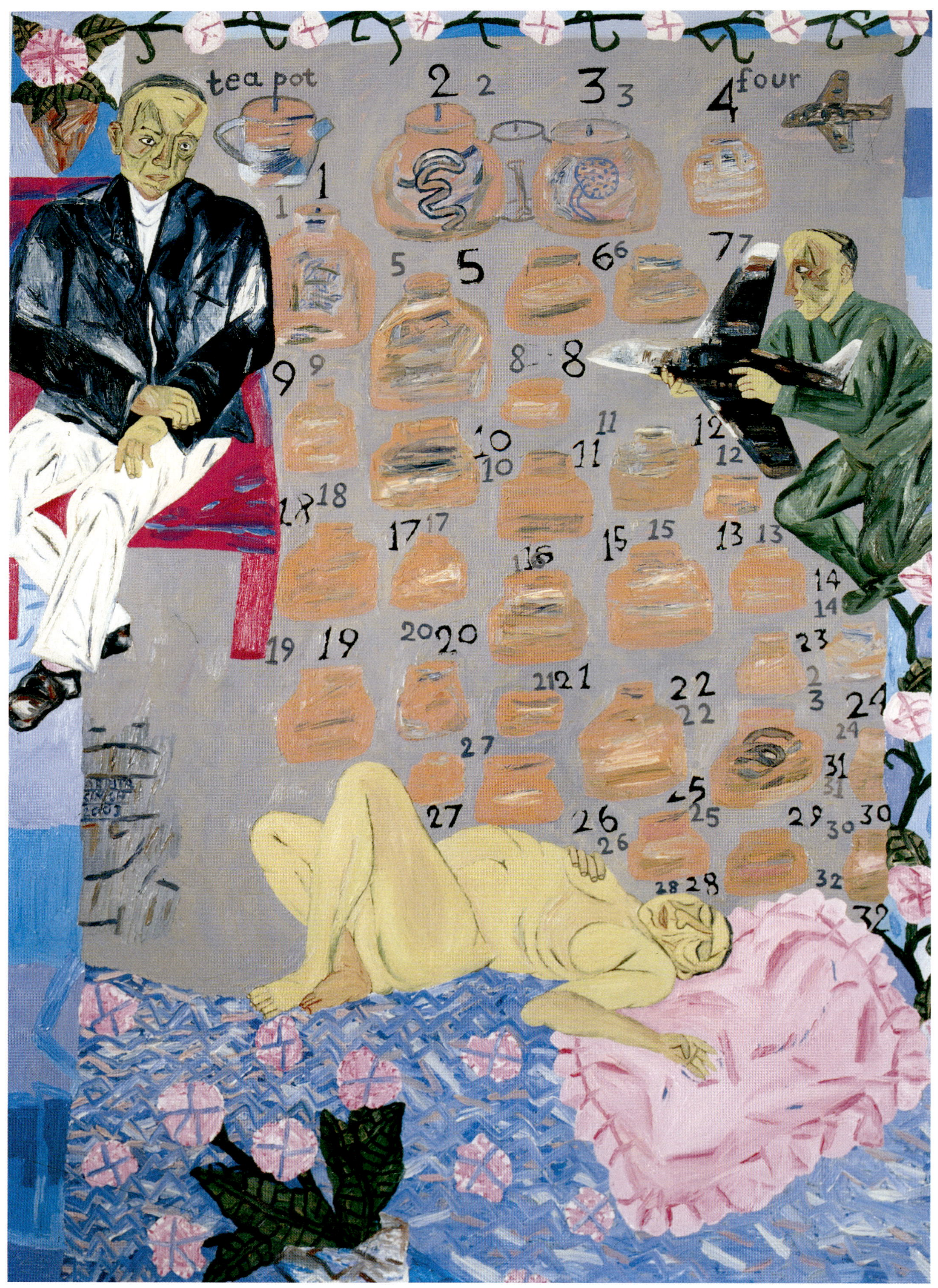

tea pot
2 2 3 3 4 four
1 1
5 5 6 6 7 7
9 9 8 8
10 10 11 11 12 12
18 18 17 17 16 16 15 15 13 13
14 14
19 19 20 20 23 23
21 21 22 22 24 24
27 31 31
27 26 26 25 25 29 30 30
28 28 32 32

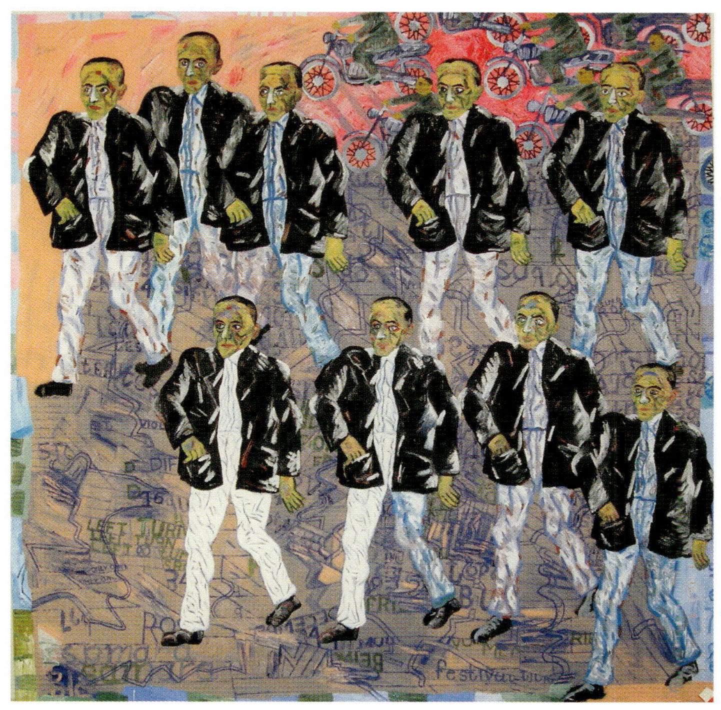

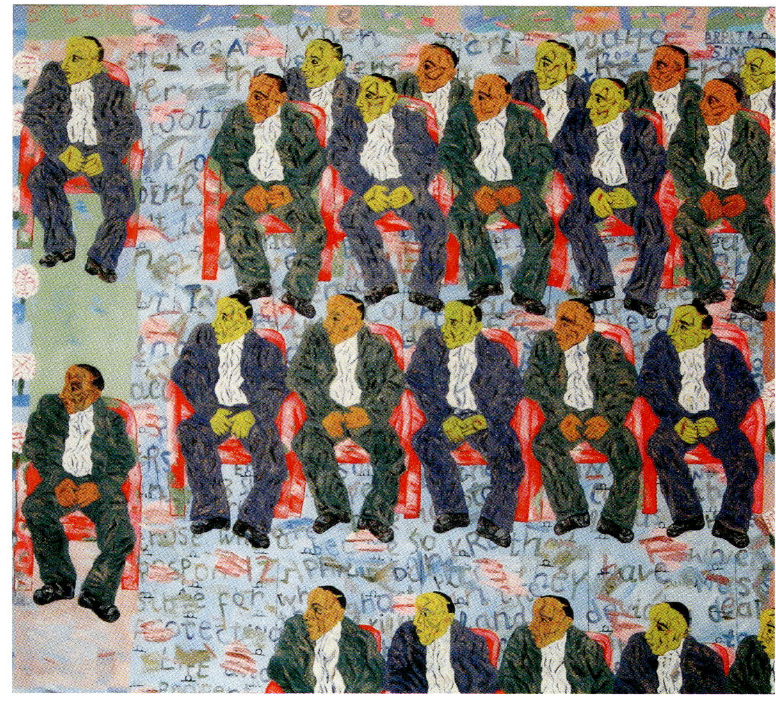

Arpita Singh. *Evening Walk*, 2004.
Oil on canvas; 60x60 in.
Private collection.
Photography: Betty Seid.

Above right:
Arpita Singh. *Watching*, 2004.
Oil on canvas; 60x66 in.
Private collection.
Photography: Betty Seid.

The workings of Singh's mind—memories, fear, pain, love, grief and sadness—swirl around her in bird's-eye perspective. Like dreams or memories, her story is fragmented, allowing the artist or the viewer to construct a narrative. Pieces of a life story emerge: a young couple, haloed with a garland of blossoms, is seemingly blessed (although a dagger dangles forebodingly between them); an older couple shares a bench; a crouching woman (her entrails streaming) is supported by her braid that morphs into her spine. Along with several portrait busts (ancestors, perhaps), two competing objects repeatedly punctuate the background text—rotund pink blossoms and glimmering sharp daggers that could be weapons or surgical instruments. They spar symbolically with each other: female and male, life and death, comfort and foreboding. Here again, like the hem binding on a tapestry, the border bears a supplementary story. The right side is decorative, but death lurks on the left: two corpses, a man and a woman, arms crossed on their chests, are laid out for final rites. In the corner below, a mourner covers his grieving face. If a life can be symbolized by a year, *Summer Months* provides a comfortable time to look both forward and backward, enjoying a final flowering before the onslaught of autumnal darkness and winter death.

Memory Jars is also organized around a cycle of time. In this painting, a single month of a calendar (oddly having 32 days, each day having duplicate numbers) indicating that "all this" will happen again. It serves as a memory cabinet, the mnemonic device used by Medieval and Renaissance scholars, where the means to remembering was to visualize rooms or drawers in a cabinet as individual storage units for a particular idea. Singh has employed jars on a calendar to the same purpose. We are allowed glimpses into only the first three vessels. A teapot stands alone on day one. A large jar with a piece of intestine follows. Another with a flower comes next. We know that the voluptuous dreamer at the bottom of this picture has experienced the contents of each. In contrast to the somber gray calendar and brown jars, she has retreated into a contented dream space, as evidenced by her erotic languor and self-caress on a bright pink ruffled pillow. She has escaped the potentially violent world of

men in suits, with their authoritative attitudes (seated man on the left) or their violent
wars (man with war plane on the right). Her haven is decorated with flowers, stylized
little wheels that indicate continuity.

> . . . I believe that, after all, I am not the first or last human being, I am part of
> a chain.[1]

Evening Walk and *Watching* look like cops, goons, politicians or
lawyers, in their uniforms of conformity. They have become the repeat unit of choice
in two of Singh's paintings from 2004. In earlier paintings, she has used familiar
household objects, but here, her familiars are her bogeys: men in suits. She is
visualizing the enemy and, in so doing, takes away some of *their* power and *her* fears.
"There is a growing sense of danger and insecurity in our society. Life is no longer safe
and it is visible in my paintings."[2] The repetitive uniformity of the figures, whether
strolling with right hands reaching into pockets (for knives or guns?) or seated in red
power chairs, has diffused their threat. The walking men seem benign enough as they
trod what appears to be a gray map that includes directions to turn left and the word
"festivelle." Are they on parade? Closer inspection reveals that the vibrant pink
background is filled with roaring motorcycles, Singh's all-purpose flowers serving as
their wheels, like the roses in the anti-war song *Guns and Roses*. The seated men are
grounded in gibberish, words and alphabets whose story has been lost. They sit, hands
in laps (protecting genitals?), facing expectantly to the left.

Luscious color and thickly applied oil paint might entice the viewer to
think Arpita Singh's paintings are "easy on the eye." But that sensuous skin is just
visual seduction, inviting the viewer to go beyond the surface and delve into the
artist's psyche, to know intimately her emotional state, her fears. "These paintings
reflect the way I am emotionally and spiritually, and accordingly I try to create a
language, a process."[3] Her upbeat color scheme is often in stark contrast with the grim
content of her narrative.

BS

---

1   Arpita Singh quoted in Neville Tuli, *Indian
    Contemporary Painting* (Ahmedabad: Mapin,
    1997), 248.
2   Arpita Singh quoted in Apinan Poshyananda,
    Contemporary Art in Asia: Traditions/Tensions
    (New York: Asia Society, 1996), 41.
3   Arpita Singh quoted in Tuli, 388.

In both of these site-specific works, *This space between you and me* and *Mum-my*, Hema Hirani Upadhyay explores her relationship with her family, filling the "space between" with creative endeavors that strive to close the gap. Using fiber—*ragi*, an indigenous grass, or crochet yarn—to lengthen the umbilicus of her familial connections, the artist weaves a tale of emigration—separation from home—with and without choice. Her parents were forced to leave Pakistan; she chose, in turn, to leave them for the life of an artist in Mumbai. In both cases, striving to locate and affirm her identity is the subtext.

Letters have long been a form of narrative, with their tales of travel, youthful adventure, revelations of love and romance, and longing for home. Beyond being a means of merely "staying in touch," they provide opportunities for emotional openness that might not be comfortable in face-to-face (or voice-to-voice) communications. A letter does the same thing as a telephone. It connects people who are not currently sharing physical space. The difference is time. Time adds several luxurious features that are missing in the use of a phone: thoughtfulness in composing the message, the physical materiality of a writing implement and paper, the lack of an immediate response. A letter is not a conversation.

Pages 48–49:
Hema Hirani Upadhyay. *This space between you and me*, 2002.
Photo documentation of site-specific installation using *ragi*, dimensions variable.
Collection of the artist, Mumbai.
Photography: Courtesy of the artist.

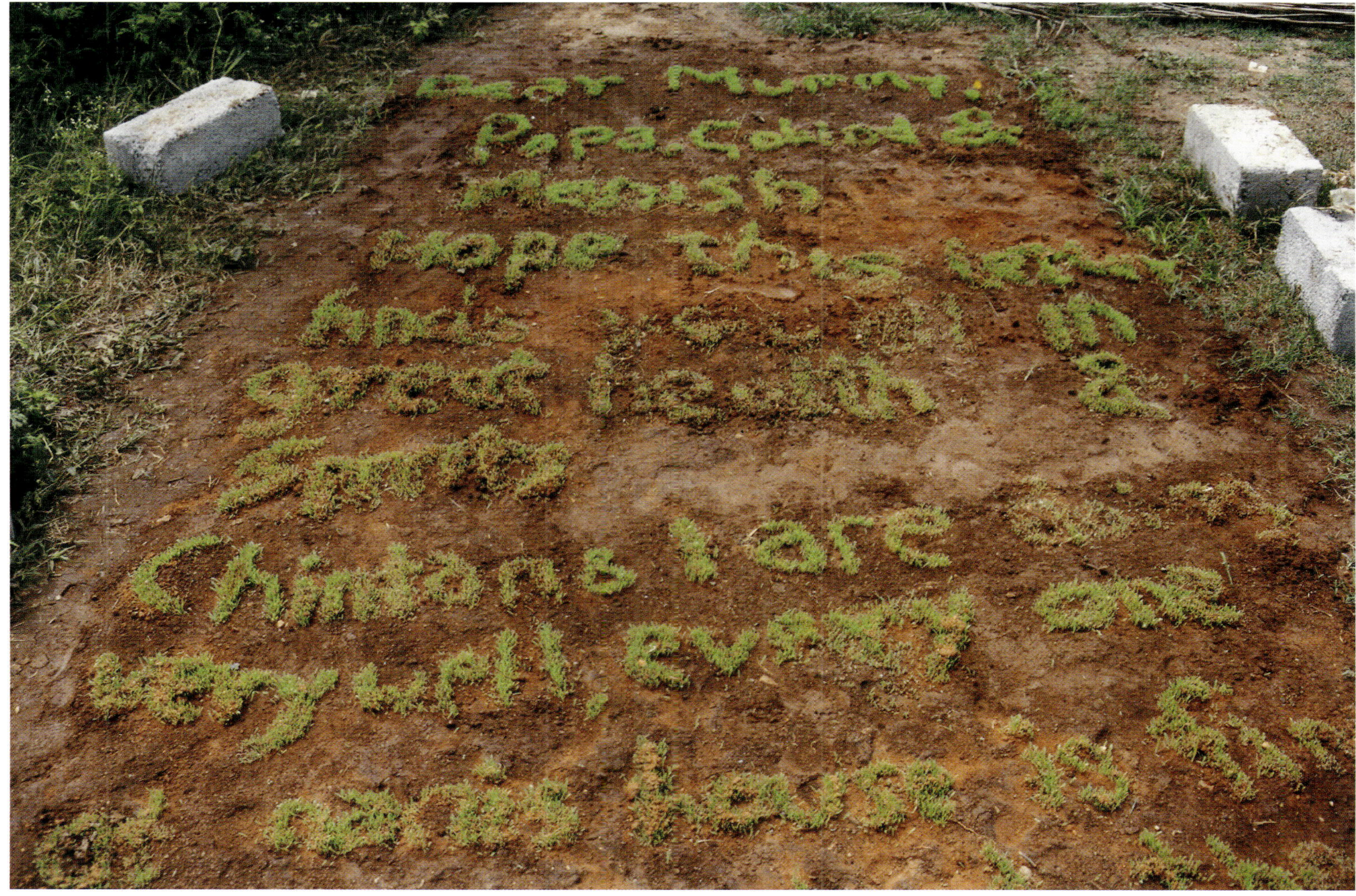

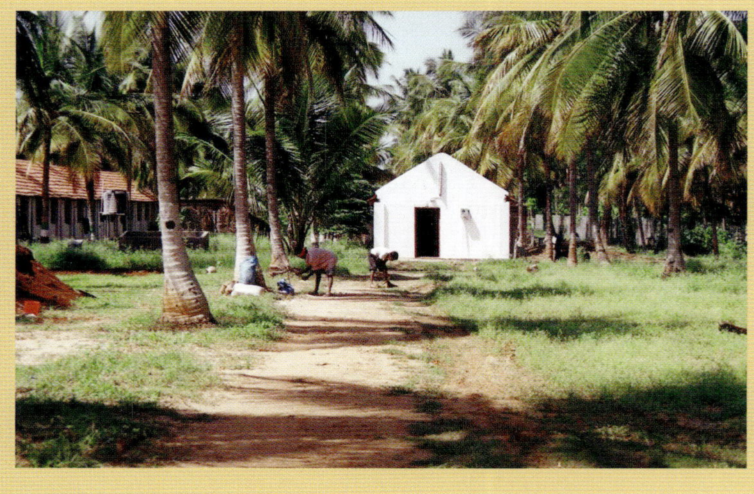
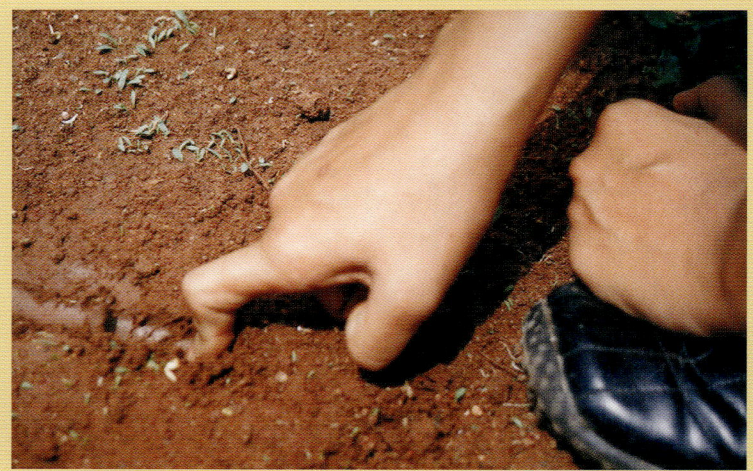
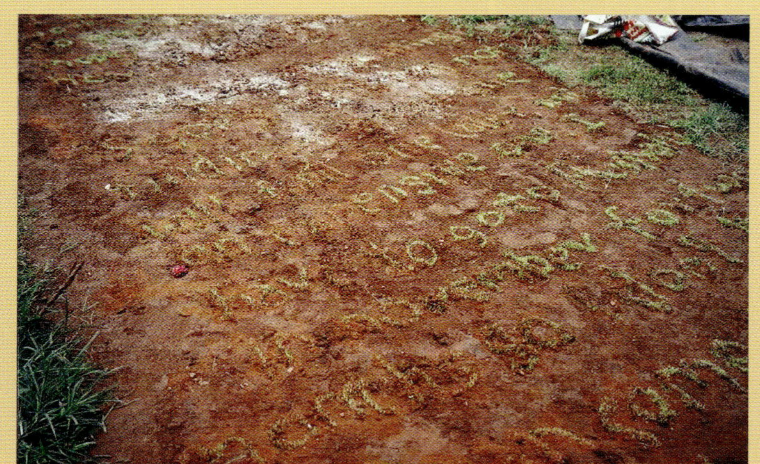
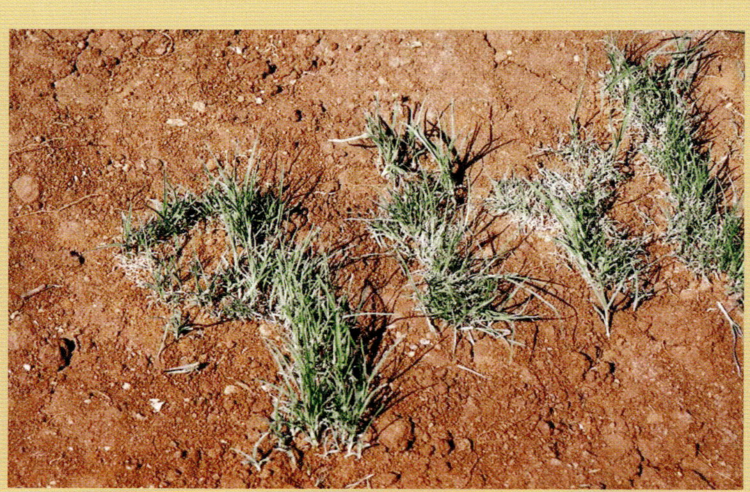
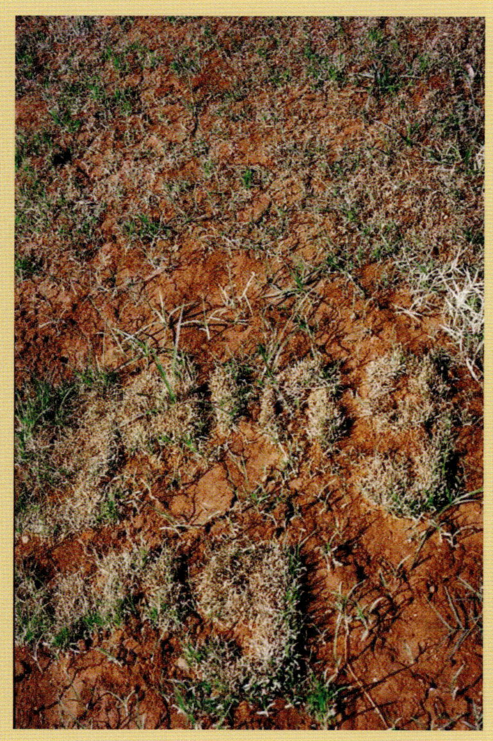
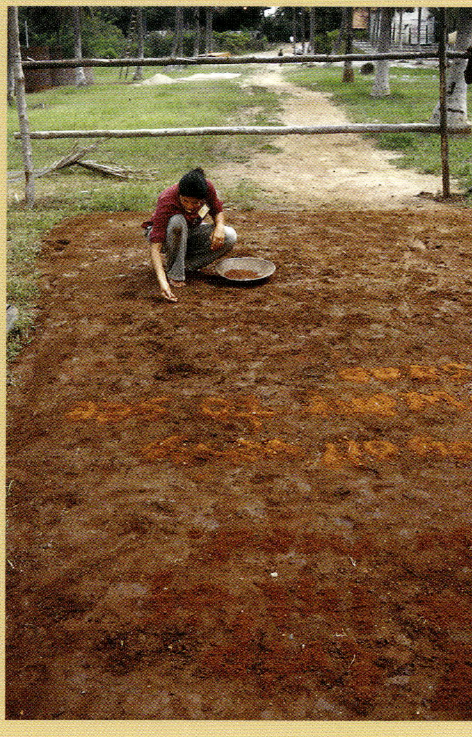
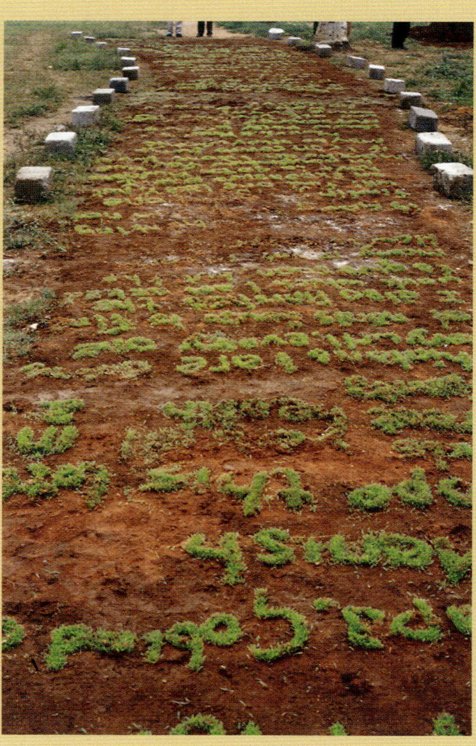

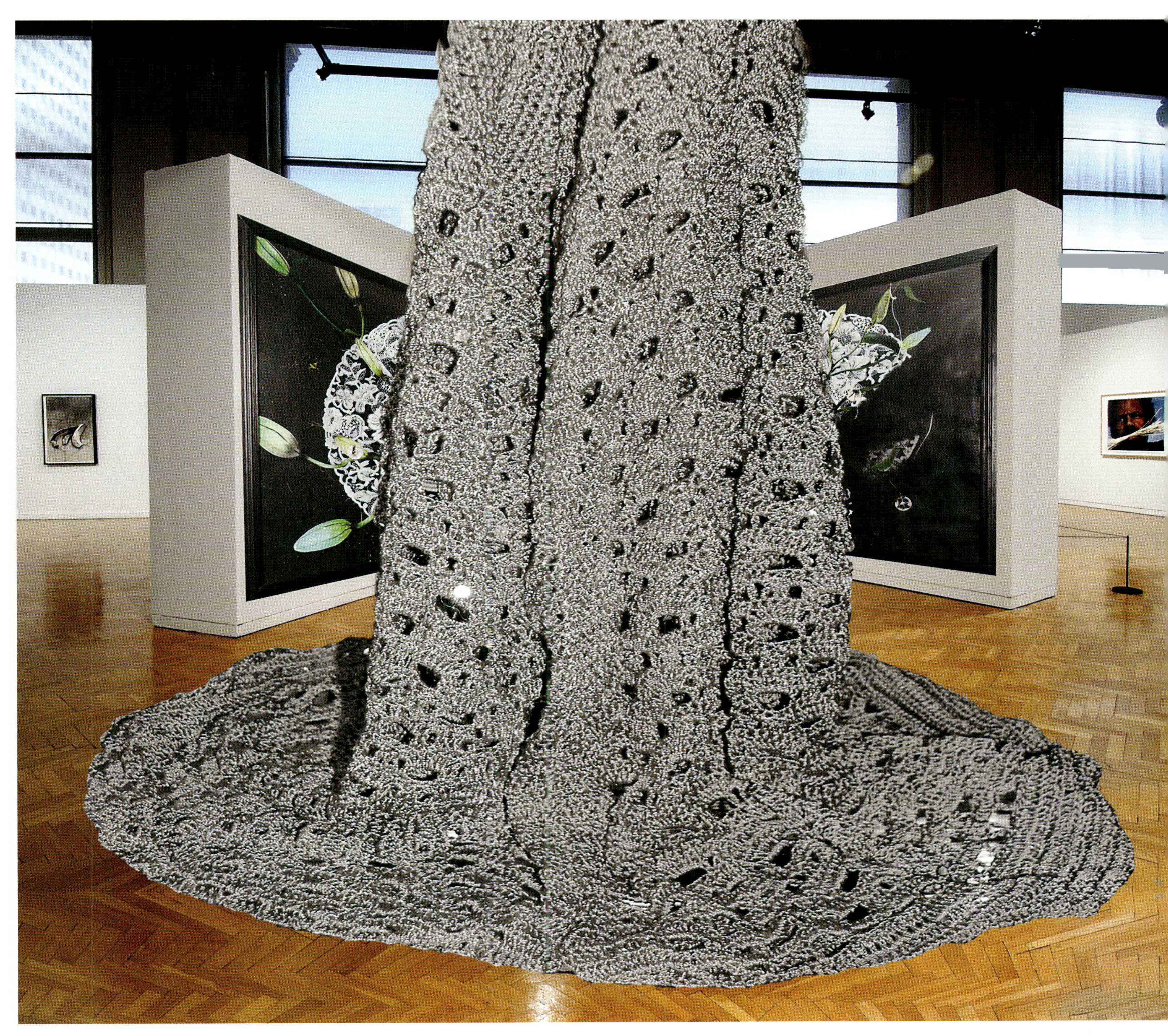

Hema Hirani Upadhyay and Bina Hirani.
Mum-my, 2007.
Installation of four works on paper: acrylic,
gouache, dry pastels, graphite and photographs;
chandelier and cotton thread crochet; size variable.
Courtesy of the artists, Mumbai.
Photography: Courtesy of the artists.

Upadhyay had never written a letter to her parents prior to her participation in the Khoj International Artists Workshop in 2002. As a child of the media age, she connected with them via telephone wires (or cable, to continue the linear metaphor), but more likely via mobile phone satellite transmissions. With the Khoj project, in an outdoor space near Mysore, Upadhyay chose to "plant" a letter home on a path that led to a small white house (an obvious metaphor). Recognizing that connections to one's family are akin to one's connection to the earth, she opted for a medium that would need nurturing in order to survive. Using *ragi* seeds for ink and the earth itself for paper, she laboriously inscribed each letter with her finger in dampened ground, and into each crevice she planted her message. There was, of course, the risk that her words would never sprout. With constant care the message eventually did surface; however, it would ultimately disappear . . . return to the earth.

Mum-my further extends the artist's desire to fill "the space between . . ." Here she has collaborated creatively with her mother, Bina Hirani, creating a home-like environment—with a rug on the floor, pictures on the wall, a handcrafted tablecloth—in a place neither of them knows, an exhibition hall in Chicago. The thread of connection is more obvious: the mother's hand has created a crocheted cloth to protect her daughter's painted carpet. Upadhyay recalls that after marrying, her mother used crocheting not only to keep herself busy, but also as a means of distraction from disturbing issues. She would drift into her own world, appearing at peace with herself. But her daughter believes that her mother's surface serenity merely masked the deep roots of an active mind.

In her work, Upadhyay has nurtured her very personal story to the surface, using metaphoric materials and processes that imply blanketing or covering (a bed of grass, a tablecloth, a carpet), but she is always aware of the roots that support her efforts.

BS

VIVAN SUNDARAM

The passage of time gives a natural chronological flow to personal narrative. But what if one could shuffle the deck a bit, have people meet at different points in their lives? What adult child has not wanted to go back and rewrite his family history—whether to change the course of events, work out unresolved family issues, or merely imagine how it might have been if things had been just a tad different? In the fertile mind of an artist, with access to the photo archive of his esteemed family and the latest Adobe Photoshop software, this sort of narrative manipulation allows for the creation of inventive—albeit ghoulish—collaborative picture-making. Like a god in Hindu mythology controlling the great cycles of time, Vivan Sundaram has shifted his family lineage out of chronological linearity. Yet, at the same time, he wants the viewer to know that he is the ultimate entry in this venerated lineage of artists.

The artist is the nephew of Amrita Sher-Gil (1913–41), the first professional woman artist in India and one of the country's earliest modernists. She died tragically in the prime of her career. Sundaram's grandfather was Umrao Singh Sher-Gil (1870–1954), an aristocratic Renaissance man whose avocation was photography. Over a period of about sixty years he produced approximately eighty

Vivan Sundaram. *Sisters Apart*, 2001.
Digital photomontage; 15x14.4 in.
Courtesy of Walsh Gallery, Chicago.
Photography: Courtesy of the artist.

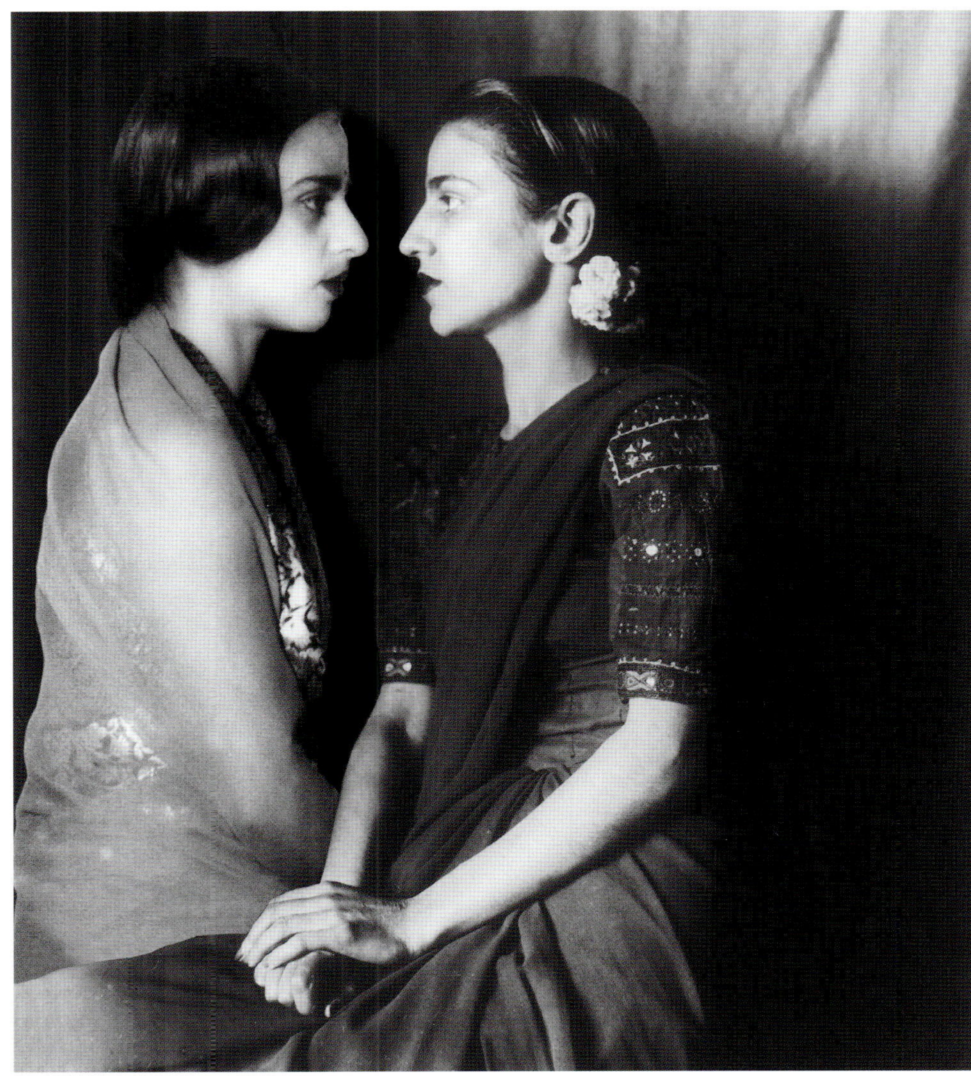

Opposite page:
Vivan Sundaram. *Father-Daughter*, 2001.
Digital photomontage; 19x14 in.
Courtesy of Walsh Gallery, Chicago.
Photography: Courtesy of the artist.

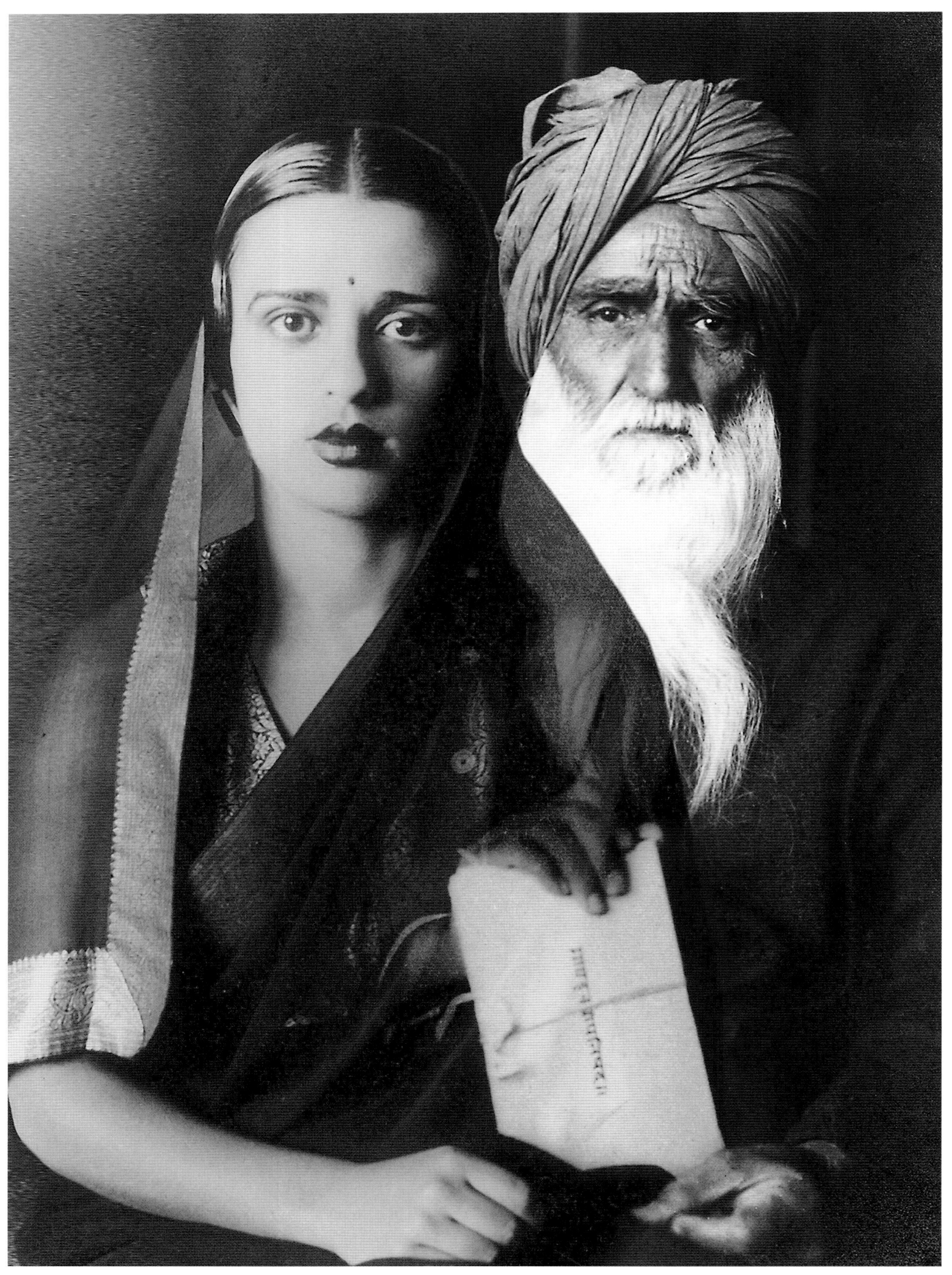

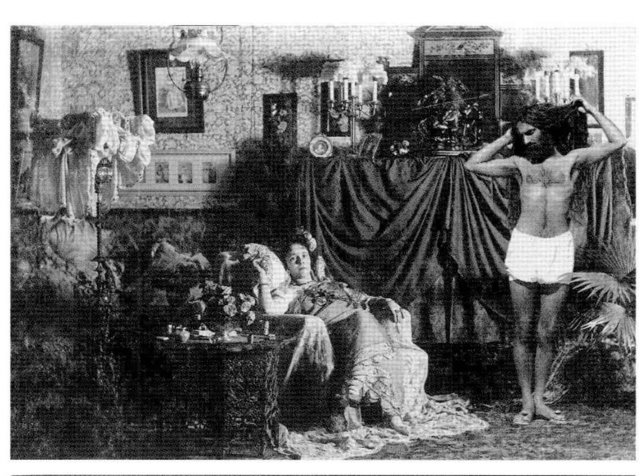
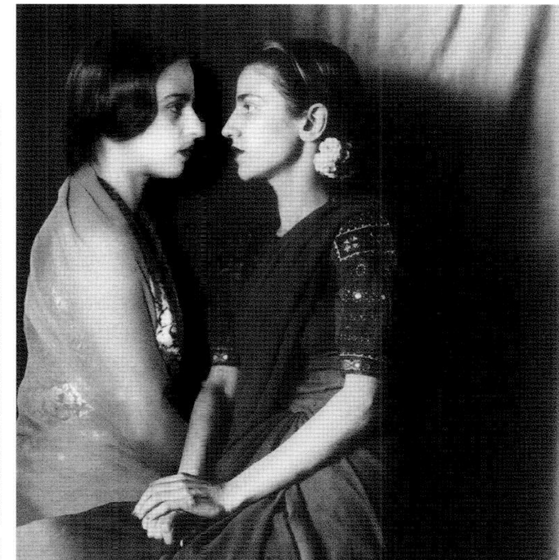
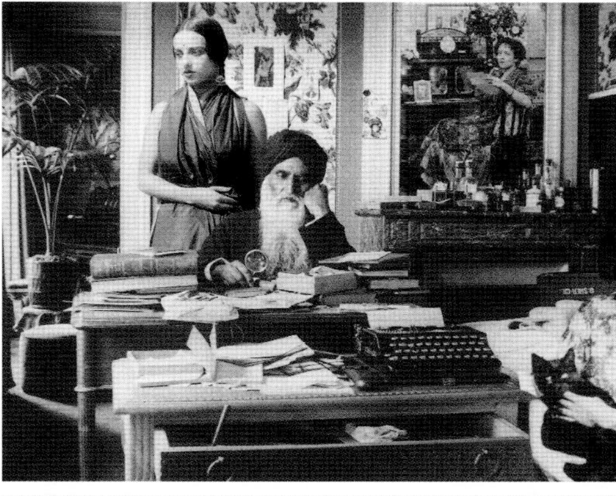
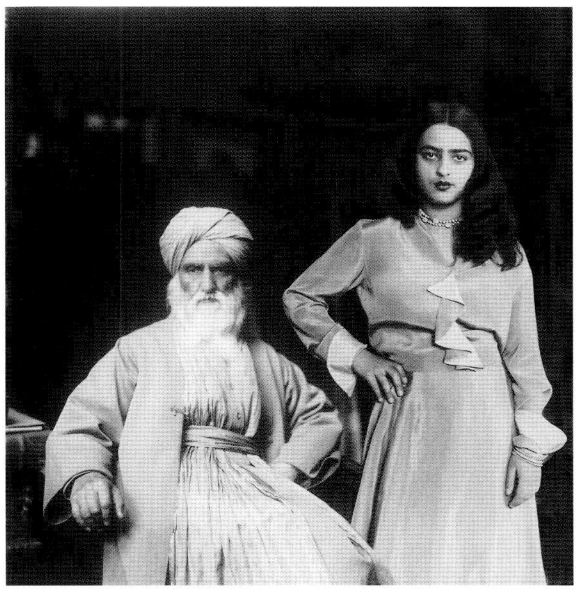
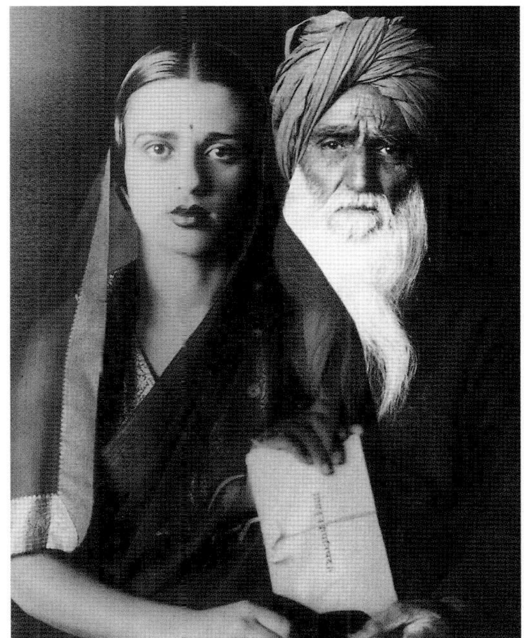
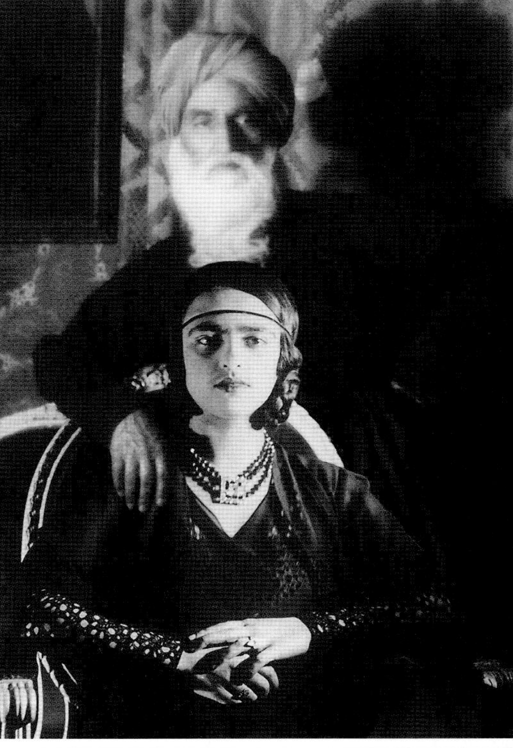
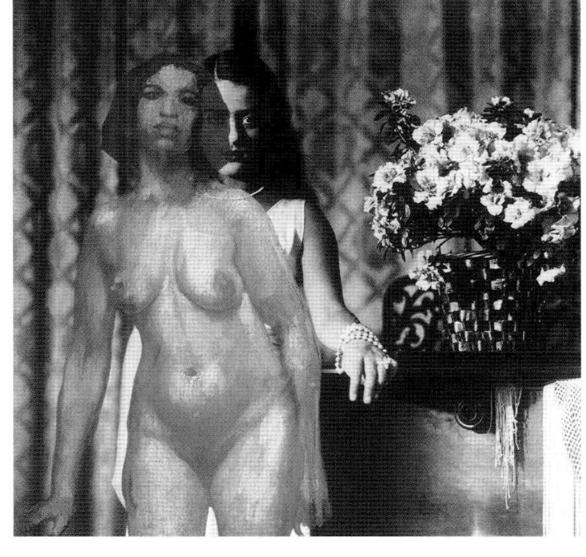
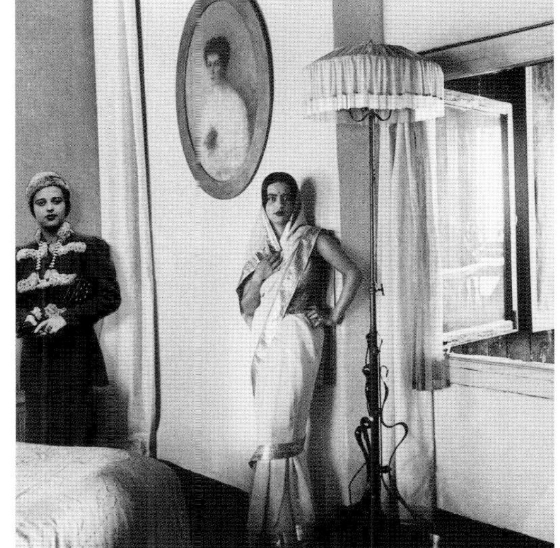
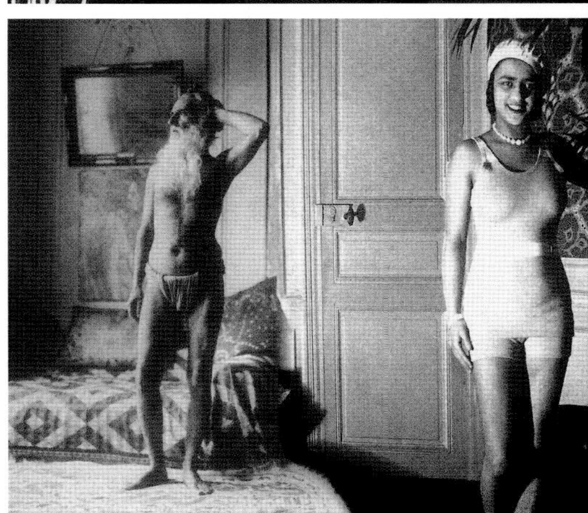

self-portraits. His self-inspections bordered on extreme narcissism, but capture nonetheless his proud physical being, intellect, moods and aesthetic talents. Sher-Gil's European wife, Marie Antoinette, and daughters, Amrita and Indira (Sundaram's mother) were often posed before his camera.

Sundaram has been involved with what he calls the Sher-Gil project for more than thirty years. Visually placing himself as observer and prominent member of this artistic and intellectual family, Sundaram wants the viewer to know that he is now the artistic director of this narrative lineage. It is from Amrita that he wishes to draw his private family tree, making it photographically possible in a "twinning" faux mirror image of his mother and his aunt. (Had they been twins, he would be genetically even closer to Amrita.)

Earlier in his career, Sundaram documented the Sher-Gils with paint. But his motive in *Re-take of Amrita* is much more intimate. "I see seduction as central to these images."[1] "I enter the space of the Sher-Gil homes to explore and amplify the family scenario, and then make them enact (and re-enact) a moment under my direction."[2] These re-enactments seem more tabloid than tableau, with images of his four-person cast pasted into impossible settings. Sundaram has defied time and space by visually suggesting the coexistence of youth and age, life and death. He has also disrupted rules of familial propriety in a sensational manner, by digitally "coupling" (the artist's word of choice)[3] his virile grandfather with his nubile aunt. Could the artist be the imagined product of this Adobe-contrived incest?

BS

---

1 Vivan Sundaram, *Re-take of Amrita: Digital photomontages* based on *photographs by Umrao Sher-Gil (1870–1954) and photographs from the Sher-Gil Family Archive* (New Delhi: Tulika Books, 2001), 50.

2 Vivan Sundaram, quoted in "A Re-take of the Sher-Gil Archive: Stills from 'Amrita,' 2001," http://www.gallerychemould.com/vivan.htm.

3 Vivan Sundaram, quoted in "A Re-take of the Sher-Gil Archive: Stills from 'Amrita,' 2001," http://www.gallerychemould.com/vivan.htm.

"
I see seduction

as central
"
to these images.

Vasudha Thozhur

Some symbols are obvious, others, obscure suggestions in Vasudha Thozhur's self-referential, multiple-panel paintings. All are revelations of her inner and outer self, her personal history narrated in symbols. Adding an overlay of political commentary, she addresses the plight of women, the caste system, religious riots. They all find their way on to Thozhur's canvases in both subtle and unsubtle symbolic form.

"Untouchable" is a politically charged word in India. Beyond the obvious focus on those beneath the caste system, Thozhur uses that association to represent "other forms of marginalization . . . [and] subordination . . . My focus is on the idea of the untouchable as someone falling outside the hierarchy . . . but useful as [one] who provides access to the darker . . . forces of life."[1] She might just mean an artist, i.e., herself.

The first panel of *Untouchable* is formatted to look like a letter, but without legible words; it could be easily mistaken for a page of music. The artist has deliberately made it inscrutable. Yet, that very inscrutability is embellished with precious media—vermillion and gold. The two most powerfully narrative images in this group of four panels are those that deal with loss and purification. Thozhur has exchanged her own face and body for that of a man in a newspaper image that she saw after the Gujarat earthquake in 2001. Thus, she is seen having *her* head shaved in preparation for rituals of death and mourning. The artist has borrowed this image of grief and made it personal—widowhood and the shaving of one's head is associated with a loss of sexuality. A disembodied leg floats in the final panel, an image also inspired by a news story. A girl, crushed under architectural debris, scratched a message on her leg to her would-be rescuers that she wished to be "let go." [Hindi: "Don't stop the one who is going."]

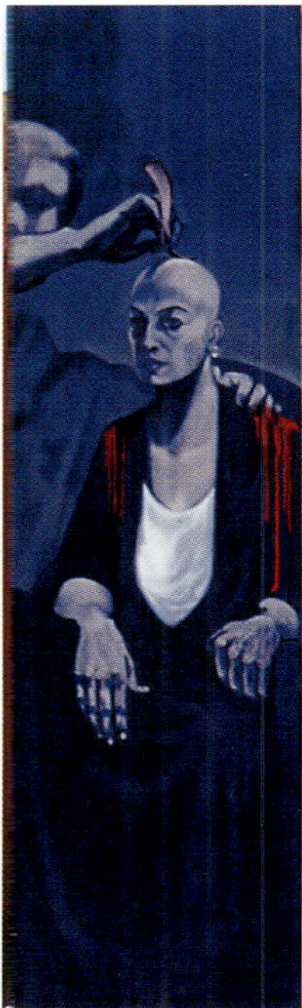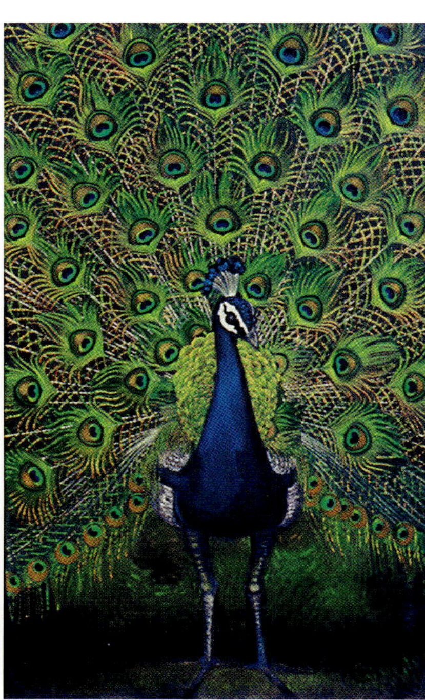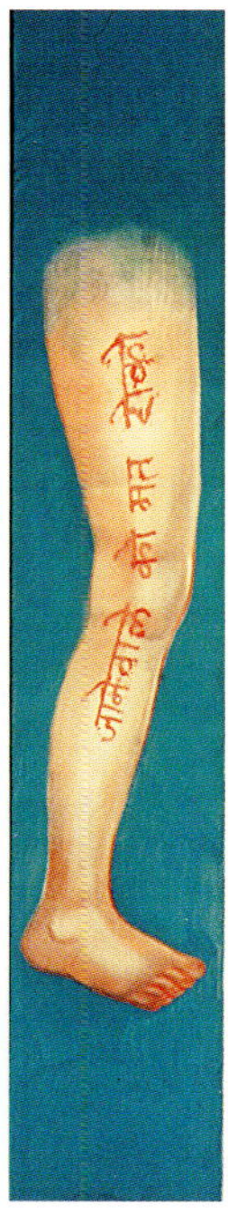

Vasudha Thozhur. *Untouchable*, 2002–3. Oil on canvas; 96x132 in, all four panels. Collection of Neville Tuli, New Delhi. Photography: Courtesy of the artist.

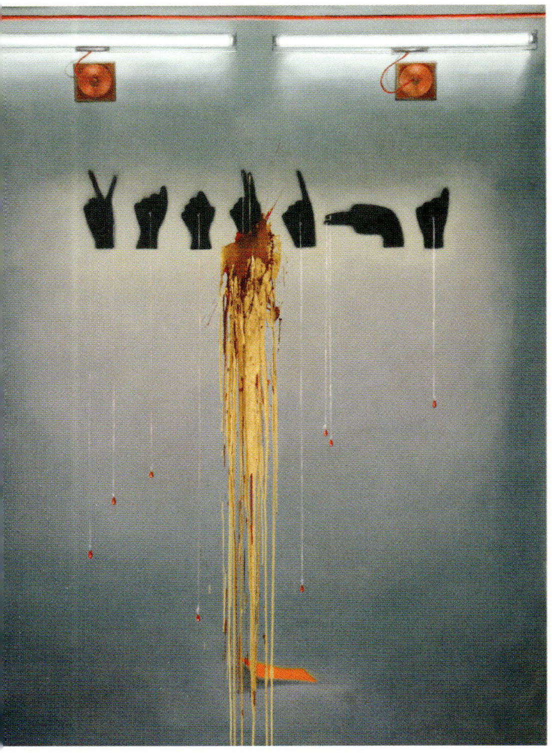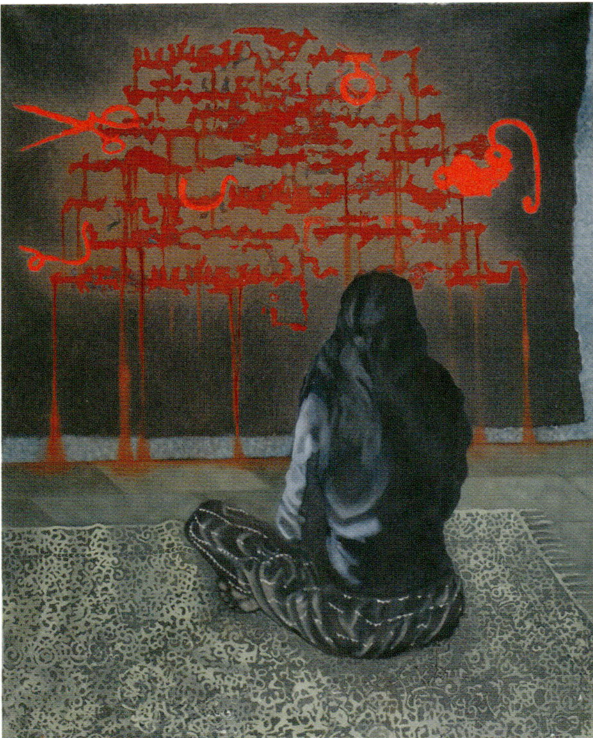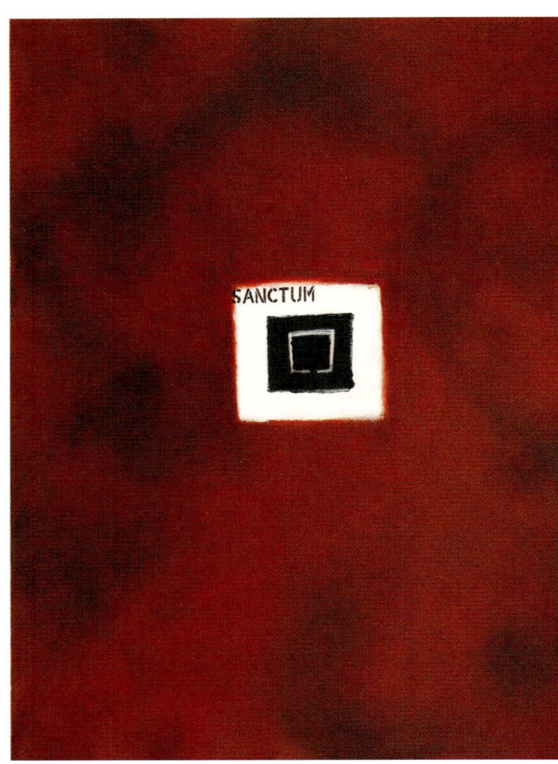

The peacock, national bird of India, a preening male that dominates the Indian terrain, also dominates the four *Untouchable* panels. Using an intentional cliché, the artist implies that the issues of loss and marginalization go beyond personal pain and should be addressed nationally.

With her triptych, *Sanctum*, Thozhur has revisited a youthful desire to find a personal sanctuary in art. In the central panel, she has depicted herself sitting meditatively. The wall she faces is marked by red paint suggesting spat betel juice, some writing (again inscrutable) and various graphic symbols. Flanking that panel on the left, the artist has spelled out her own name with hand signs. Then, with dualistic purpose, she has desecrated that panel (again the betel spittle) and simultaneously rescued it with a worshipful addition of gold. Her ultimate peace is found in the eponymous "Sanctum" panel on the right, where she merges two cherished memories from her art student days: one, looking at architectural plans of Hindu temples in which the innermost sanctum, obscured in reality by exterior structure, becomes serenely available; and two, bringing that association to the viewing of Mark Rothko paintings at the Tate Gallery in London.[2]

BS

Vasudha Thozhur. *Sanctum*, 2006.
Triptych, oil on canvas; 84.25x67 in each panel.
Courtesy of the artist, Vadodara.
Photography: Himanshu Pahad.

---

1   Vasudha Thozhur, notes on *Sanctum* and *Untouchable*, 11 September 2006.

2   Vasudha Thozhur, notes on *Sanctum* and *Untouchable*, 11 September 2006.

Jayashree Chakravarty

Jayashree Chakravarty's *Personal Space* recalls of the scrolls unrolled by storytellers to illustrate mythical—and now contemporary—tales in her native Bengal. On her monumental scrolls of glue-stiffened paper, patched and painted on both sides, she maps a narrative of personal journey. At the same time, she invites the viewer to be guided along paths she has delineated on their multilayered surface. They are painted in an earthy neutral palette, luminously punctuated with white and seemingly random bursts of gold. We are easily enticed to enter.

Monumentality here comes not merely from sheer height and dimension, but also from the organic layering of material and imagery. Graphic markings enliven Chakravarty's topography. They appear to be directional—recognizable names of streets and lanes, railroad lines and waterways—but just as often are radio circuit boards, arbitrary graffiti, a jagged readout of an EKG, calligraphic meanderings and even guidance for New Age self-improvement. Physical roads for Chakravarty are emblematic of life's path. Human circulatory and nervous systems are suggested as equivalent to the roads we need to navigate her lush semiotic forest—easy to enter, difficult to leave. In fact, the symbolic body is present in an occasional

Jayashree Chakravarty. *Personal Space*, 2003.
Acrylic and glue on multilayered paper and
fabric; 11x42 ft. and 11x16 ft.,
installation space, variable.
Courtesy of the artist, Kolkata.
Photography: Sunny.

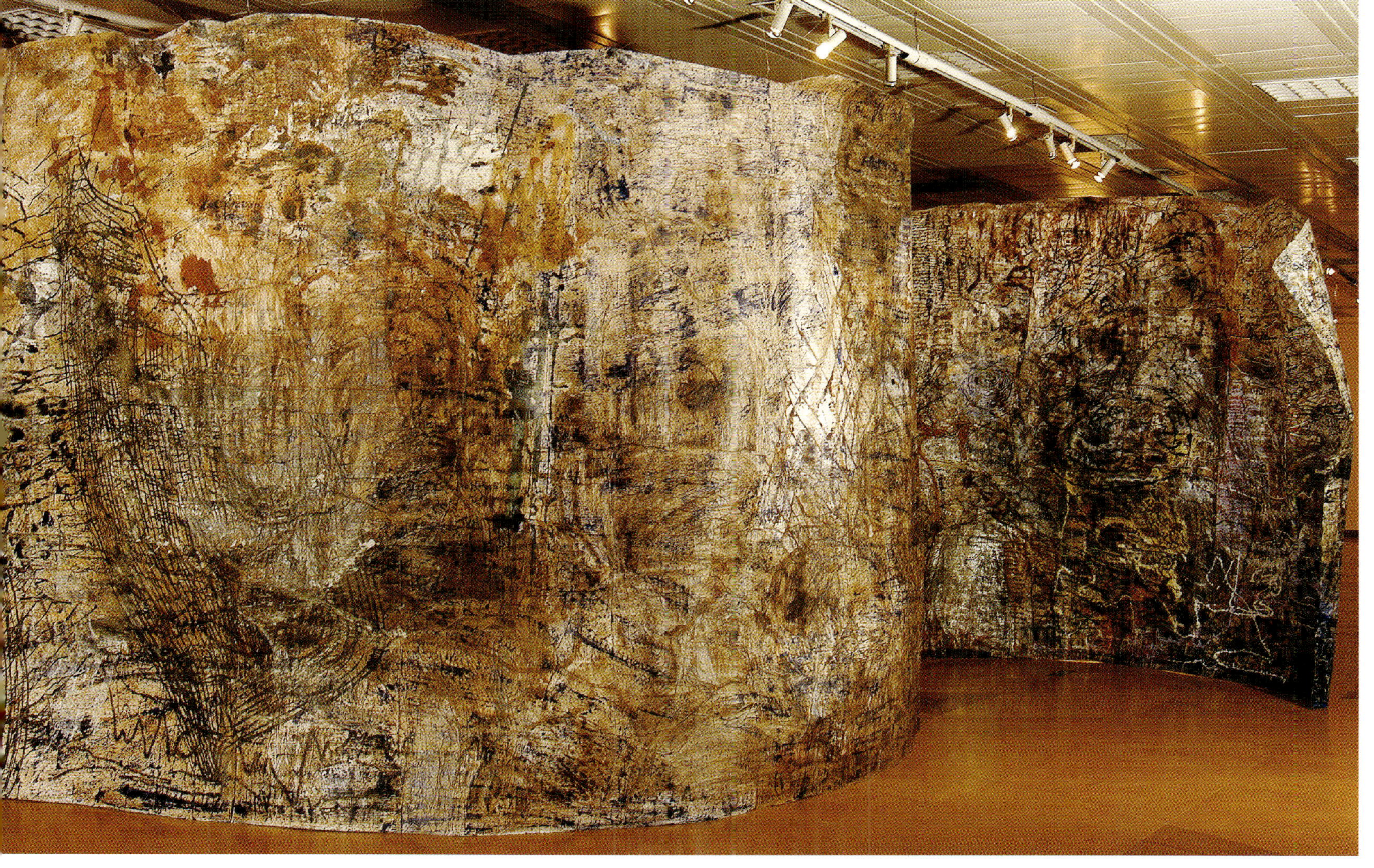

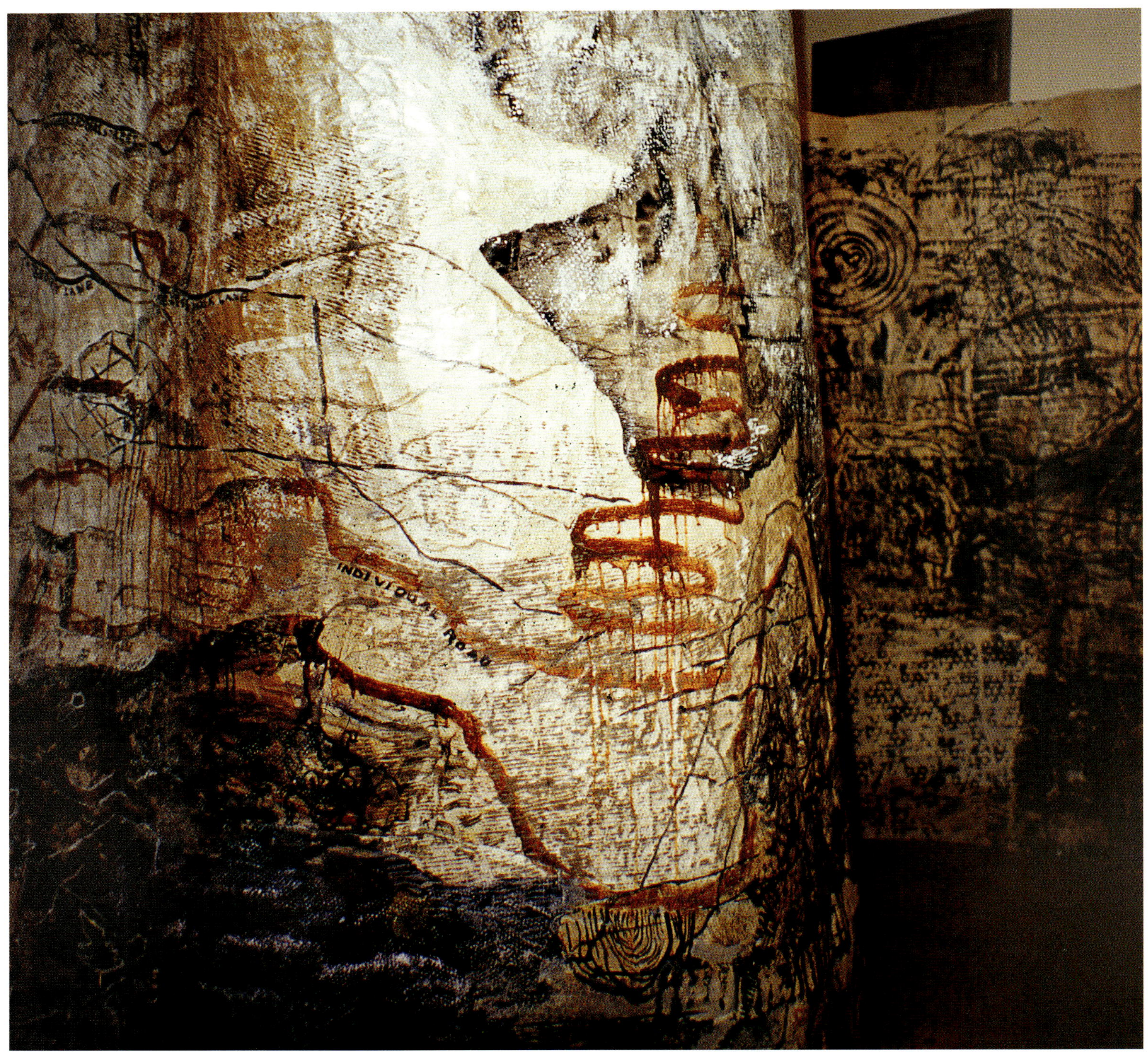

mandala that might be read as merely a maze, or a fingerprint, or concentric ripples of a stone thrown into a pond.

Jayashree Chakravarty. *Personal Space,* 2003. Detail, see page 58.

       Chakravarty's private journey into the depths of this encrusted terrain is a bit like mountain driving, with meandering roads changing suddenly to sharp switchbacks. It is both monumental and intimate, but the artist has agreed—sort of—to show us the way. There are so many paths to the ultimate destination of self-awareness, and unlike Robert Frost, she does not ponder "the road not taken." She conceals and reveals and then lures us to plumb the visceral and psychological pentimenti with her guidance.

BS

ANJU DODIYA

Existing stories, or those fabricated during dreamtime, provide much of the narrative substance in Anju Dodiya's paintings. Her "canvas" is a brocade-upholstered foam mattress, which by its very nature is rife with associations. It is the arena for sex and dreams, physical and psychological encounters, pleasure and pain. Dodiya takes advantage of these dramatic possibilities by focusing her powerful personal narrative through the lens of dreamtime. The viewer is invited to be a voyeur—mediated by Dodiya's conscious manipulation of the images that inhabit her waking and sleeping mind. The mattress provides the metaphor; the images tell the story.

Anju Dodiya. *The Path of Berries*, 2005.
Acrylic on mattress; 78x46x7 in.
Shumita and Arani Bose Collection, New York.
Photography: Courtesy of Bose Pacia Gallery and
the artist.

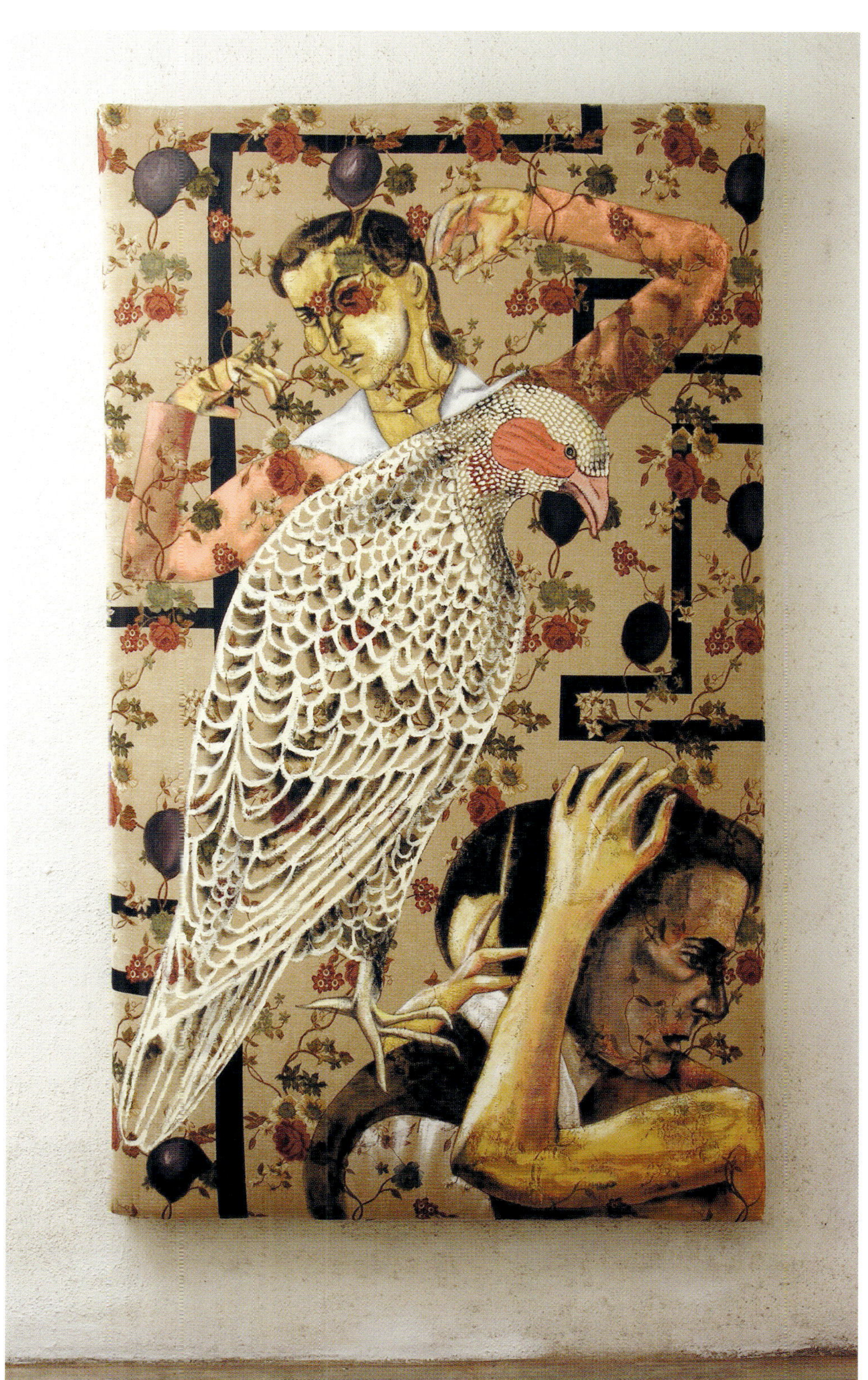

Opposite page:
Anju Dodiya. *Cloud Hunter*, 2005.
Acrylic on mattress; 78x46x7 in.
Collection of Mr. Prshant K. Lahoti, Hyderabad.
Photography: Courtesy of the artist.

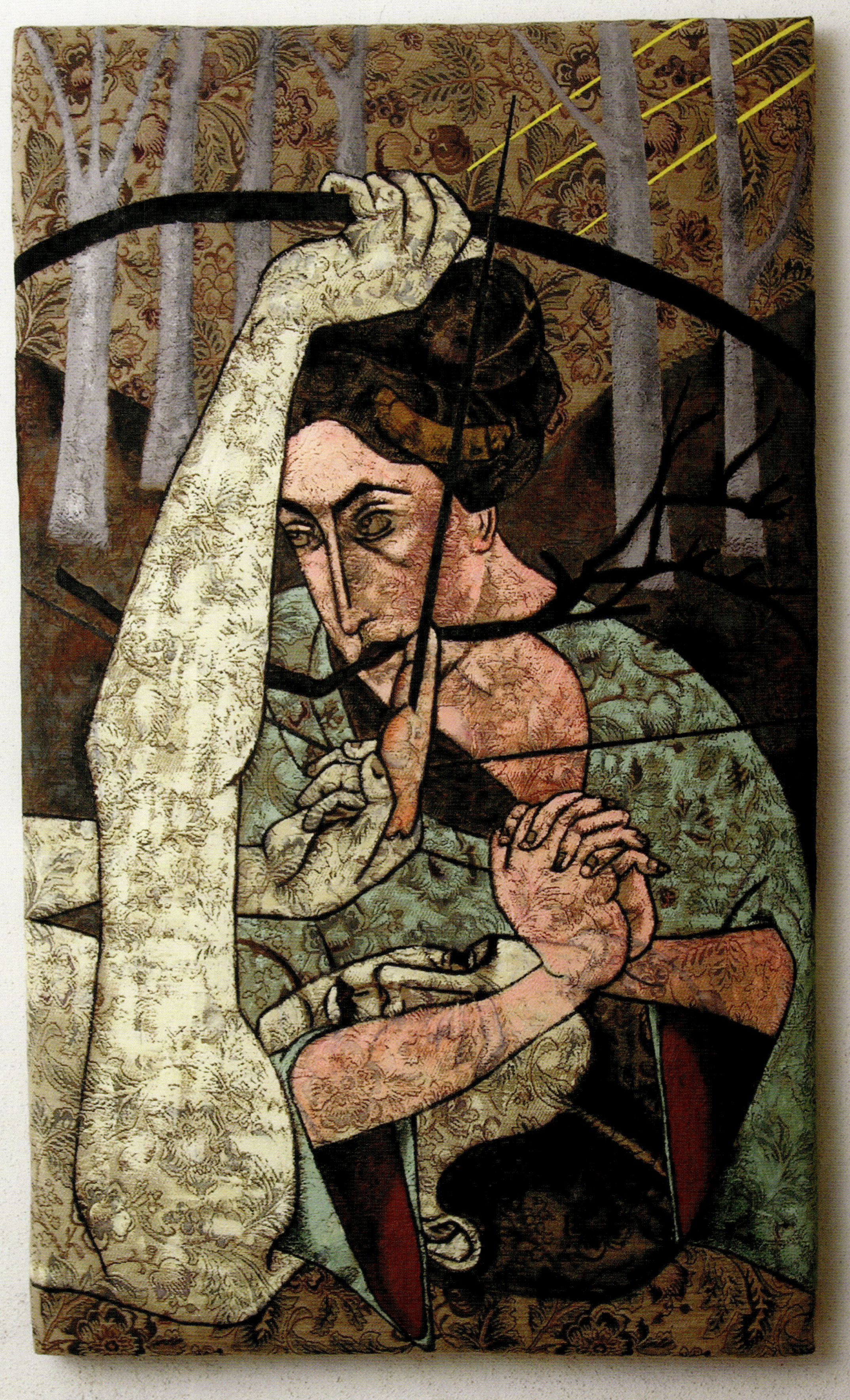

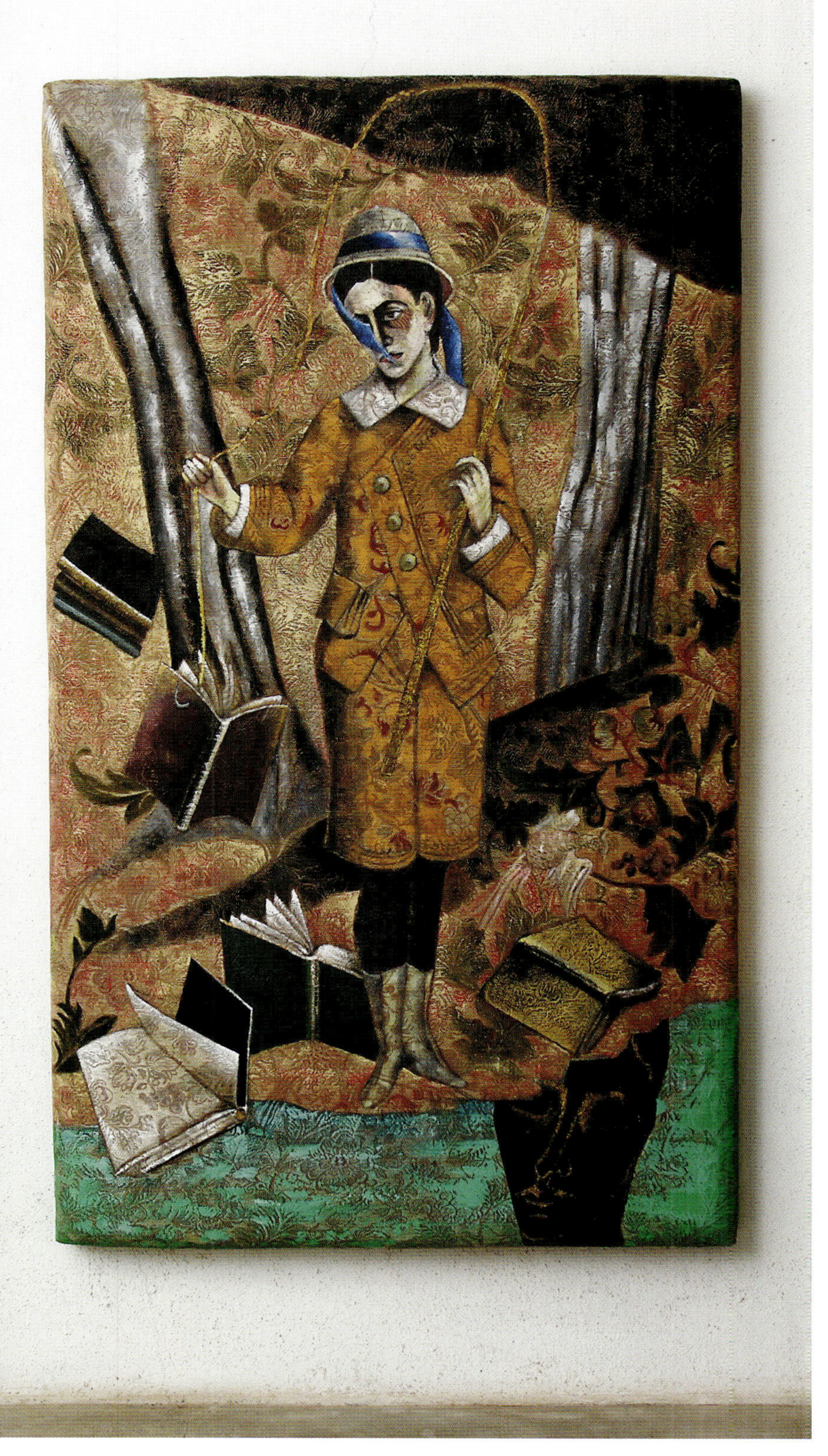

Anju Dodiya. *Island of Greed*, 2005.
Acrylic on mattress; 78x46x7 in.
Collection of Lalit Goyal, New Delhi.
Photography: Courtesy of the artist.

In *Island of Greed*, the protagonist (assume it's the artist—so much of her work is self-dramatization) is androgynously masquerading in stiff European-style clothing, unbefitting an island adventure. She stands cautiously at the shore, fishing line in hand. She has just hooked a book. With Jungian attention to the odd conjunction of dream images, Dodiya presents the expansion of her consciousness as a consequence of dreaming. Is her catch another literary source for her imagery? (Dodiya has an impressive library of literature and art books.) But the pages are blank—a reference to Dodiya's "terror of white," i.e., the blank page or canvas[1], alleviated here by the already existing pattern on the mattress. How can the artist survive on her island with only empty books to feed her mind? Or is it her own mind in which she is trolling? The island may exist only as the dream/nightmare emerging from the dark head that precariously supports it. Can the dark goddess (Dodiya's Doppelgänger?) whose head supports the whole island manage the weight of all that emptiness? Is it avaricious to love literature? Is that whip-like fishing line also a disciplinary instrument to punish the deadly sin of greed? But greedy about what, too many books? Too strong a desire to fill them? Consume them?[2]

Cloud Hunter quotes the familiar Hindu myth of Shiva and Shakti, the enlivening active female energy, without which Shiva is but a corpse. Their union is about awakening the passive male energy to its creative purpose by his active female counterpart. She is pink, pigmented by the life-blood coursing beneath her skin. He is white—*shava*, a corpse—the empty page that Dodiya fears, yet is drawn to.

In addition to the obvious coiffure and fingernails often seen in *Ukiyo-e* prints, the artist has employed the verticality of Japanese formatting to express a vertical narrative. The union of Shiva and Shakti symbolizes the spiritual unity that her "cloud hunter" is seeking. Clouds are celestial, evanescent as dreams, removed from the earthly realm. In the tense, mystical moment before the arrow is released from the hunter's taut bow, the upraised arm is phallic, indicating an erotic parallel to the spiritual quest.

Beyond the mystical, Dodiya recognizes in this classic narrative the power of the feminine. Returning to an *Ukiyo-e* motif to demonstrate the exquisite anguish and ecstasy of earthly love-making, her heroine is biting on a twig to stifle a moan. The artist acknowledges that mind as well as body are involved in this most intimate of physical encounters. A glimpse of neck where the kimono falls open is the only revelation of flesh. Erotic enough, the artist seems to say. Thus, her female subject has denied not only her lover, but also her viewers, the much despised "male-gaze" at her nude body. Her own gaze is distant; her expression neutral and one of sublime detachment, removed from the activity at hand.

Dodiya has said *The Path of Berries* is about waiting, specifically the legendary twenty-year wait of Odysseus's faithful wife. The mythic Penelope told the suitors who courted her during her husband's epic absence that she would make a decision only when she had finished her weaving. Each day she worked at her loom and each night unraveled her day's labors. Struck by the duality of this process, Dodiya has centrally placed an image of a falcon—a bird with the most regal masculine associations—in the center of her painting, delineating its white feathers as if they were crocheted loops that could be undone with the pull of a single thread, its power undone by the wiles of a woman.

Penelope waits at home, while her man travels the world. Dodiya's personal affinity for this story is simple: her own husband, artist Atul Dodiya, often travels while she waits at home. Another is that since childhood the artist has suffered from leucoderma, a skin disorder that causes loss of pigmentation. She has spent much of her youth " . . . waiting for the white to turn into brown and now . . . waiting for the brown to turn into white . . . ; . . . looking at the white marks on my body I think of maps and then again of Odysseus and his travels . . . "3

Skin is a potent theme in Dodiya's paintings. The mattress membrane, in addition to offering tapestry-like texture, provides diversity. Her stories each have their own distinct derma. Whereas in *Island of Greed* and *Cloud Hunter* she employs the dense floral brocade as part of the forested backdrop of her drama, in *The Path of Berries* the flowers are lightly strewn over the surface of the bed. Dodiya lets their random placement mimic her own skin ailment. One strategically located bloom may even be a "rose-colored glass" through which the waiting woman at the top looks at the world. She stretches languorously, waking amid a bouquet that will ultimately perfume a reunion with her lover (at the bottom of the painting). The sleeves of her modest garment more resemble flesh than her own. In the embrace of her lover, her arms reveal the same sulfuric pallor of her face and hands.

BS

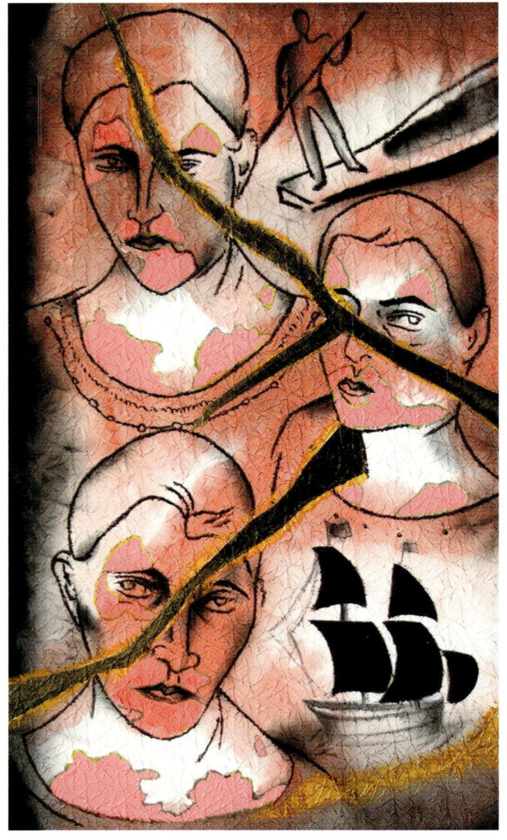

Anju Dodiya. *Pink Clouds (for Penelope)*, 2006.
Acrylic on fabric; 72x42 in.
Private collection.
Photography: Courtesy of Bose Pacia Gallery and the artist.

1   "Gieve Patel talks to Anju Dodiya," *Anju Dodiya* (New York: Bose Pacia, 2006).
2   The artist's original intention was to create a series based on the seven deadly sins. Although that has not materialized, this reference to avarice remains. From the author's conversation with Anju Dodiya, October 2004.
3   "Gieve Patel talks to Anju Dodiya," *Anju Dodiya* (New York: Bose Pacia, 2006).

"
… looking at the

white marks

on my body

I think of maps

and

then again

of Odysseus

and

his travels …
"

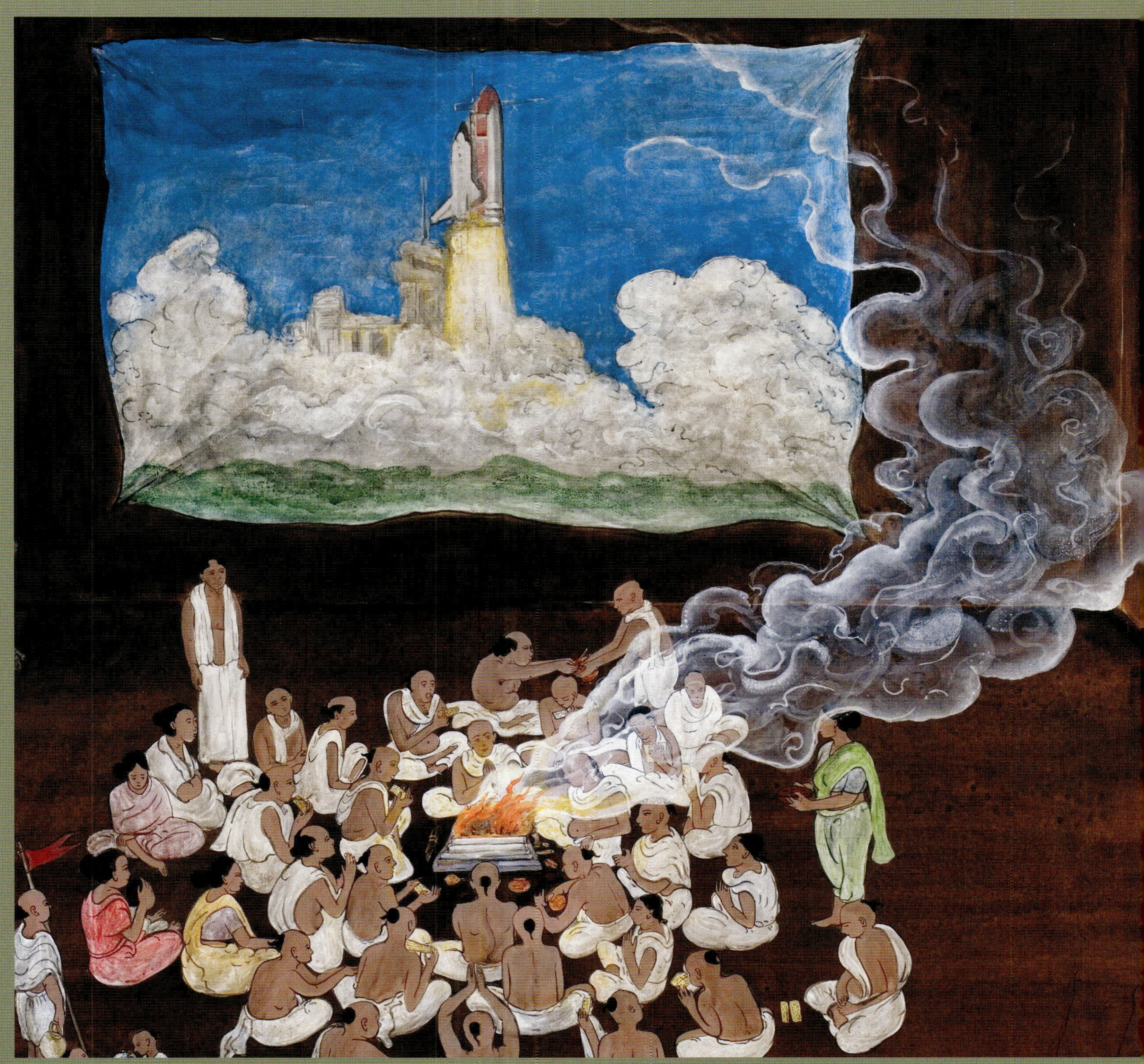

N. S. Harsha. *Smoke goes up, smoke goes down*, 2005. Detail, see page 72.

LOOKING OUTWARD
Contemporary Observations

Reena Saini Kallat

·

Subodh Gupta

·

N. S. Harsha

·

Nalini Malani

·

Jitish Kallat

·

Shilpa Gupta

·

Ranbir Kaleka

·

Single-channel Video Art

Reena Saini Kallat

Alamkara, embellishment per se to just the right degree—neither subtle nor garish—is a key factor in the aesthetics of India. Foreheads are marked with *bindi*s, hair parts are stained with *kumkum*, hands and feet are painted with henna, fingers and toes are manicured and pedicured. Mere decoration. Markings of the sort that Reena Saini Kallat uses are stronger signifiers—authoritative blue-ink stamps of approval, the necessary franking that enables the bearer to pass freely into the next phase of existence. Kallat has taken the omnipresent stampings of bureaucratic India, and ironically calls them "blueprints," a double entendre on grand plans. Is not the grand scheme of one's life in India marked in one way or another by the larger plan of one's karma? The stamp on a pregnant belly announces that the unborn child is already carrying the lineage of caste and the weight of karma. A stamp on a breast indicates that breast milk is safe for consumption. Some of the imprints are on body parts that are usually hidden from view, allowing the bearer the opportunity to pass undetected. But, like Lady Macbeth's blood-stained hands, these tattoos do not wash away. Others are blatant: a government seal where a Shaivite *tilaka* would be, or a calligraphic line that mimics a carefully arched eyebrow. A viewer in the West will recognize the irony that this genre of authoritative marking on human flesh looks remarkably similar to what is used to grade butchered meat in the United States.

Every individual body is a part of the larger body politic to which it belongs. The narrative of one's life as outlined by Kallat is defined by the multiple stamps and franked documents that allow passage from one phase to the next.

BS

Pages 66–67:
Reena Saini Kallat. *Blueprint: Birthmarks and Tattoos*, 2005.
C-prints; 64 prints, 11.25x15 in each;
edition: 2/5.
Courtesy of Walsh Gallery, Chicago.
Photography: Courtesy of Walsh Gallery.

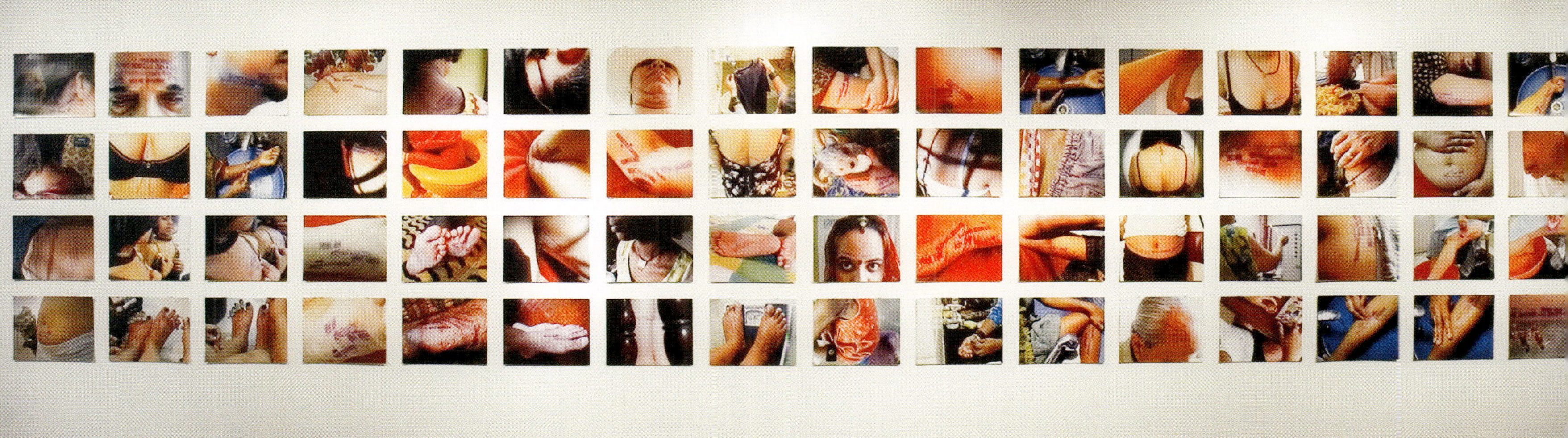

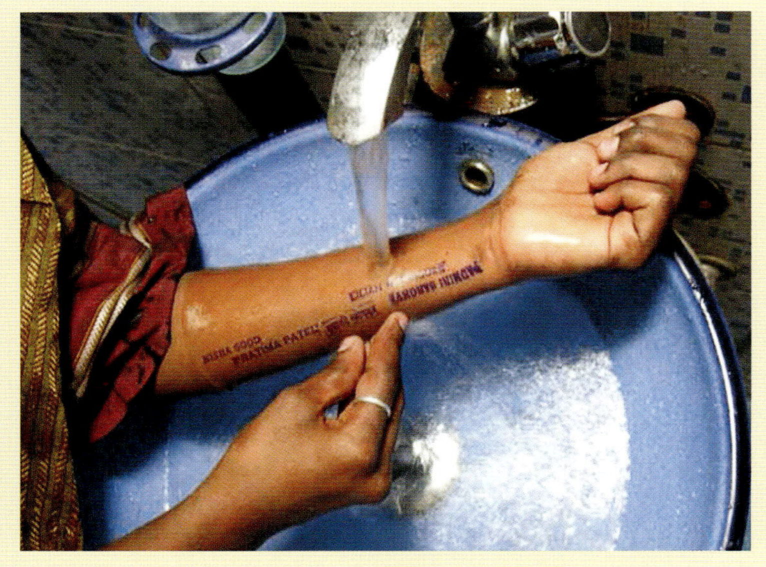
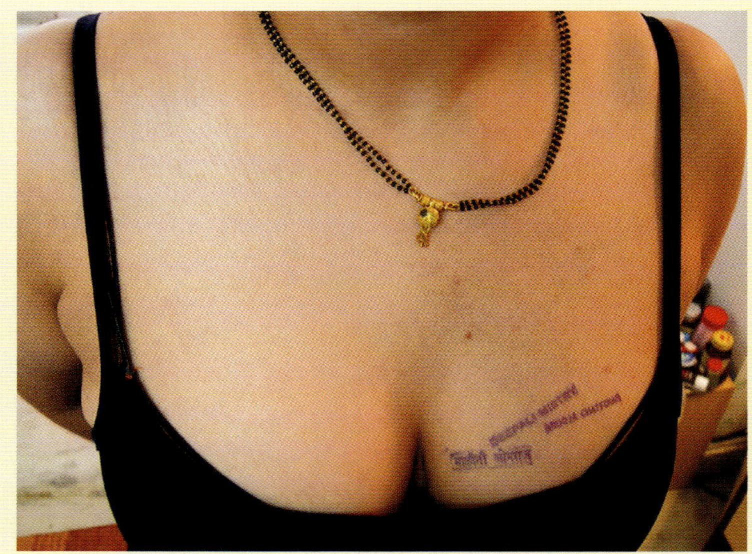
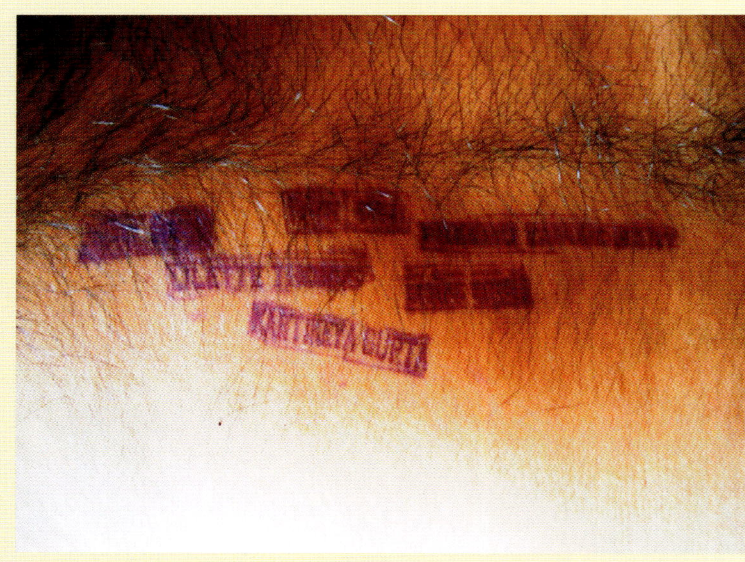
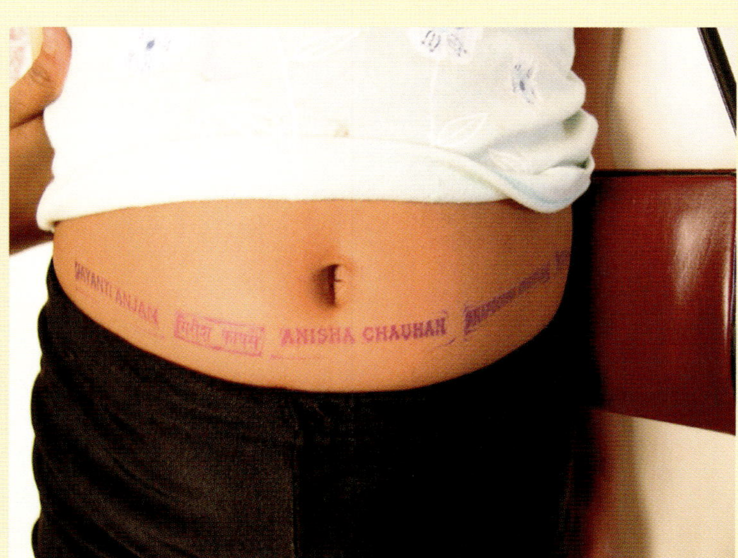
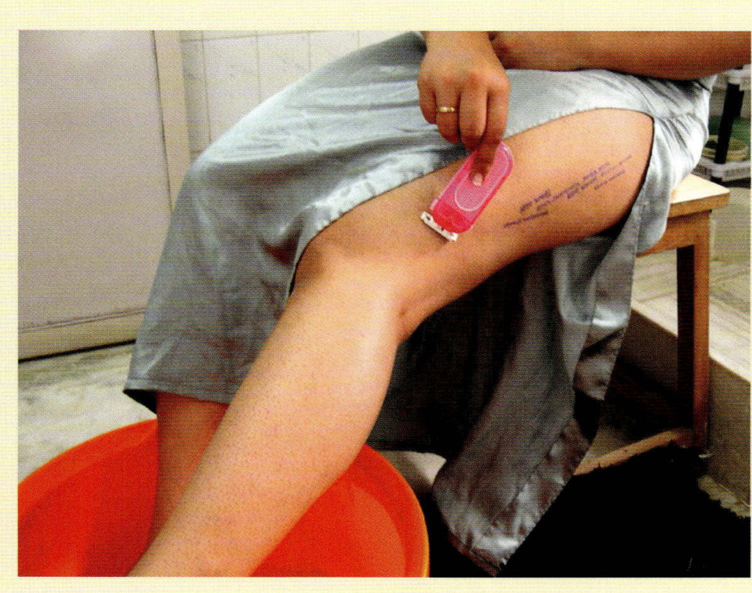
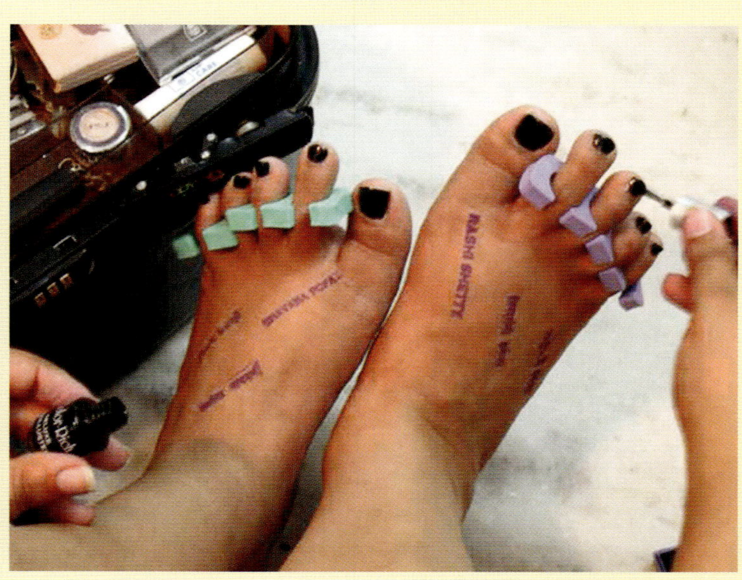

Subodh Gupta

With his invocation of that most ubiquitous of Indian symbols, the sacred cow (and particularly the fluids associated with it), Subodh Gupta incorporates the concept of nature's cycles into his artistic output and puts his own spin on it. His fascination with the liquid flow of nature has led him to seek its source—as in the source of a river—finding it allegorically embodied in the cow. The bodily fluids of the cow—specifically milk and feces—connect it with the water, rain and sap of the cycles of nature. All are essential for agrarian fertility. Kamadhenu, the sacred cow, is an integral part of Hindu mythology. She is the cow of plenty, Mother of all cows, granting wishes and desires, her abundance a measure of prosperity.

Gupta casts in bronze the humble bicycles and motorcycles of the *doodhwallah* (milkman). He calls them cows and loads them with milk cans, acknowledging that they provide urbanized delivery of fresh warm milk in their galvanized metal udders. Gupta's medium is as much the message as is the cow. He has incorporated actual cow dung into his paintings. The cow *pat*s in *Every Day Is Less* are even gilded, indicating their preciousness.

Subodh Gupta. *Three Cows*, 2003.
Cast bronze bicycles and chrome-plated cast bronze milk buckets (set of three); life-size.
Shumita and Arani Bose Collection, New York.
Photography: Courtesy of Bose Pacia Gallery and the artist.

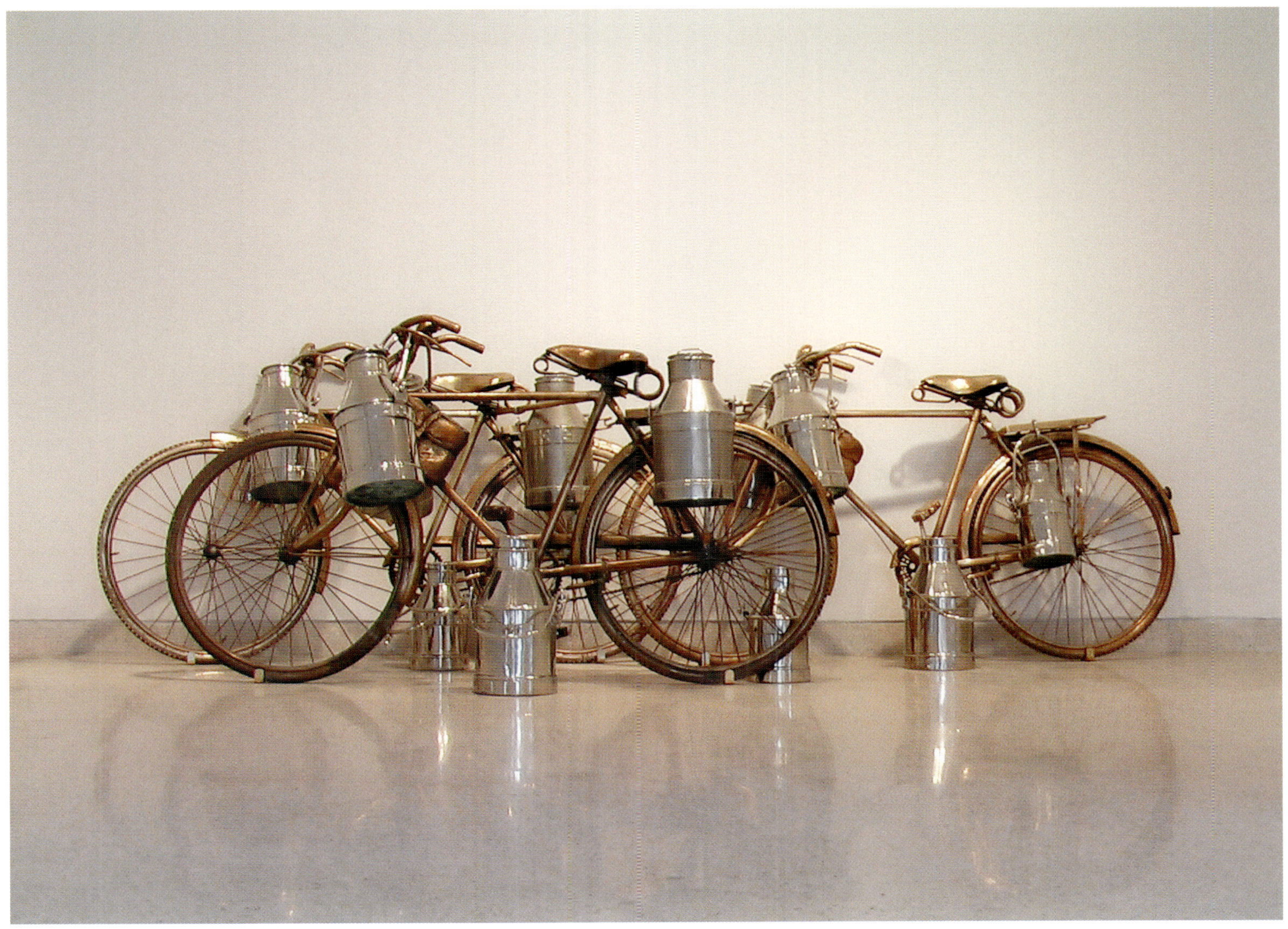

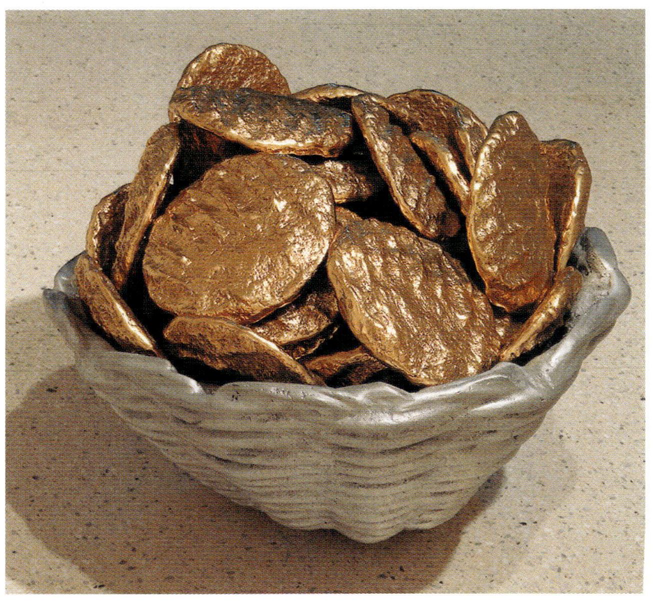

Subodh Gupta. *Every Day Is Less*, 2003.
Bronze and aluminum; 22x19.2x20 in.
Collection of Larry Warsh, New York.
Photography: Courtesy of the artist.

Subodh Gupta. *Gauri 2*, 2000.
Oil and cow dung on canvas; 66x90 in.
Collection of Anupam Poddar, New Delhi.
Photography: Courtesy of Devi Art Foundation.

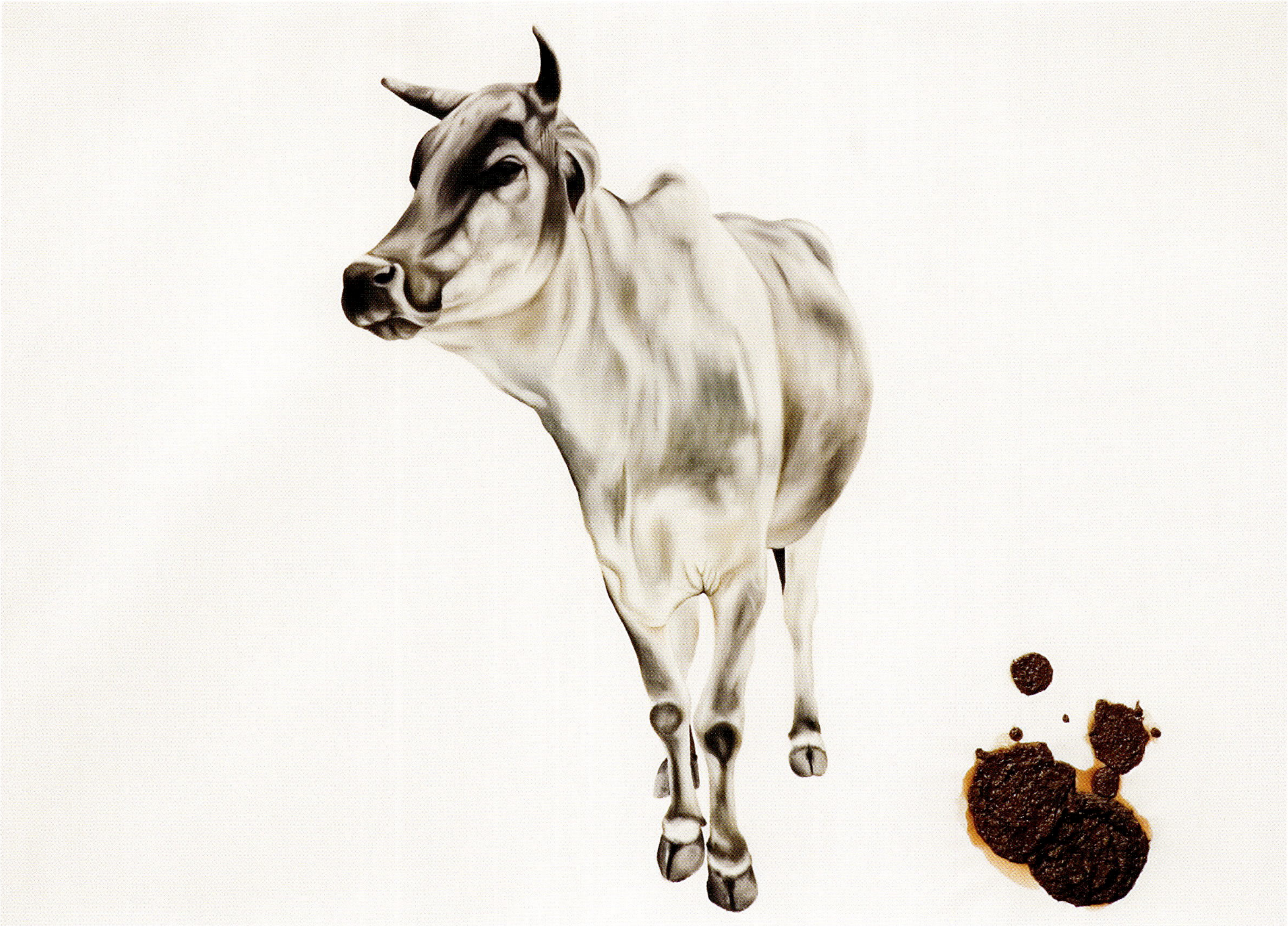

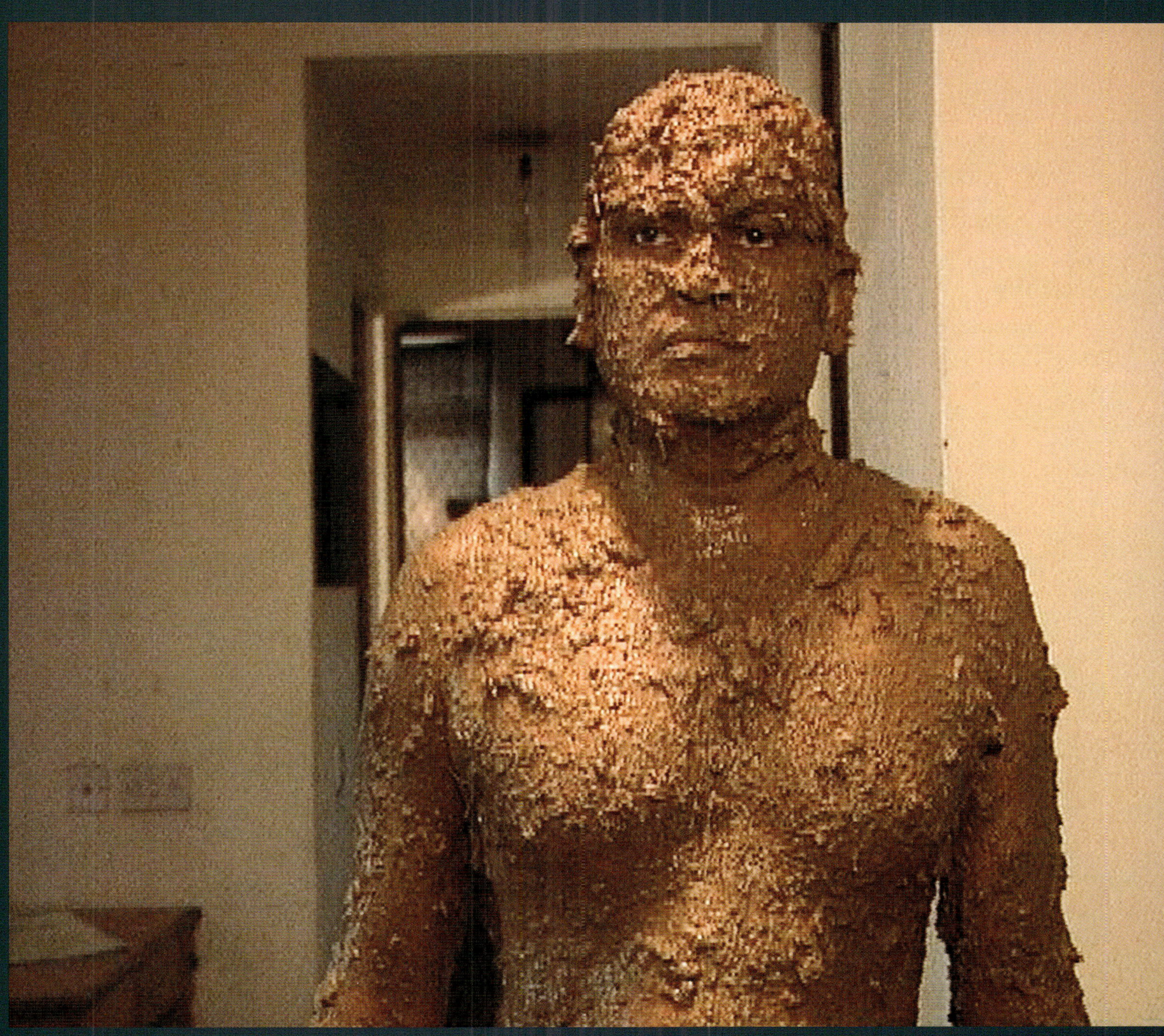

Subodh Gupta. *Pure*, 2000. DVD (silent), 9 min.
Collection of the artist, New Delhi.
Photography: Courtesy of the artist.

In a sense, Gupta recognizes the irony of the cow's holiness: this four-legged, equal-opportunity garbage disposal chews, digests and defecates in a form that linear thinkers might call the end of the line. But in India, cow dung is but a stage in a great regenerative cycle. Refuse passes through this bovine conduit and returns in liquid form to replenish the earth and sustain the billions who inhabit it. With his imagery, Gupta proclaims the cow's potential as a vehicle of transformation, purification and union with the fluid circuits of the physical and cosmic universe.

Cow dung is used for building bricks, a sort of non-white whitewash on walls and fuel for cooking fires. Moreover, it is a cleansing agent. Gupta recognizes all of this, and puts it to a further purpose: cow dung cues the viewer that the artist literally has immersed himself in this cosmic process. As he did with his bronze urban "cows" in his video *Pure*, Gupta sets up a rural/urban dialog. It expands even into conceits of what is private and what is public, acknowledging that with the numbers of people living on the streets of India, many private activities are of necessity public.

The idea that cow dung is inherently clean is ingrained in rural India. There, it is a purifying element, both ritual and symbolic. In *Pure*, Gupta takes the "detergent" concept literally and has filmed himself taking a shower in cow dung. Then he removes his "cleansed" body from the private shower to a public elevator. His private/rural ritual is repulsive in the public/urban domain.

By re-consecrating—and thus elevating—the symbolic clichés of India into art, Gupta insinuates that the mobility of art in our global age might be nothing more than the excrement of cows, or indeed, might be analogous to the grand fluid cycles.

BS

N. S. Harsha

N. S. Harsha has said, "I am not sure if an artist can consciously work out a balance between tradition and modernity."[1] Putting that uncertainty aside, he has created in his twelve-painting series, *Charming Nation*, an ironic narrative of just how the omnipresent elements of tradition in India do or do not fit in contemporary life. With a witty eye toward local concerns in a global age, he investigates the dualities—and attendant politics—that occupy one's existence: access versus exclusion, food versus hunger, aspirations versus obstacles, dreams versus reality. Harsha takes the current human condition personally. These paintings are about the relationship of the self to the world. He has said,

> I am living with this investigative eye, which is always searching for values in these rituals which are relevant to our contemporary lifestyle. On the one hand, I have all this personal experience of local practices; on the other, my exposure to other cultural practices from far-off lands—via the booming communications media—keeps on challenging the local beliefs. I am constantly trying to negotiate a space which defines this complex situation.[2]

Each of the paintings in this series is one meter square, with a faux wood finish and a *trompe l'œil* illusion of depth. Lined up, they look like a series of dioramas in a history museum. Each contains a small dramatic tableau, often including a painting within the painting—telling a story within the story—as the backdrop for the depicted narration. A banner with a cynical inscription pointing out the separation of desire from reality headlines the action. Harsha has thoughtfully chosen his media and style to enhance his concept: the disparity between the expectations of traditional practice and the reality of contemporary life. Art within art, stories within stories are visual and psychological devices for furthering the illusion of distance. Each lyrical painting develops his wry commentary.

The title work, *Charming Nation*, is a biting look at accommodation. Harsha acknowledges that India is perceived as "charming" in a quaint, exotic way. The multitudes that throng there annually to "do" India, for business or pleasure, have made this their reality. But the charm that has attracted the world to India—via tourism, outsourcing, the art market etc.—is being destroyed to accommodate those very attractions. Historical sites are bulldozed to make room for hotels with amenities. Phone centers in India are now outsourcing *themselves*, hiring young Westerners seeking sojourns in charming India. Harsha recognizes that much of what has made India so enticing initially is being sacrificed in the interest of global, homogenized services.

Opposite page:
N. S. Harsha. *Charming Nation*, 2005.
Acrylic on canvas; 38x38 in.
Private collection.
Photography: Courtesy of Gallery Chemould and the artist.

N. S. Harsha. *Charming Nation*, 2006.
12 paintings, oil on canvas; 38x38 in. each.
Dispersed in private collections.

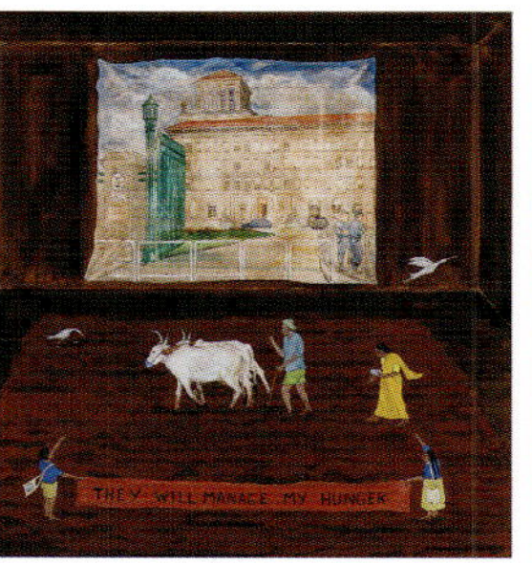
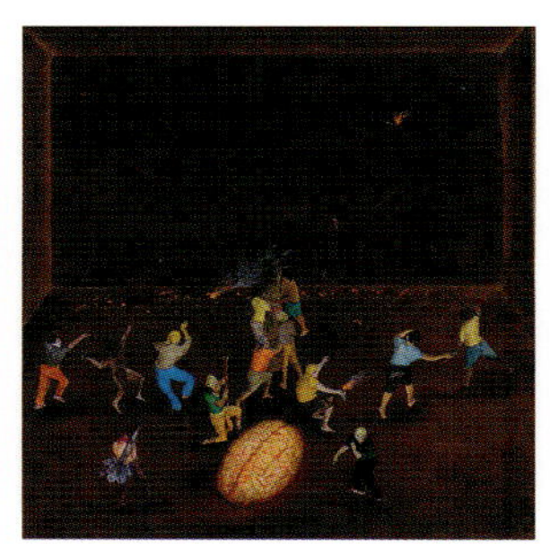
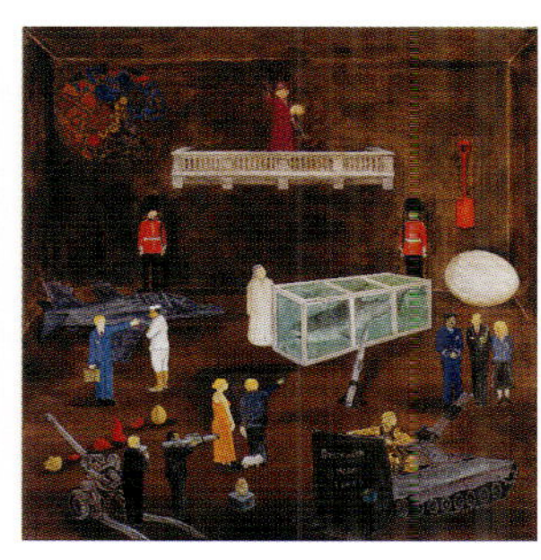
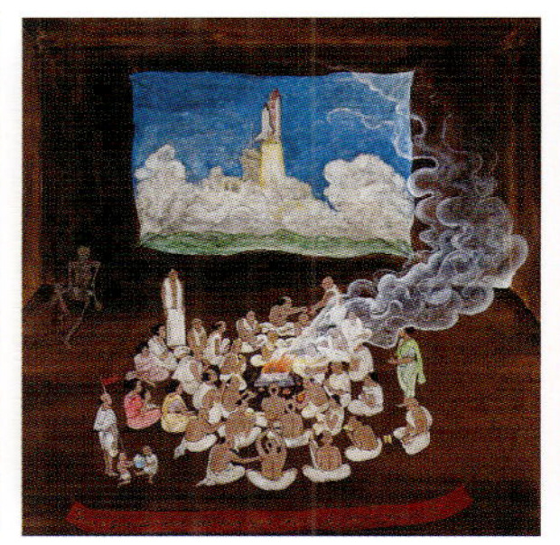
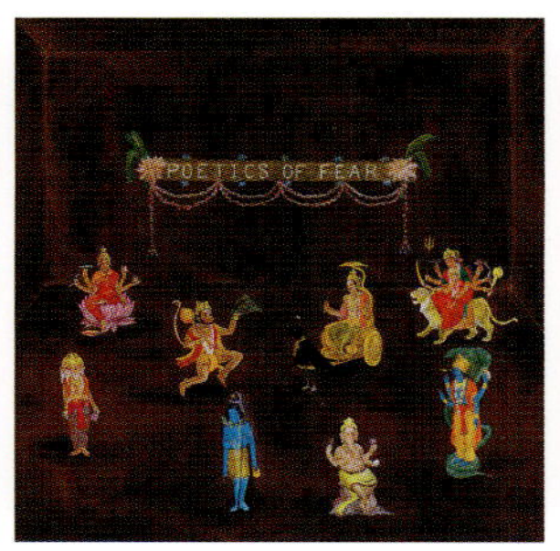
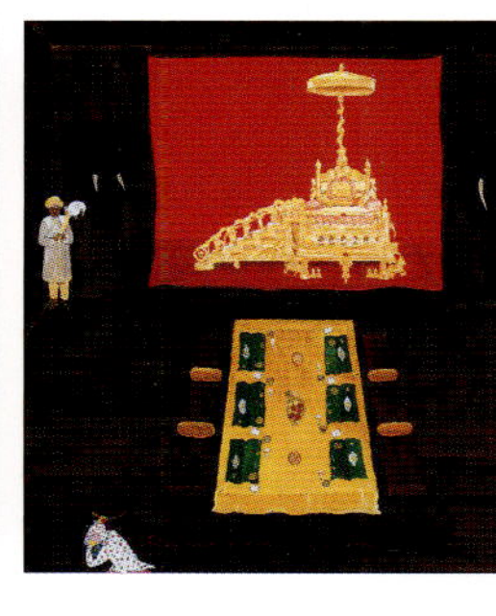

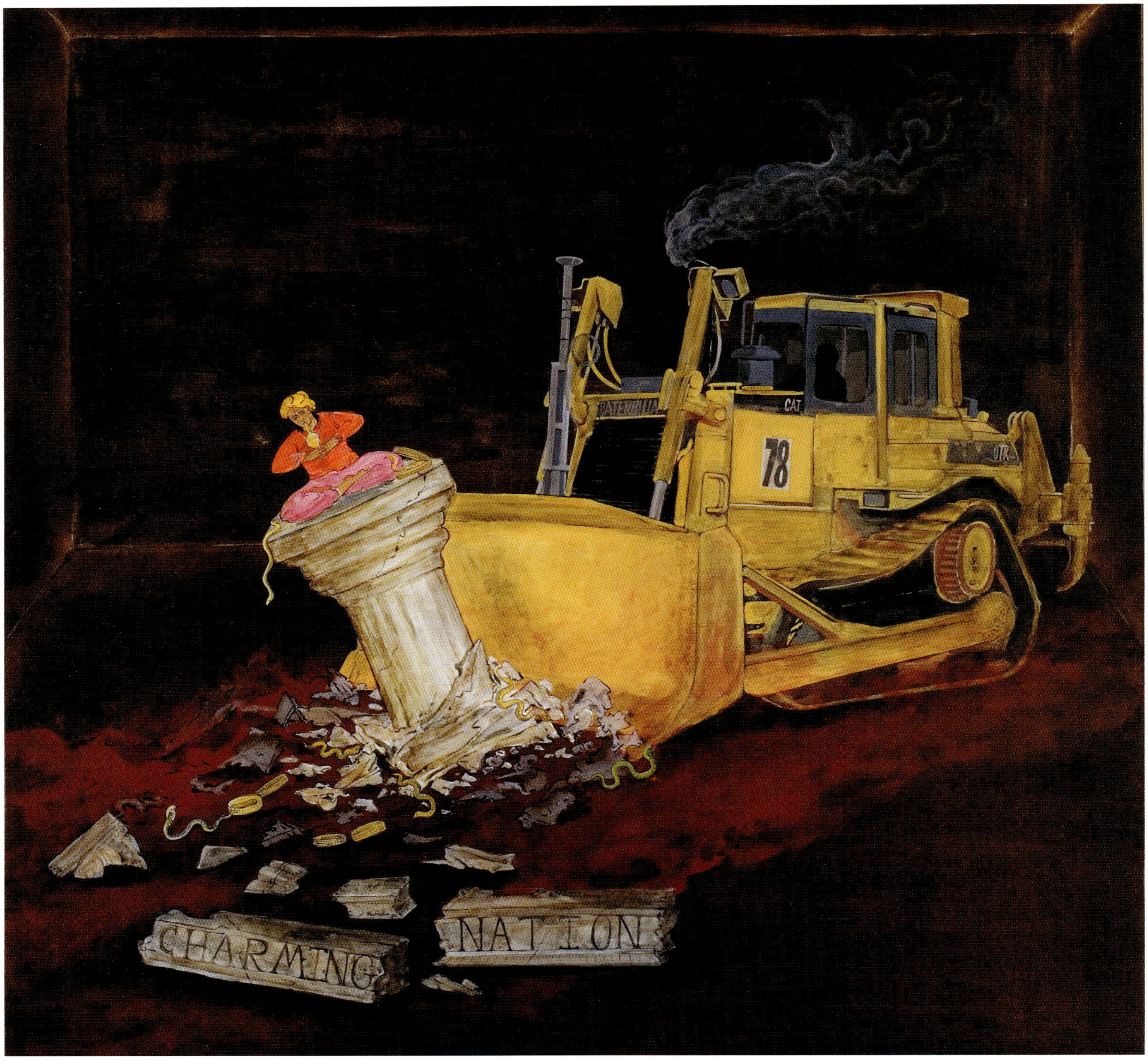

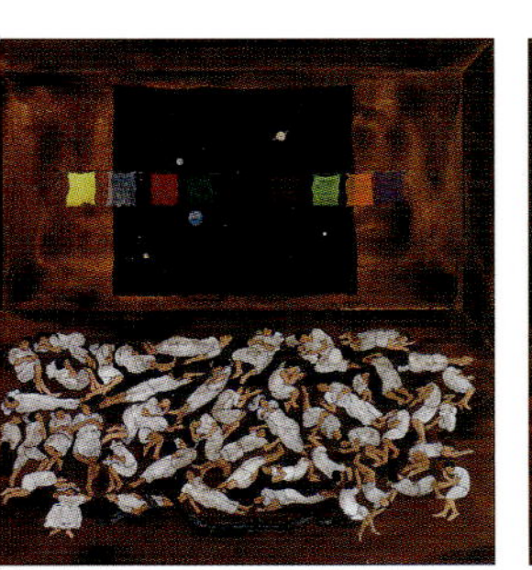 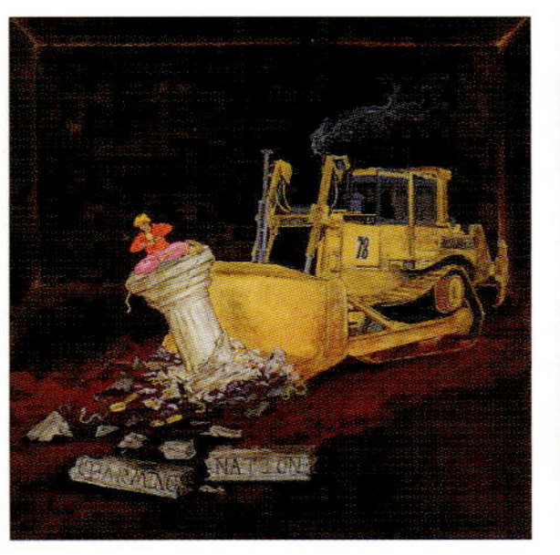 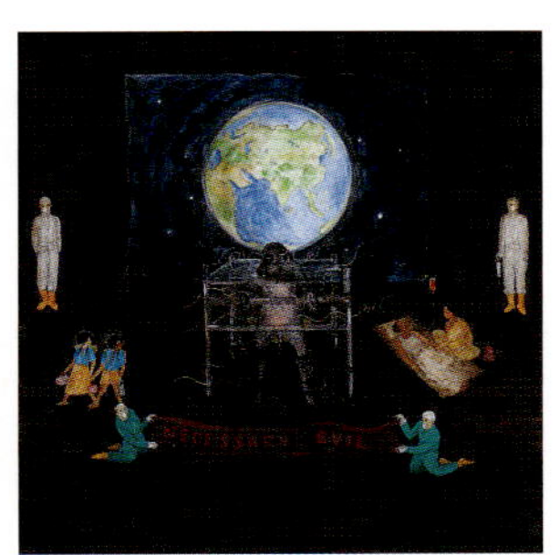 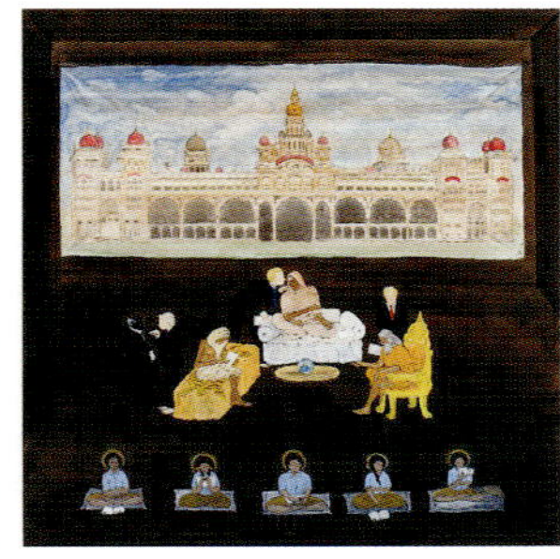 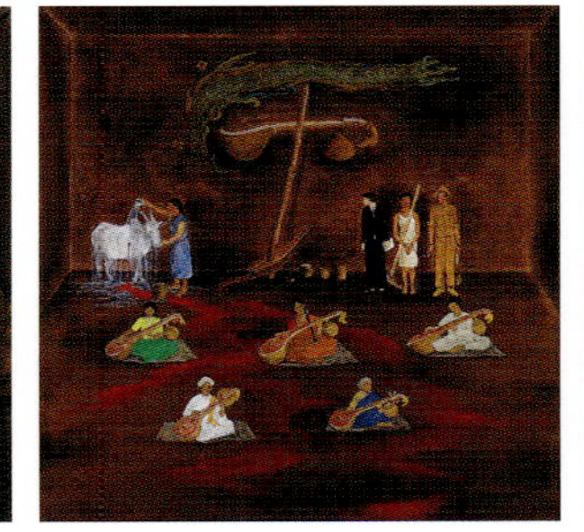 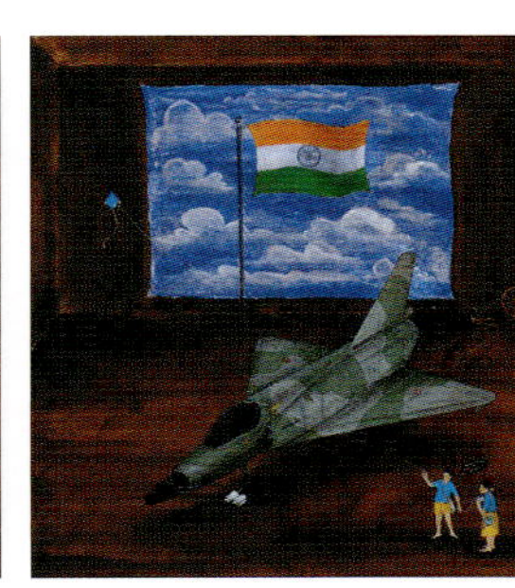

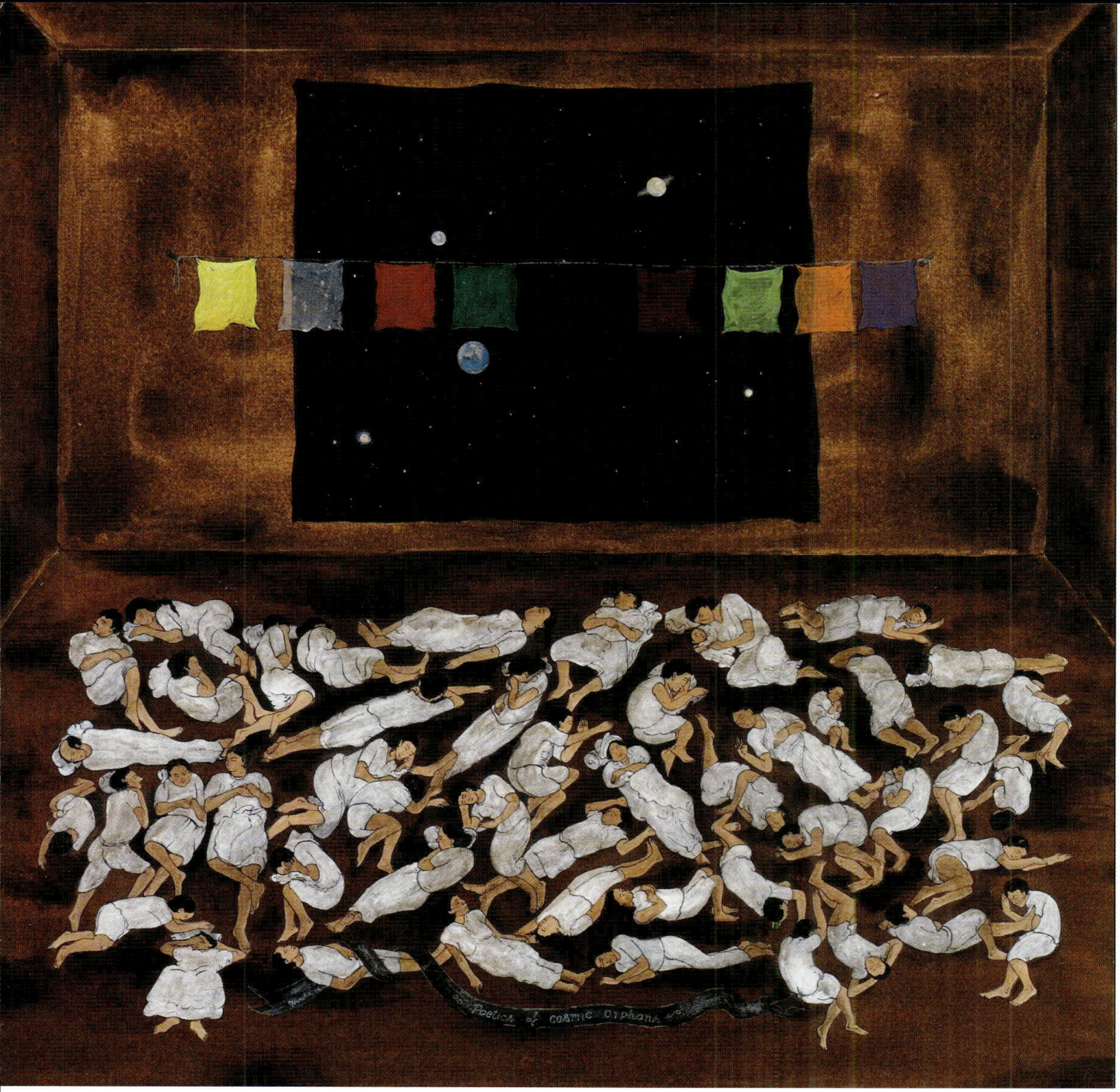

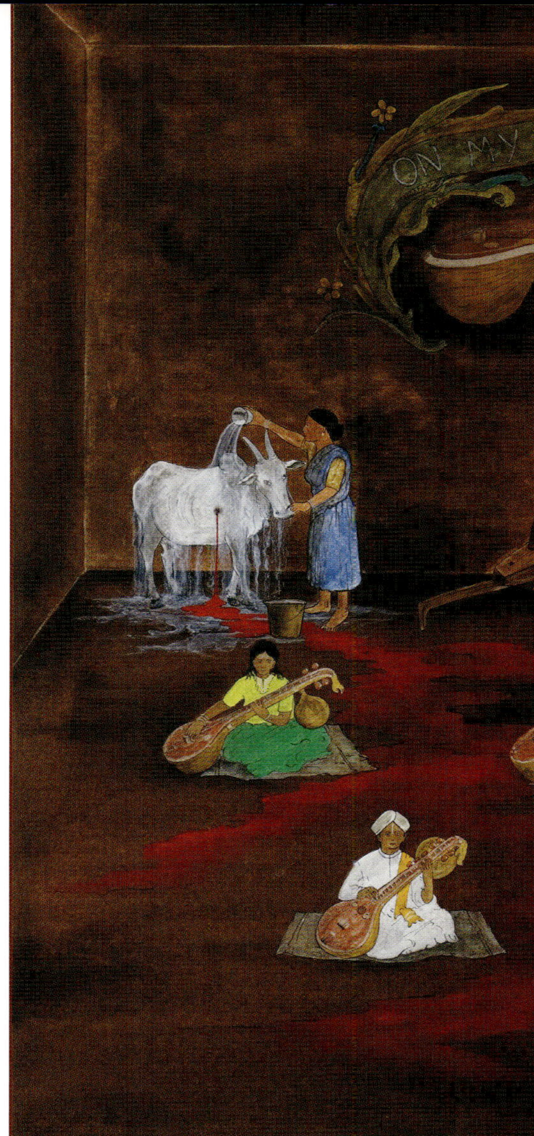

N. S. Harsha. *Poetics of cosmic orphans*, 2006.
Acrylic on canvas; 38x38 in.
Collection of Gallery Chemould, Mumbai.
Photography: Courtesy of Gallery Chemould and the artist.

Right:
N. S. Harsha. *On my way to museum*, 2006.
Acrylic on canvas; 38x38 in.
Collection of Sangita Jindal, Mumbai.
Photography: Courtesy of Gallery Chemould and the artist.

Harsha is a master of ironic wordplay. For him, it was a short hop from "charming" to snake charmers. The artist has literally knocked the snake charmer off his pedestal. The irony of fearsome reptiles being overturned by a caterpillar (a mere larva, indeed) visually sums up the loss of mythic power when traditions are decommissioned. Like a statue of a deity defiled, their potency is gone. The snake charmer sits serenely piping his melody, as his snakes slither hither and yon. His charm—as well as his exalted perch—has been toppled.

Harsha's message in *On my way to museum* is that harmony is a relic, only to be preserved in a museum along with an oversized model of a *vina*. His ensemble of musicians in traditional costume is related to the famous painting by Raja Ravi Varma, *Galaxy of Musicians*, an oil painting that was exhibited at the Parliament of World Religions in 1893, in Chicago. Both seek to demonstrate how harmony can be achieved through the careful orchestration of diverse—even discordant—sounds. The more mordant elements of this picture, however, are the living relics, also relegated to mere artifacts: the sacred cow, hemorrhaging so profusely that no amount of traditional lustrations can staunch the bloody flow; and the farmer in his *dhoti*, being escorted out of his traditional existence by the twin powers of business (the "suit") and the military (the "uniform"). The whole museum display has been oversimplified for public consumption.

Since ancient times in India, sacrificial fires have been the ritual vehicles for offerings to the gods. Clarified butter feeds the flames that send oblations

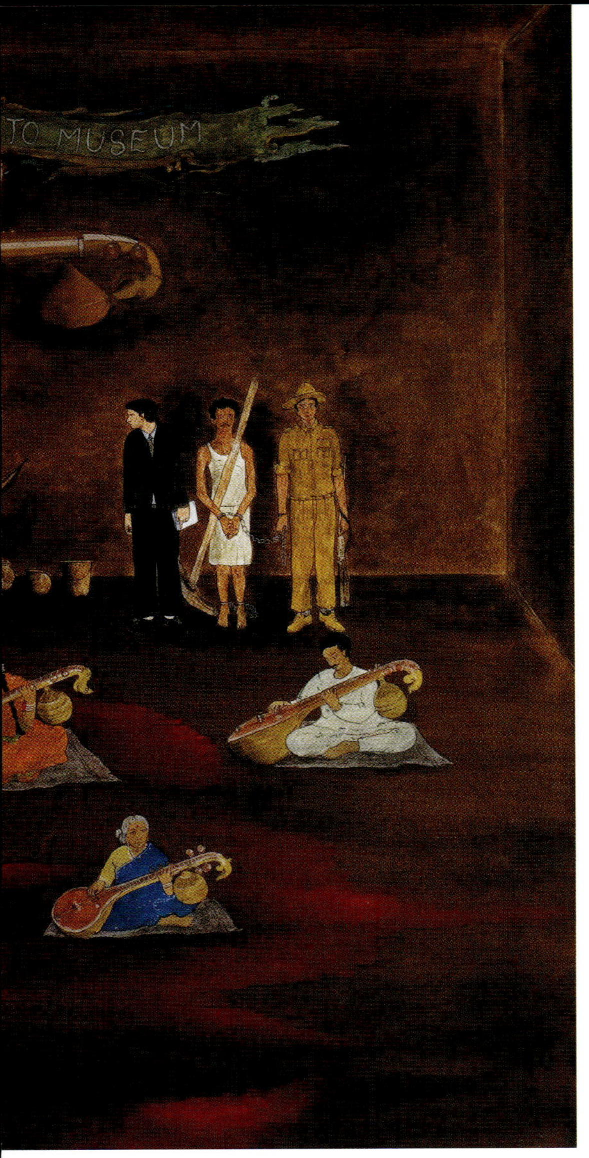

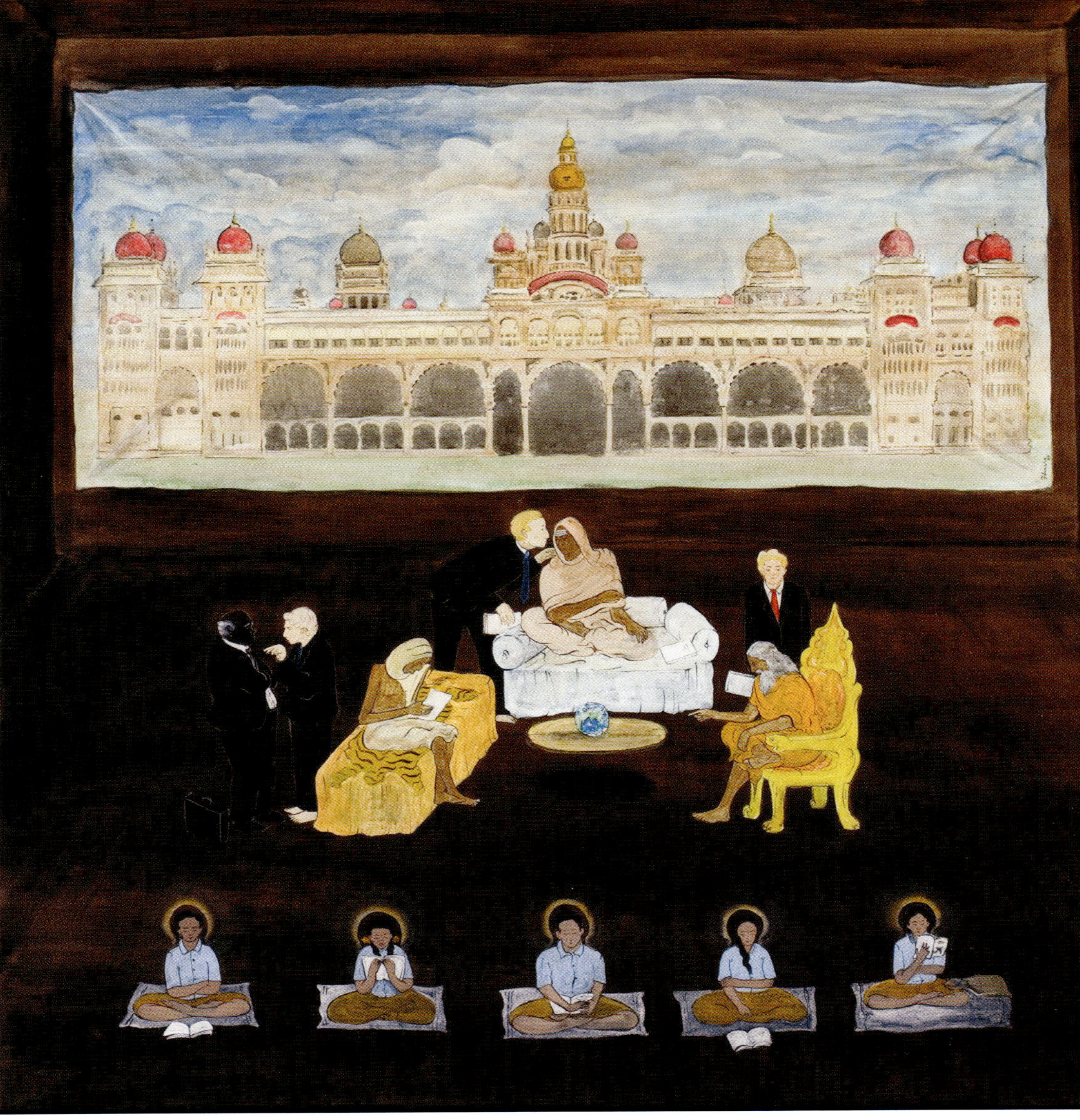

heavenward. In *Smoke goes up, smoke goes down*, Harsha has turned the quest for the cosmos upside down. The traditional transport to the heavens is, in our techno space age, merely the after-burn, as rockets roar into the sky. The full inscription reads: "Smoke goes up, smoke goes down. Your search for me is always on." Children on the periphery of the Brahmin gathering play innocently with a ball that resembles Earth. What have they been taught? What do they know?

Several dozen white-garbed people slumber in *Poetics of cosmic orphans*, the most ethereal of the paintings in Harsha's series. They are nestled together like pieces in a jigsaw puzzle. The fragile vulnerability of sleep is evident in each individual's unconscious position. In dreams, it seems, anyone can achieve a state of cosmic bliss. And so it appears in this painting. It is only after a moment that we notice this is no ordinary rooftop dormitory; the illuminated night sky beyond includes the planet Earth. The artist makes the sardonic point that the heavens, whether conquered spiritually or physically, will always have the homeless sleeping on rooftops, with laundry and stars for a canopy.

BS

N. S. Harsha. *Negotiated heritage*, 2005.
Acrylic on canvas; 38x38 in.
Private collection.
Photography: Courtesy of Gallery Chemould and the artist.

1   N. S. Harsha and Naomi Siderfin, E-mail conversation with N. S. Harsha and Naomi Siderfin, *Drawing Space: Contemporary Indian Drawings; Sheila Gowda, N. S. Harsha,* *Nasreen Mohamedi* (London: inIVA [Institute of International Visual Arts], 2000), 74–85.

2   Harsha and Siderfin, 74–85.

Nalini Malani

The video installation *Unity in Diversity* places us in the pleasant surroundings of a pre-Independence Nehruvian upper-class house, with its typical furniture, lamps and crimson red walls. A period before the birth of the new nation, where during the Gandhian years there was passionate hope of building up an egalitarian society—even for those at the lowest rung of the caste hierarchy like the Hindu widows. In a bourgeois gold frame a video plays—this is a take on the oil painting *Galaxy of Musicians* by the late 19th-century Indian court artist Raja Ravi Varma that originally represented the different cultures living in harmony together in the Indian subcontinent. His work was shown for the first time at the Parliament of World Religions in Chicago in 1893, where the philosopher Swami Vivekananda addressed the dangers of orthodoxy in religions.

Pages 76–78:
Nalini Malani. *Unity in Diversity*, 2003. Installation, livingroom setting with flat screen in golden frame on a crimson wall, two lamps and a framed photograph, sound, 7 minutes. Collection of the artist, Mumbai. Photography: Courtesy of Johan Pijnappel.

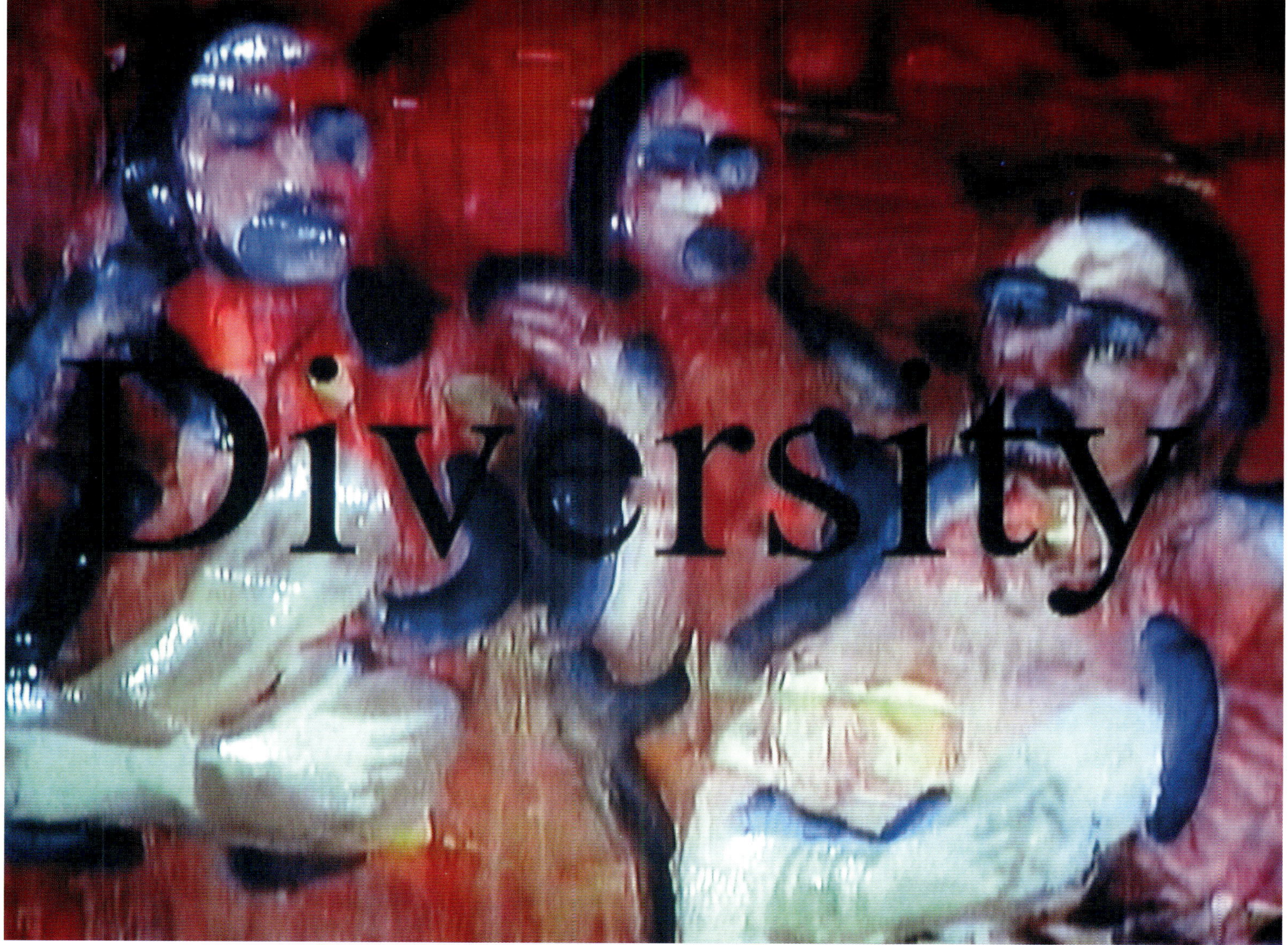

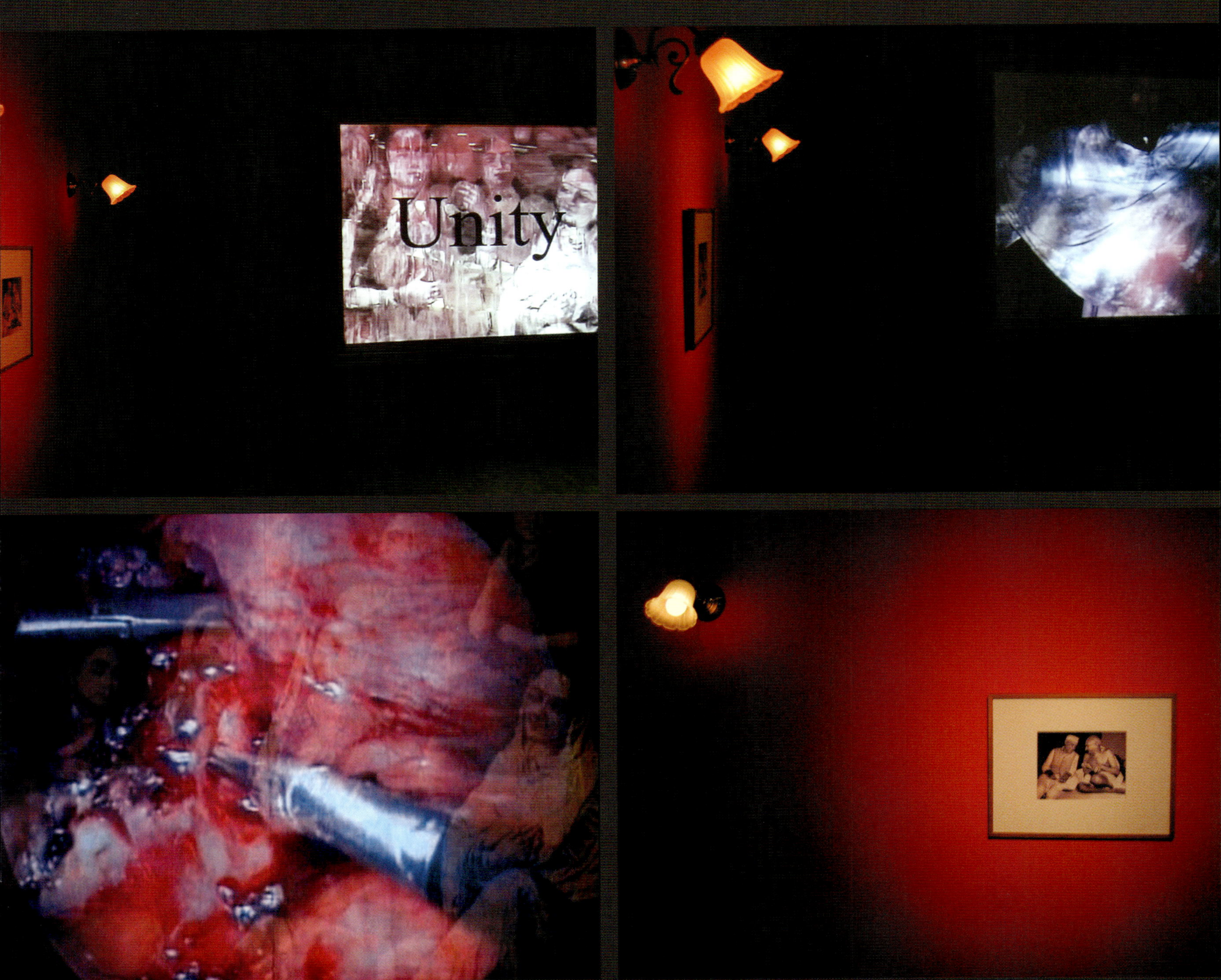

Unity

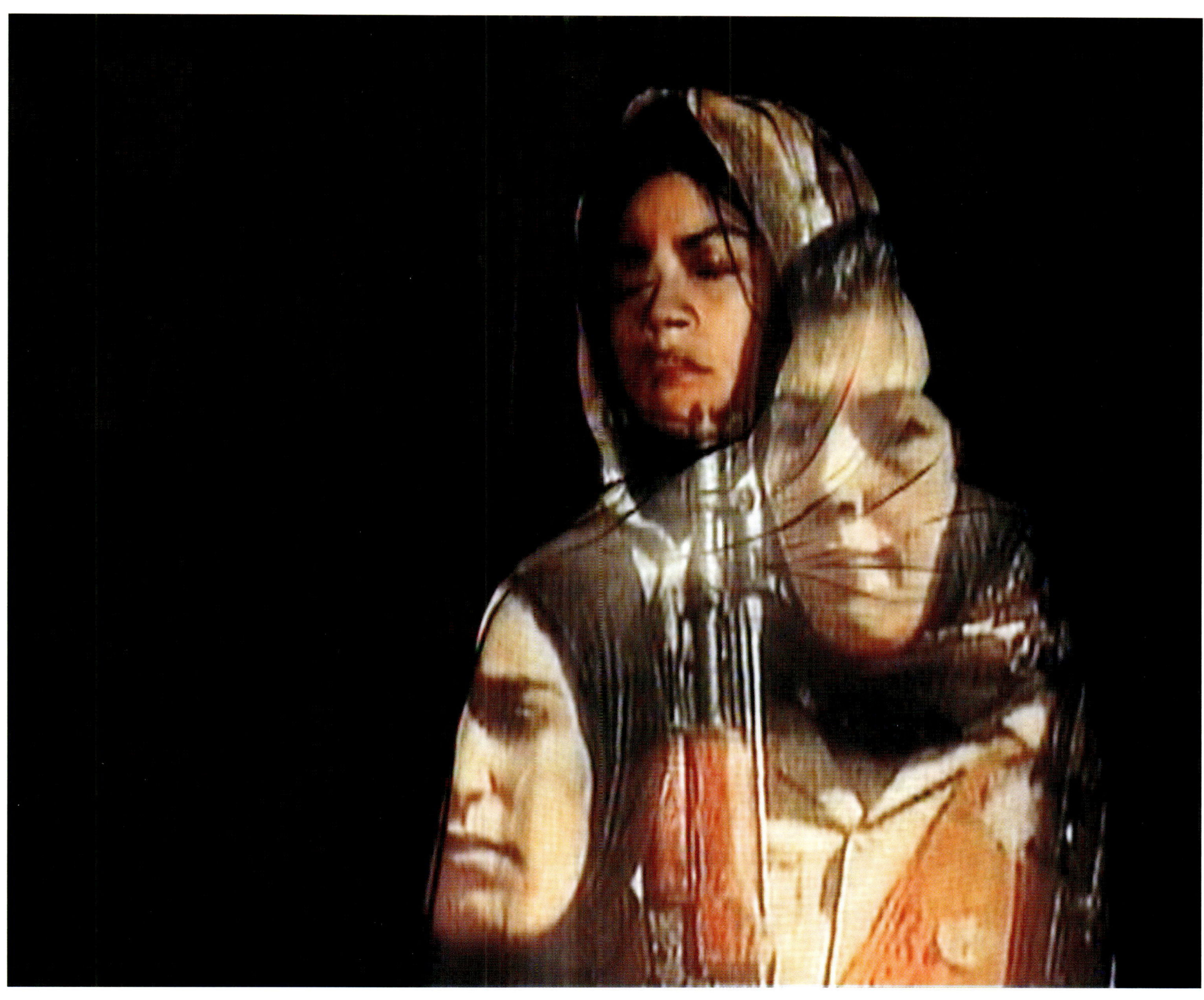

In Malani's version, the painted female musicians are startled out of their languorous state by the sound of a gunshot a century later. The new *tablecux vivant* in which they find themselves trapped develops into a macabre, bloody setting. What follows is a collage that is actually taking place in the minds of these female protagonists in the form of projections of memories, broken dreams and fears—cathartic experiences in a twilight zone. In an antagonistic and intensely psychological exchange we are witness to these desperate women and their helpless attempt to survive in a post-Nehruvian political landscape. Painful emotions are combined with intriguing text fragments from Heiner Mueller and Veena Das. Together they create a setting that is simultaneously repulsive and attractive. As Malani recounts: "I work between the scratch and graffiti (to paraphrase Heiner Mueller) or between the cathartic and the expressionistic (to paraphrase Antonin Artaud)." Although working with elements of Western and Eastern cultures, most of Malani's visual and sound elements have a multitude of references that are deeply rooted in the cultural history of India—from the typical Nehru slogan "Unity in Diversity" to the tone of the voice of the storyteller that resembles the way the upper-class Indian society spoke.

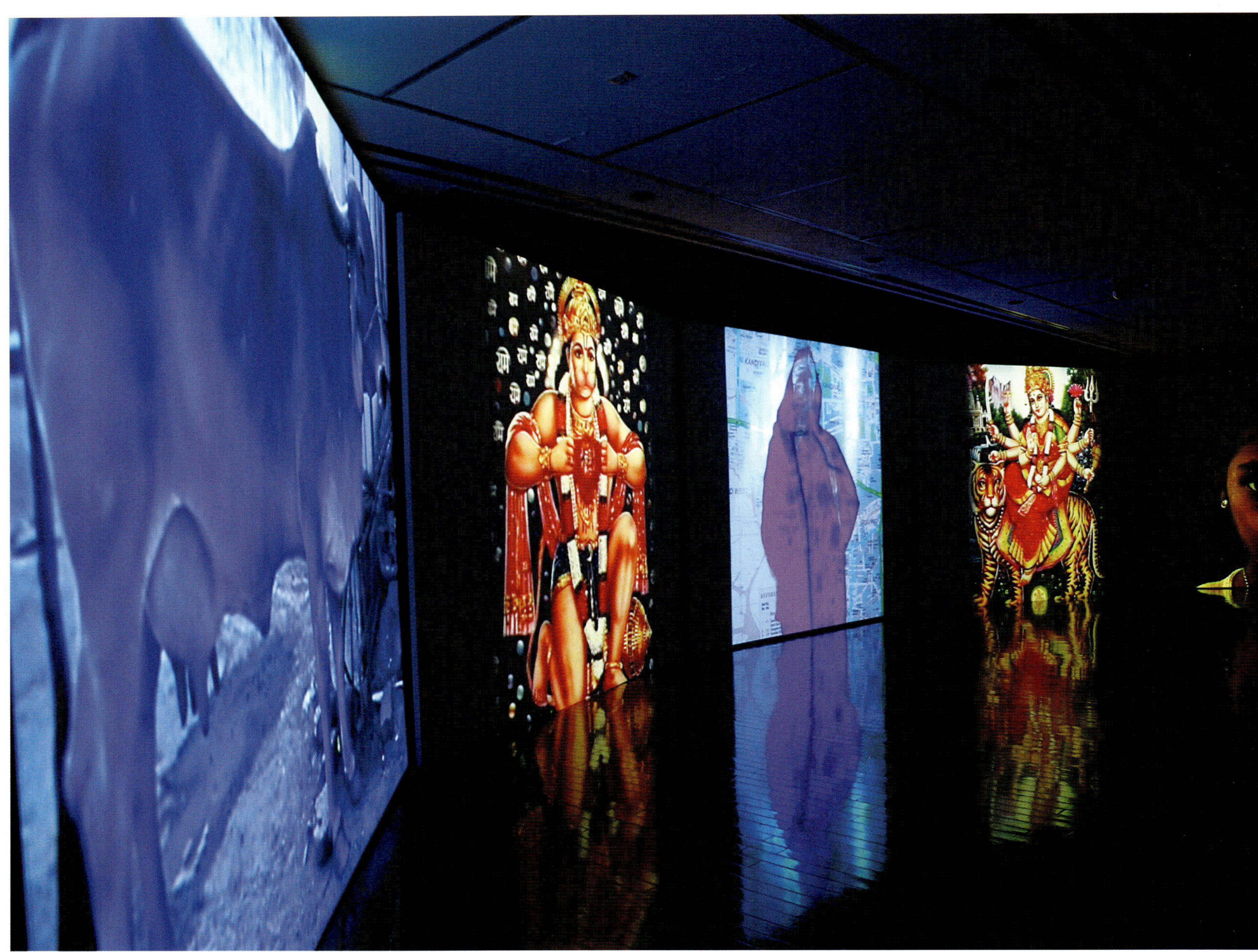

The central subject in *Unity in Diversity*—oppression and suffering—is universal and is one of the recurring elements in Malani's multilayered video installations, such as *Remembering Toba Tek Singh* (1998), *Hamletmachine* (2000) and *Mother India: Transactions in the Construction of Pain* (2005), and in her painting series *Mutants* (1994–98). India became independent in 1947; it was a moment for rejoicing, but with it came Partition, the schism of the subcontinent, and in the slipstream an ongoing series of sectarian violence ensued. In such situations, it is the powerless—the women and children—who suffer the most. So horrific was the violence that women were left speechless, their voices snuffed out. In the installation *Mother India,* the female protagonist cries out in a heartbreaking voice: "I died at the border of the new nations carrying a bloody rag as my flag."

JP

Nalini Malani. *Mother India: Transactions in the Construction of Pain*, 2005.
Five-channel video installation, sound, 5 1/2 minutes.
Installation view 5th Taipei Biennial.
Collection of the artist, Mumbai.
Photography: Courtesy of Johan Pijnappel.

Jitish Kallat

The English expression "money talks" means simply, "the man who pays the piper calls the tune." By extension, it could mean that perception changes depending on who is perceiving—rich or poor. The value of a single rupee—its purchasing power as well as the mere significance of what it meant to have or have not—varies greatly between strata of Indian society. Jitish Kallat examines this disparity with his installation *Death of Distance*. Two news reports were the source of his narrative. One told of a twelve-year-old girl who committed suicide after her mother told her she could not afford even one rupee for a school meal. The other recounted the Indian Government's announcement of the "One India Plan [which] will mark the *death of distance* as you can call from one end of the country to the other for one rupee." Hence, the ironic title of Kallat's work.

Both stories are juxtaposed in each of the five lenticular prints, forcing the viewer to see one or the other (but not both simultaneously) with a mere shift of vantage point. Neither can be read at the same time. The story changes with

Pages 80–81:
Jitish Kallat. *Death of Distance*, 2006.
Mixed media; variable size.
Courtesy of Walsh Gallery, Chicago.
Photography: Courtesy of the artist.

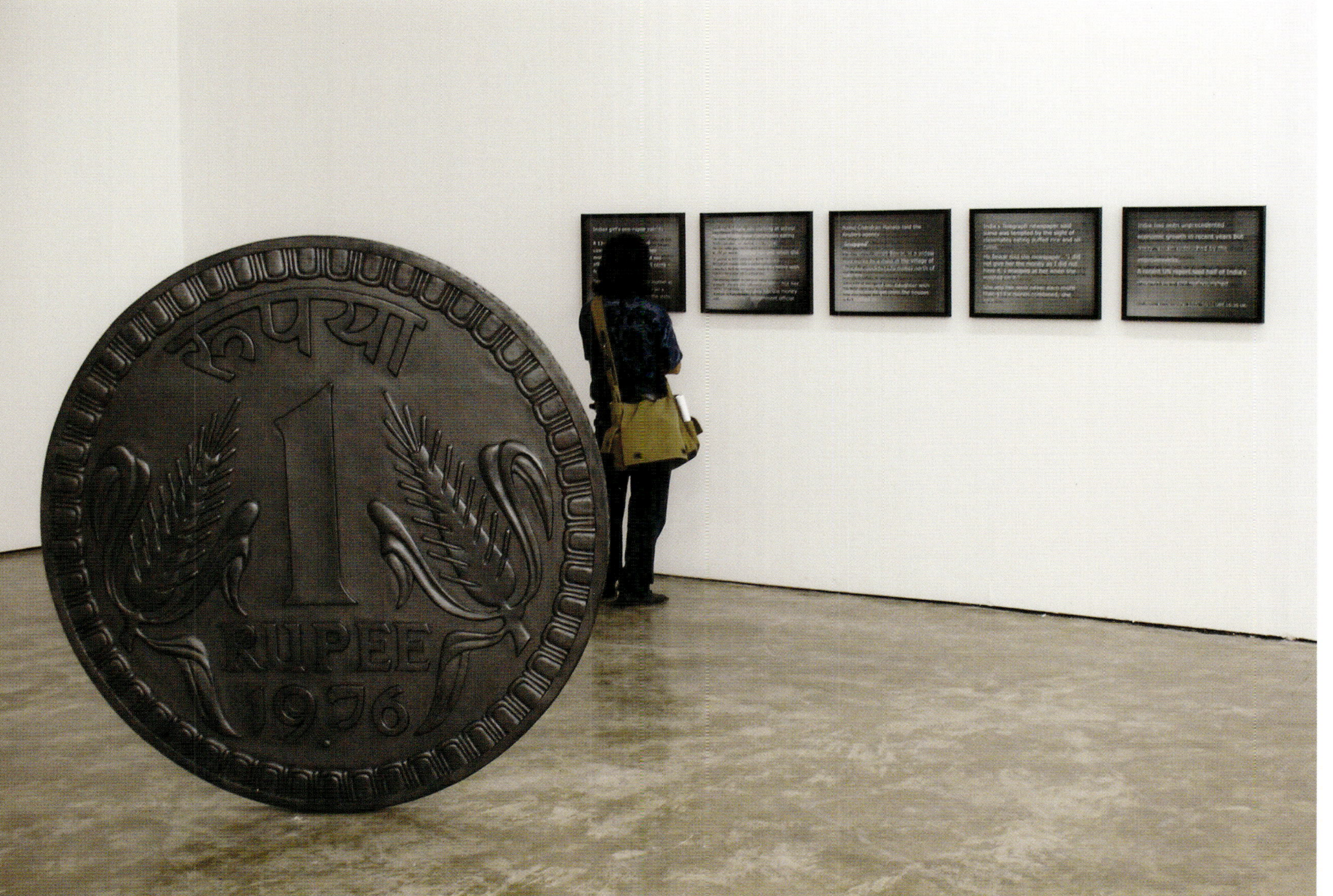

T.V. Ramachandran, director general COAI, said that this initiative by Communications & IT Minister Dayanidhi Maran, would lead to an explosion in long distance traffic as it had made STD calls affordable and within reach of each and every citizen in the country.

He added that One India was the brilliant culmination of an exercise initiated by the minister in May 2005 to demolish entry barriers for long distance calls within the country.

[Indo-Asian News Service 10 February 2006]

India has seen unprecedented economic growth in recent years but many remain untouched by the improvements.
A recent UN report said half of India's children were still malnourished.

Saturday, 24 September 2005, 14:35 GMT 15:35 UK.

how one positions oneself in relationship to the text; metaphorically, how one considers the rupee. The rupee itself is here too, larger than life, its diameter the height of an average Indian.

       Traditional museum formality informs the viewer's initial perception of *Death of Distance*. A large metallic sculpture—the emblematic lead-clad rupee—sits monumentally alone on the gallery floor. Five text panels—the lenticular prints with their hybridized realities forced into single frames—are mounted on the wall behind. One would expect the usual didactic panel with "dumbed-down," vaguely academic text. What we read however, does not jibe with our visual expectation. In order to get the message, the viewer must stop to read it; participation is essential for the perception of Kallat's narrative. Shocking the public out of its complacency is a dynamic element in the artist's commentary, his very purpose perhaps. *Death of Distance* may have been the promotional phrase used by the government in its ignorant attitude about what a rupee means to *everyone* in India; but distance—grand distance—is exactly what Kallat is showcasing here.

BS

Shilpa Gupta

Long after one has stopped playing with Shilpa Gupta's first interactive video installation, one sentence keeps on bouncing in one's mind: "TERROR TERROR TERROR—WAR FOR TERROR." A slogan that has cast a long shadow over a bright new millennium and, according to some governments, will continue to do so for the next generation. Using a wide-angle lens, one is confronted with a joyful parade of seven young women, that soon transforms into an unusual physical and mental drill with lyrics like:

ORDER TALK ORDER TALK TALK ORDER ORDER ORDER
ORDER SHOP ORDER SHOP SHOP SHOP ORDER ORDER
DON'T SEE DON'T HEAR DON'T SPEAK
SHUT UP AND BE HEY HEY SHUT UP AND BE HEY HEY
DON'T INTERRUPT PRAY PRAY PRAY DON'T INTERRUPT
AIM 1234 LEFT KILL 1234 KILL 1234 RIGHT KILL 1234 KILL KILL KILL KILL

All protagonists are the artist herself, appearing in different avatars in a "hot," "sporty," "guard," "lady," "girl," "boy" and "forty"-type of look. They all have their own identities, but share one item—the use of military camouflage cloth in their

Shilpa Gupta. *Untitled*, 2004.
Single-channel video installation, sound,
1.4 minutes looped.
Collection of Lekha and Anupam Poddar,
New Delhi.
Photography: Courtesy of the artist.

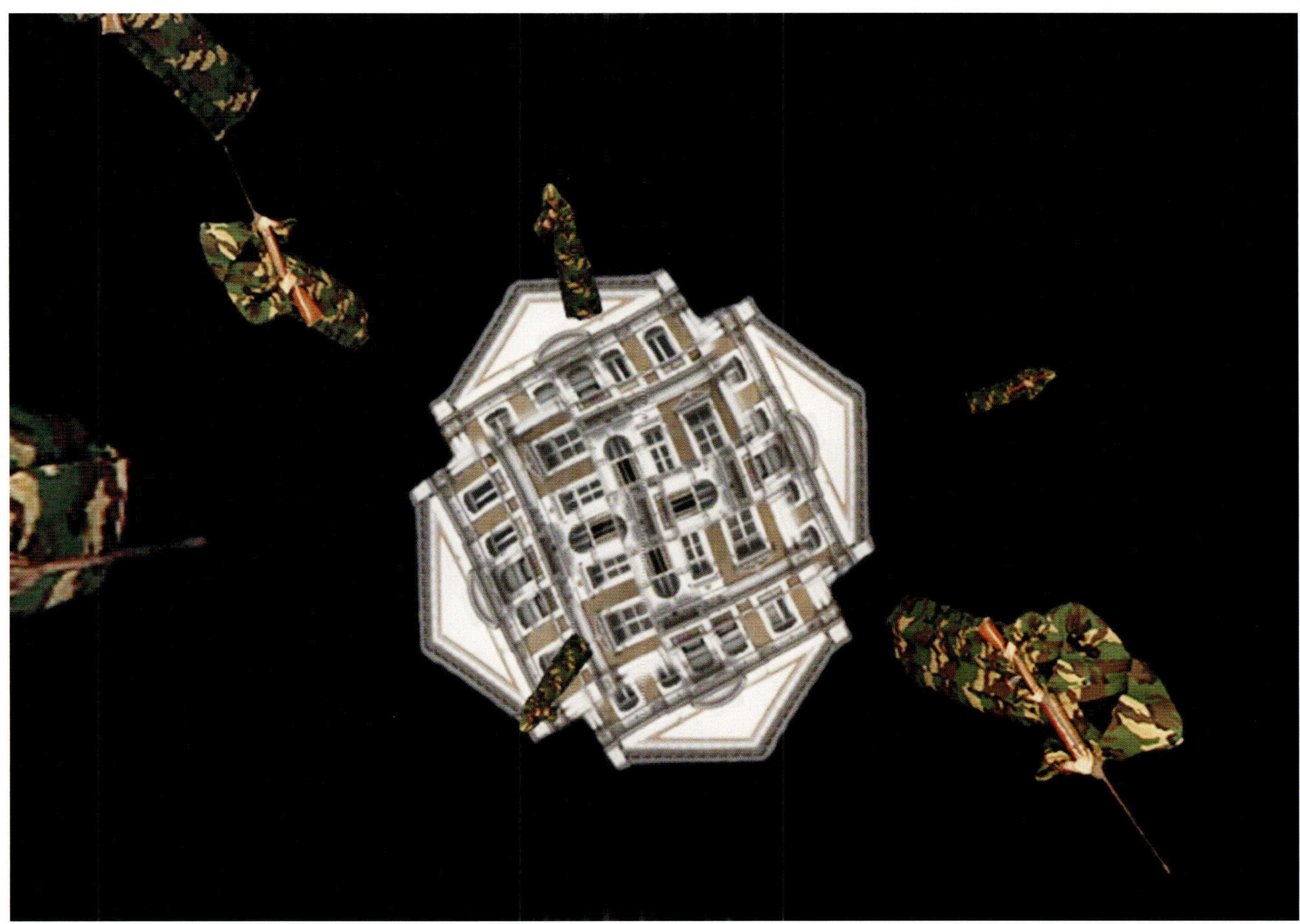

clothing, a style that has become popular among the Indian middle class since the "War on Terror," and is available at the bazaars just around the corner from where the artist lives in Mumbai. It is a fashion style that Gupta has used in several of her other works: the single-channel video installation *Untitled* (2004), in which starships created from morphing Western architecture are infiltrated by dozens of military "guards," or the website installation *blessed-bandwidth.net* (2003) in which Gupta appears as a "guard" next to a pop-up box: "Do Not Panic. You Are being Watched. Get Blessed. Feel Secure—Order Issued by the State."

Gupta's first interactive game goes back to a popular Indian nursery poem that was taught to her little niece. However, in Gupta's transformation, the subject is less innocent and relates directly to how people are numbed in society, almost "programmed." For Gupta, group movements in synchrony—for example, in marches and drills—have in the past been proven to be instrumental in indoctrinating the mind, be they rigorous State military drills, Indian RSS body drills, or Nazi mass salutes. Gupta links this idea to New Age art-of-living courses, each establishing a narrow-minded order, equivalent to the one route that leads you through her interactive game. It is a situation that resembles the "War on Terror" that employs a propaganda machine as a drill for other purposes, and in which television and other media are used as tools. It creates, according to Gupta, a state of fake/non-existent/hyper-existence, where information can exist in the understanding and not in the reality. She describes a new world order: "In the past few years, with very high technology we have been able to live through wars and violence in our living rooms, with our hands on our laps sitting on couches, while a spot of light on a black screen just destroyed a city and killed someone's father, mother, best friends, someone's child, right in front of us while we sat, while we watched."

JP

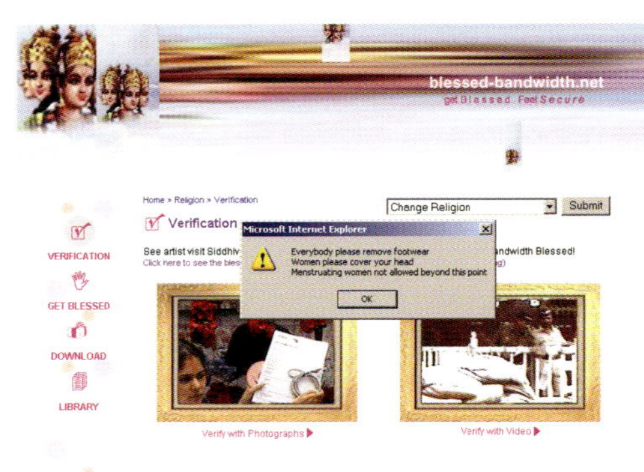

Shilpa Gupta. *blessed-bandwidth.net*, 2003.
Interactive website.
Collection of Tate Modern, London.
Photography: Courtesy of the artist.

Shilpa Gupta. *Untitled*, 2004.
Interactive single wide angle projection installation, sound.
Collection of Fukuoka Asian Art Museum and Daimler Chrysler, Stuttgart.
Photography: Courtesy of Hyung Min Moon, Seoul.

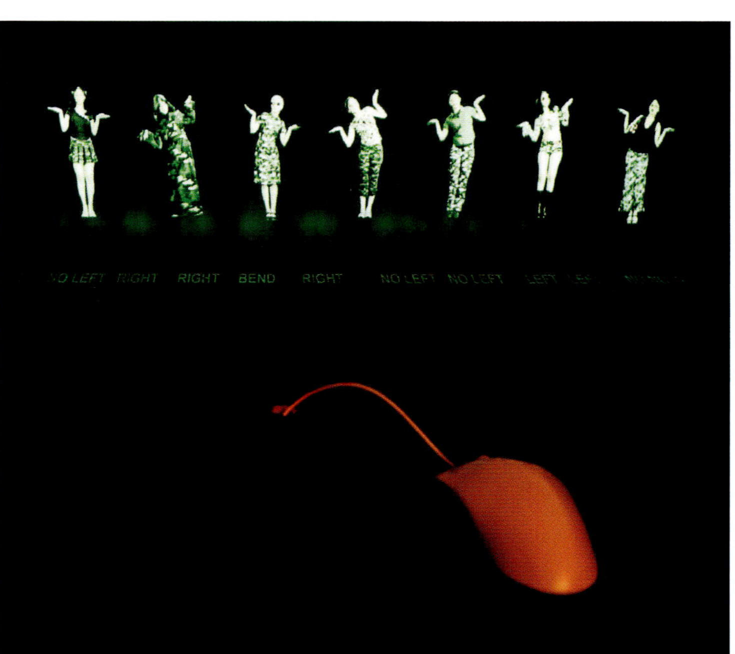

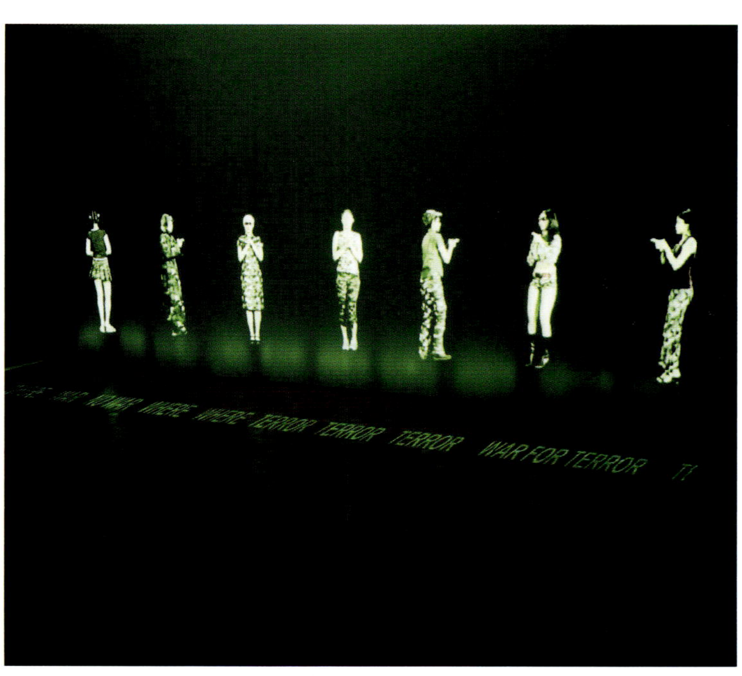

Ranbir Kaleka

Ranbir Kaleka refers to *Crossings* as: "a magico-realist drama of private lives and historical engagements with a smudging of boundaries which bring reality into fantasy and fantasy into our reality." The installation is an unusual combination of media in which a classic panorama of paintings seems to come alive. The video images on occasion move away from their painted selves leaving behind a color image or a monochromatic ghost as an "after-image." They travel to other paintings, sometimes to revisit past moments in their memories, before returning to inhabit and reanimate their "material" bodies. The stories engage us in the overlapping of both mediums that bring forth an extra dimension.

Ranbir Kaleka made his first combination of video and painting in 1999, with *Man Threading a Needle*. It shows a middle-aged working-class man sitting in a brightly colored environment focusing on his task. Nothing happens while he concentrates on threading the needle. You hear him breathing and in the distance the sound of a passing train. Kaleka's interest in this unusual combination of mediums sprang not so much from an interest in video but from his abiding passion for cinema. For it was in cinema that he found an intriguing form of intensity where a *moment could become overcharged*. This was a goal he had set for himself in his paintings but felt that this could shift to yet another level.

Kaleka has been contemplating the concept of *Crossings* for some years. He has been working the idea through in all its complexities with regard to scale, choreography and sound so it carries the "charge" he has been seeking. The video/paintings tell two intermingling stories. One is about a group of people that seem to have been rendered homeless. Without any possessions, they wait at the edge of a political/geographical/psychological boundary where they twitch, shudder, inspect

Ranbir Kaleka. *Crossings*, 2005.
Four-channel video installation with four acrylic paintings on canvas, sound, 15 minutes.
Collection of Shumita and Arani Bose, New York.
Photography: Courtesy of Bose Pacia Gallery.

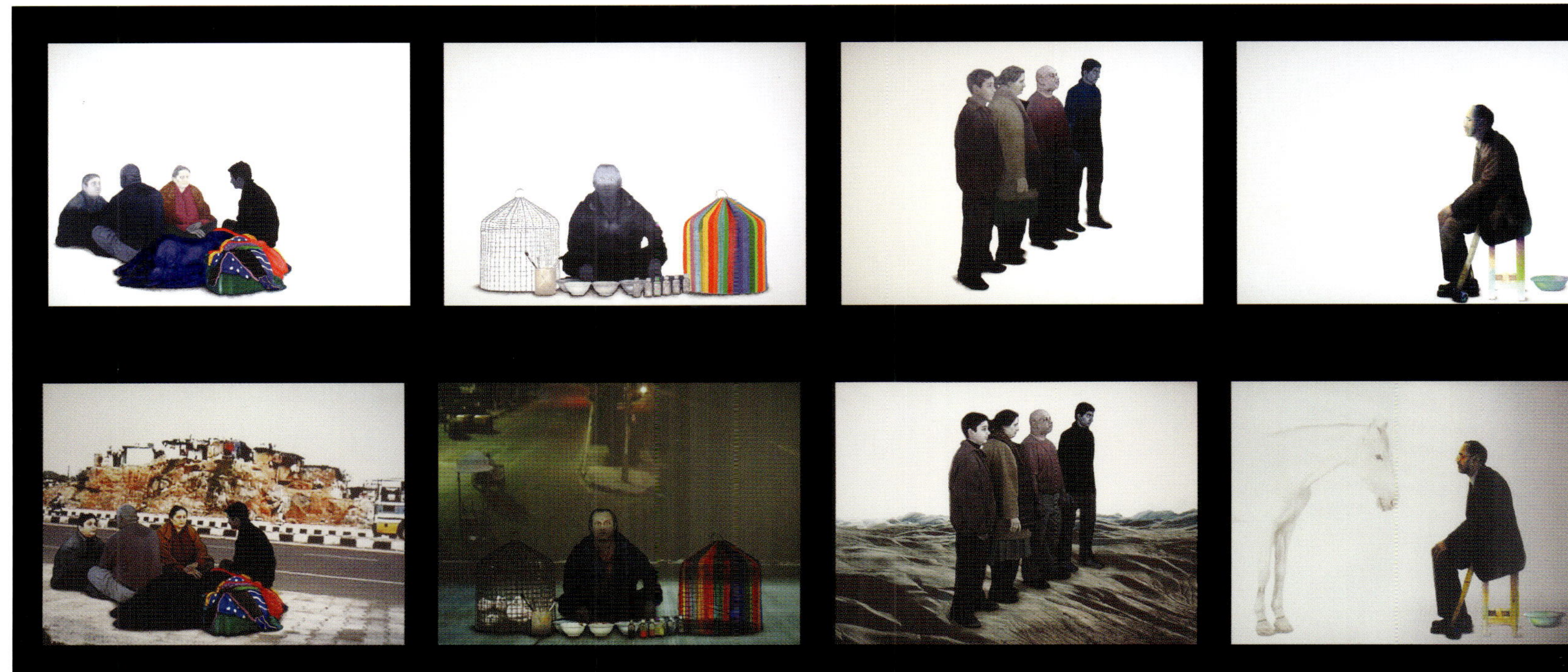

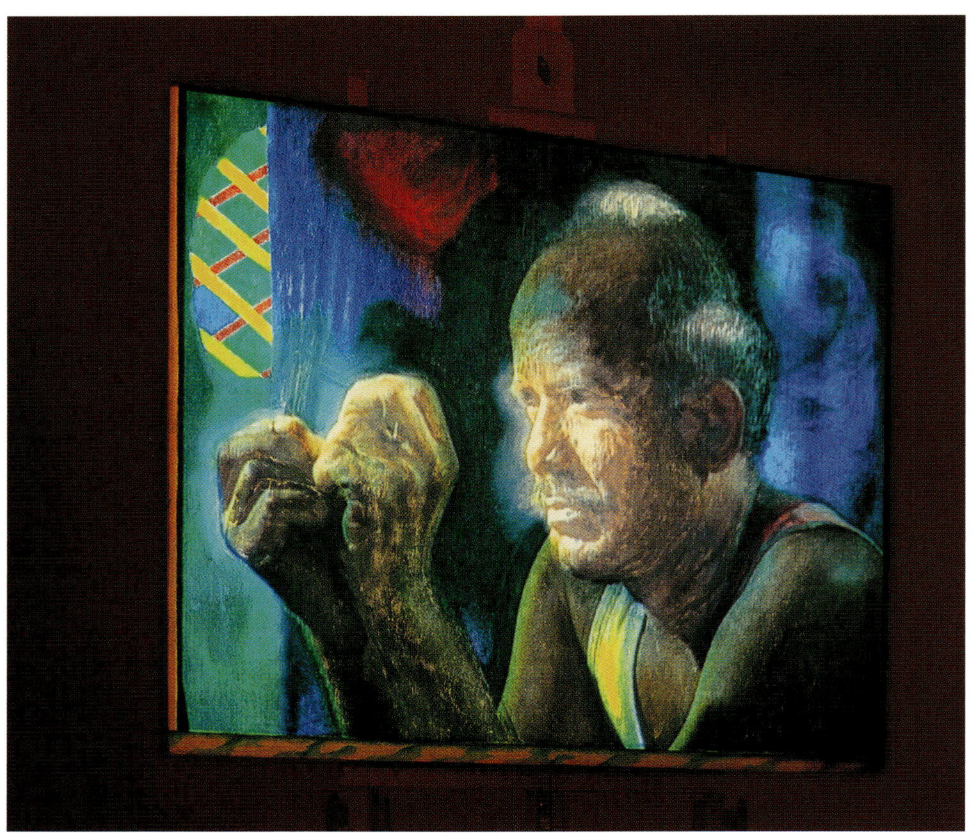

Ranbir Kaleka. *Man Threading a Needle*, 1999.
Single-channel video installation with painting on canvas, sound, 3 minutes.
Collection of the artist.
Photography: Courtesy of the artist.

one another, or occasionally holler into the distance. Among them is a sick person who sleeps in a fetal position. The second story is about a boy's "rites of passage," in which symbols of community and self-identity are passed on, in this case a Sikh turban. The turban is one of the symbols of the adult male Sikh. Here, it has not only a religious and cultural meaning, but it also gained historical significance in India after the assassination of Indira Gandhi in 1984. The older boy in the video allows the turban to be tied on his head. The second child shakes his head in refusal when offered a choice of multicolored turbans. After an extensive voyage to an alien land, the younger boy leaves the two older men who are preparing the long cloth of the turban. He runs toward windmills in a vast open landscape and the men knowingly smile at each other with a hint of admiration for the little child in his acceptance of the "inevitable." In an interview with the author, Kaleka defined the contents of this work: "It all relates to the notion of desire for a place. A psychological space that allows you a movement from one point to another. Where one space of comfort leads to another space of comfort."[1]

JP

---

1   Ranbir Kaleka in an interview with Johan
     Pijnappel, 3 March, 2006.

Single-channel Video Art

Stinging Kiss turns the male Bollywood stereotype completely on its head. In Tejal Shah's version of the usual kidnapping story, she herself acts as the male dacoit. Anuj Vaidya, the male co-producer of the video, plays the coy, kidnapped "girlfriend" in beard and sari. The hero is the great macho superstar, the one and only Amitabh Bachchan, montaged from found footage. When the superhero "Big B," for the first time in the history of Bollywood fails to rescue his girlfriend on time, this cross-gender narrative turns rather risqué as the dacoit forces "himself" on *Miss* Pretty.

Tejal Shah. *Chingari Chumma/Stinging Kiss*, 2000.
Single-channel video, sound, 8 minutes.
Collection of Lekha and Anupam Poddar,
New Delhi.
Photography: Courtesy of the artist.

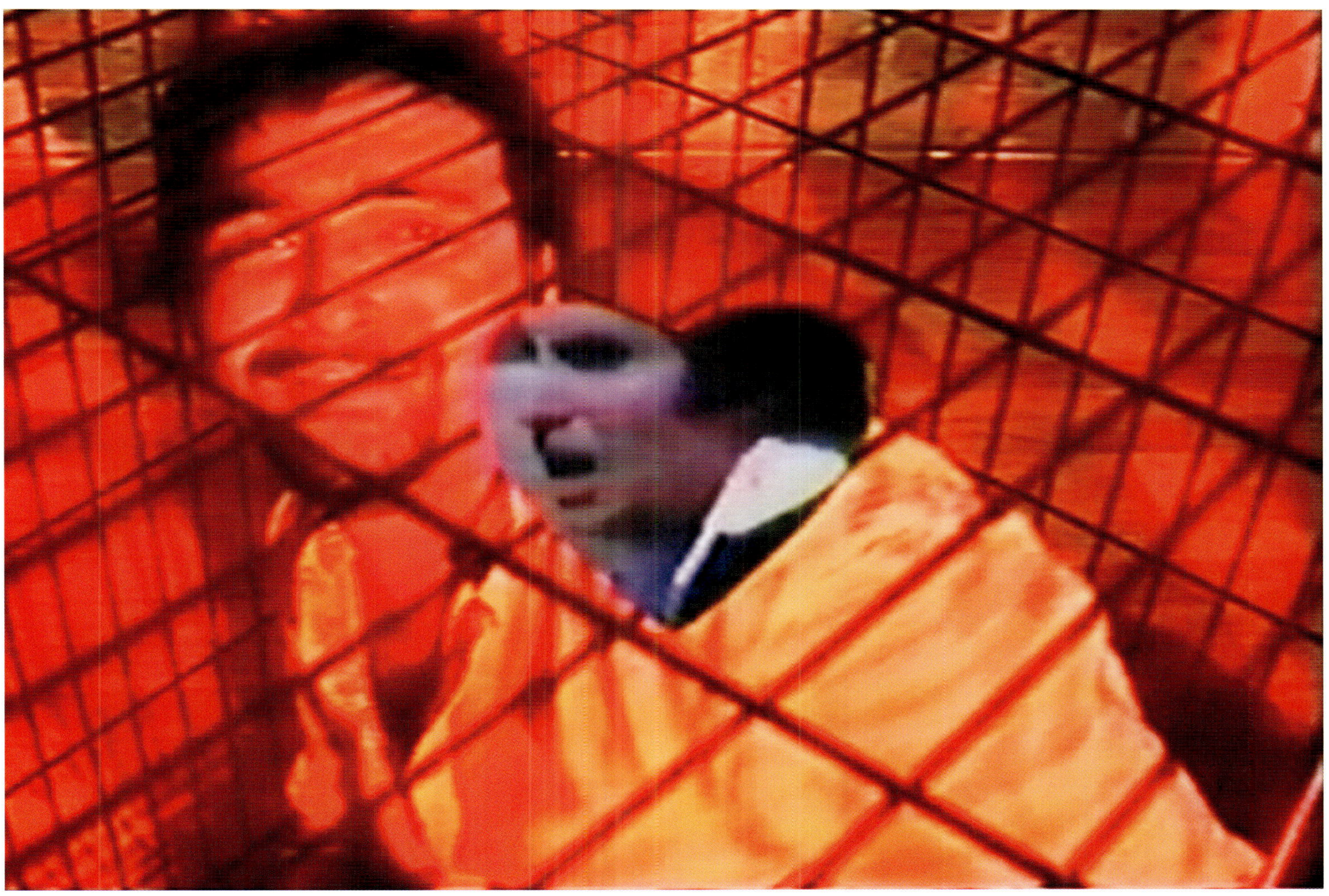

In the line of the famous Buddhist *Jataka* tales, Tushar Joag tells us his version of the incarnation of the Buddha in both human and animal form. He gives it a totally new twist when the narrator recounts, "His memory was made up of conflated images of butchery, war footage and animated cartoons." At the end of his third *Jataka* tale, Joag formulates the new state of Utopia as, "Only to be reborn as a gob of spittle, languorously sliding down the tiles of some ravaged museum. Carrying the germ of new cultures or a culture of new germs."

Tushar Joag. *Jataka Trilogy*, 2004.
Single-channel video, sound, 7 minutes.
Collection of the artist, Mumbai.
Photography: Courtesy of the artist.

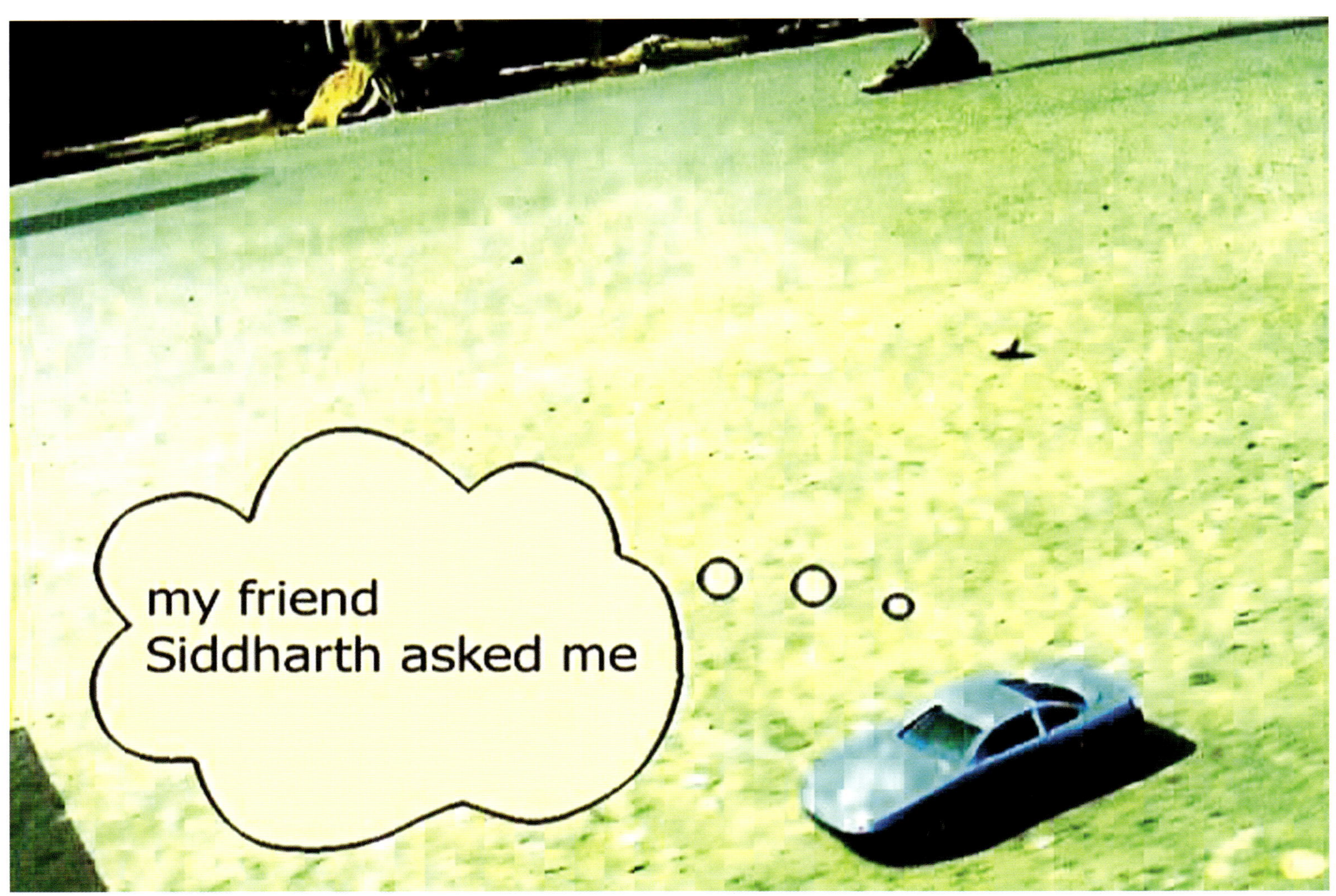

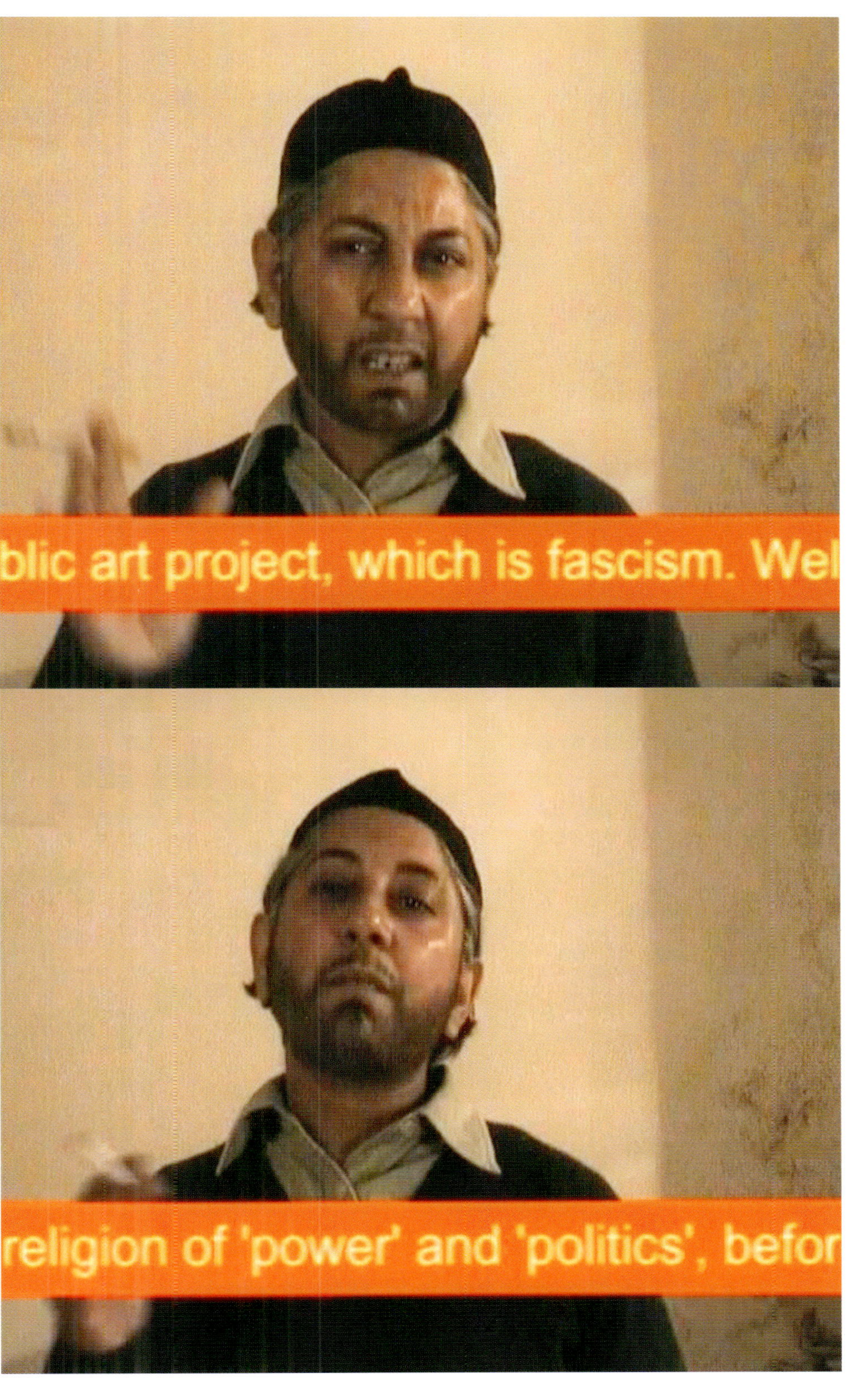

Anita Dube. *Kissa-e-Noor Mohammed (Garam Hawa),* 2004.
Single-channel video, sound, 15 minutes.
Collection of the artist, New Delhi.
Photography: Courtesy of the artist.

This seemingly straightforward video document shows the confessions of a local Muslim worker called Noor, who is offered—in the tradition of Andy Warhol—15 minutes to stand in the limelight. In his deceptively simple wisdom, the man speaks to the artist Anita Dube about his work and his daily experiences. He even has comments on politics and art, "Art cannot comprehend the spectacular power of the grotesque public art project, which is fascism." It is only when the final credits appear that the identity of the bearded, heavily smoking Noor are unveiled as being none other than the artist Dube herself.

As a cinematic tableau, this work gives us the impression of being from another era, with its blackened edges and flicker—as if it were made from archival footage or from an old training film. In a funny, touching way, Pushpamala N. portrays the ideal Indian family woven into the idea of the nation during the 1950s. While the father ponders eternal ballistic problems, his wife's existence is reduced to preparing mango chutneys from recipes. In this seemingly happy family, her political engagement reaches no further than preparing a national pudding and indigenous salad to celebrate Independence Day.

Pushpamala N. *Rashtriya Kheer and Desiy Salad*, 2004.
Collection of Centre Pompidou, Paris.
Photography: Courtesy of the artist.

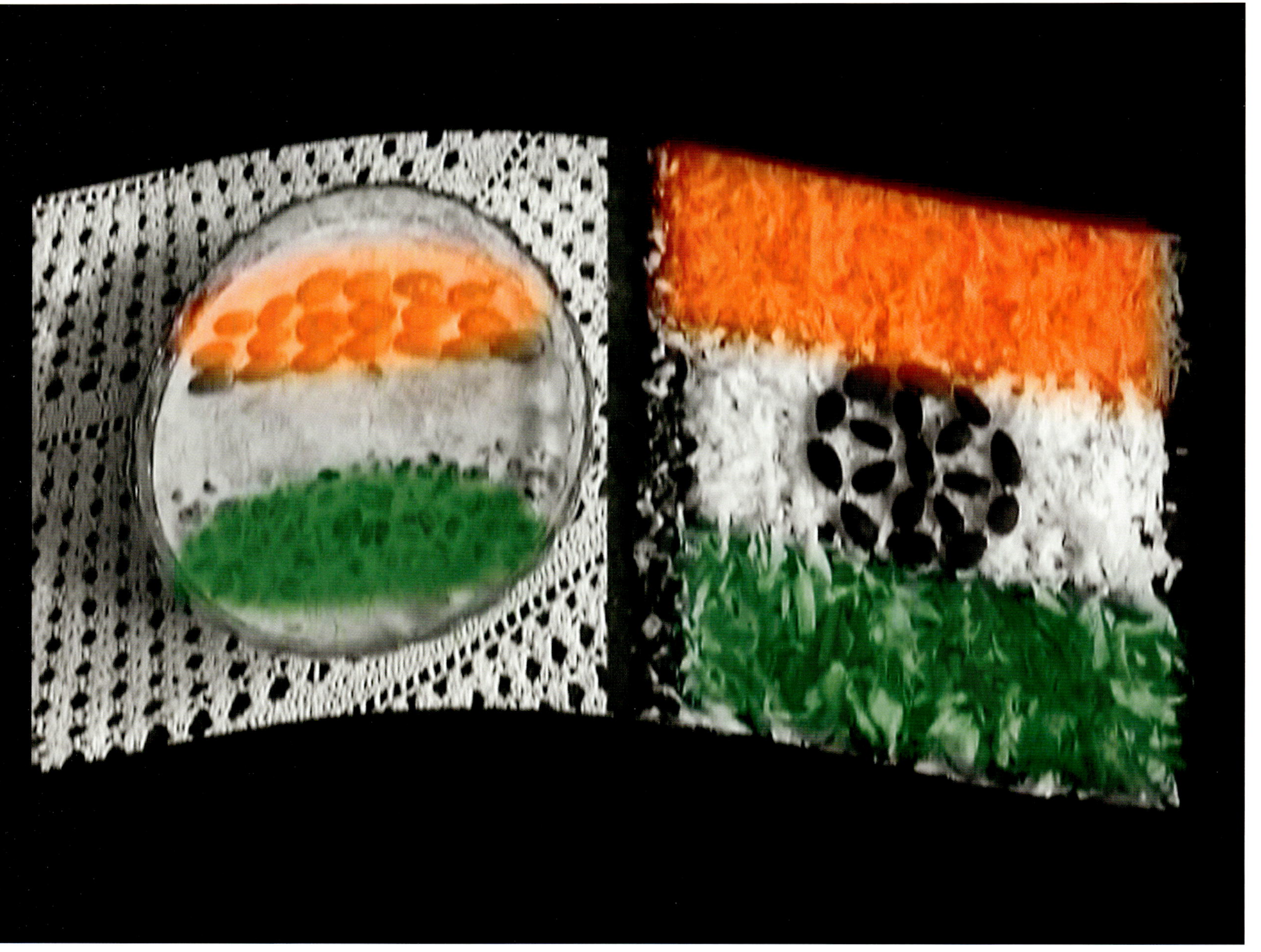

Scrolls is an appropriation from the popular TV serial, *Mahabharata*, by B. R. Chopra. After showing the introductory credits of this great Hindu epic, the war between brothers is depicted as a moral struggle with egotism, duty, selfishness, greed and deception. Valay Shende added to this the "breaking news" strip, revealing personal announcements from hospitalized Muslim victims, the need for blood donations and the "we are safe" messages from Hindu relatives. *Scrolls* was made after the Gujarat violence in 2002, about which Shende comments, "In the present state it seems men exist only for the downfall of other men."

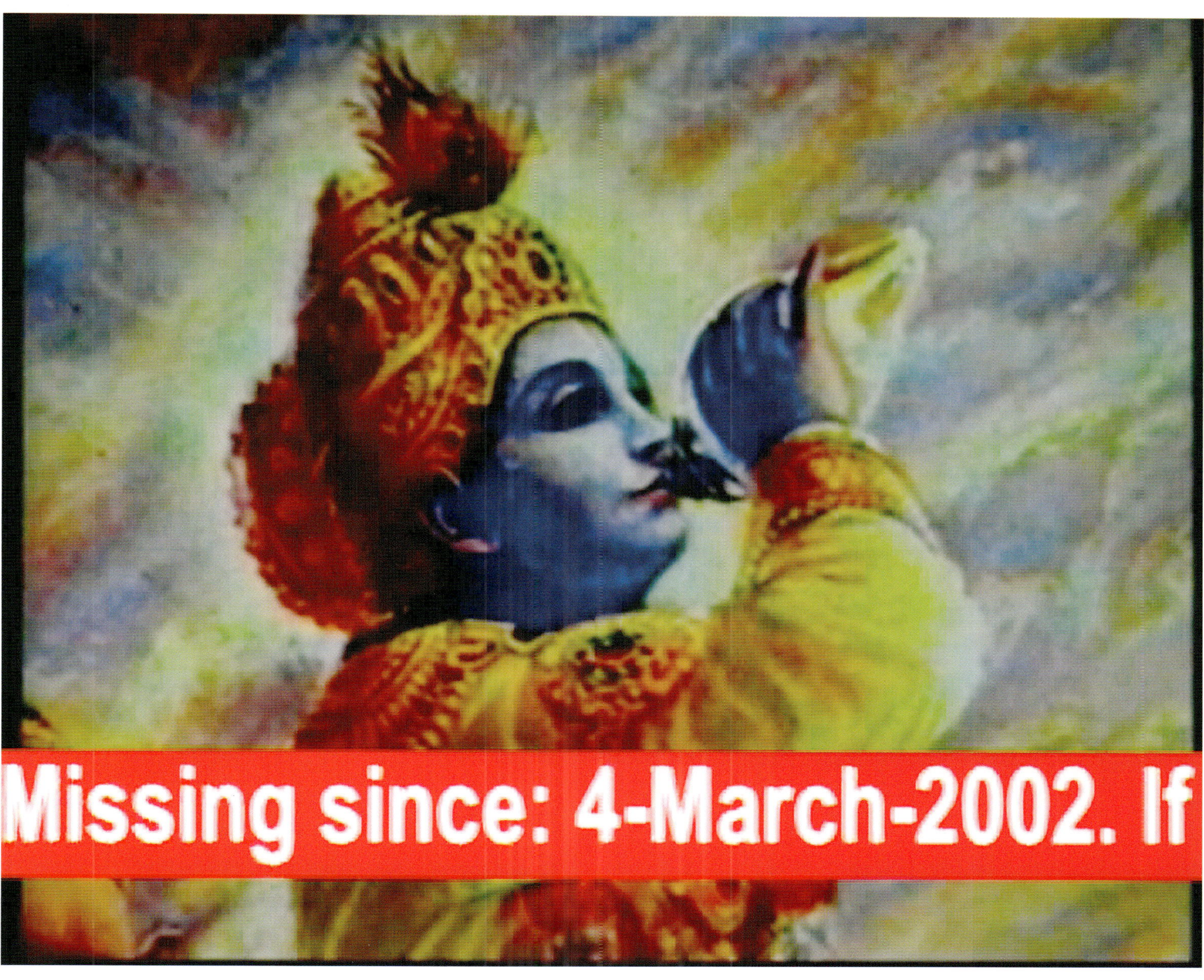

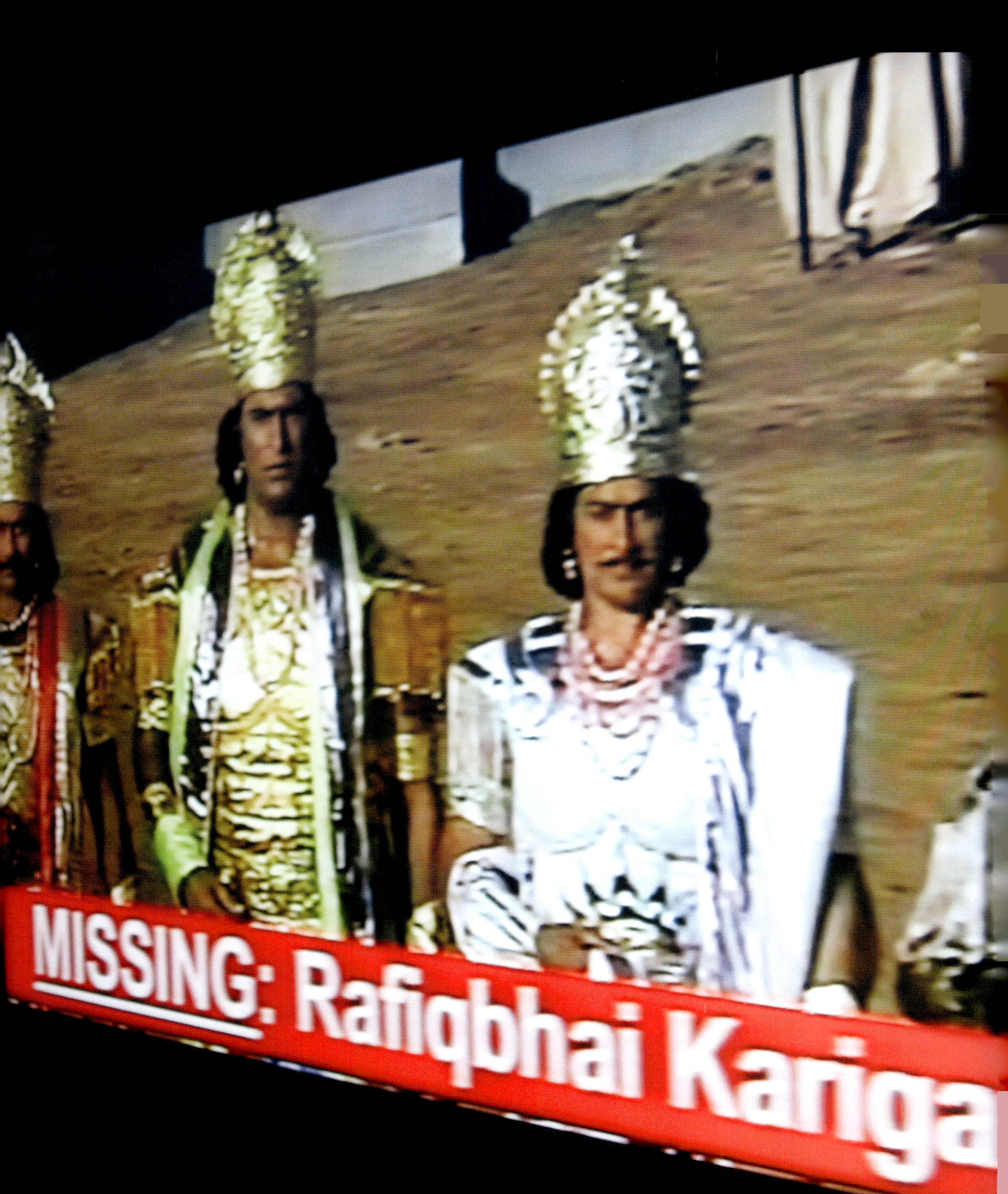

MISSING: Rafiqbhai Kariga

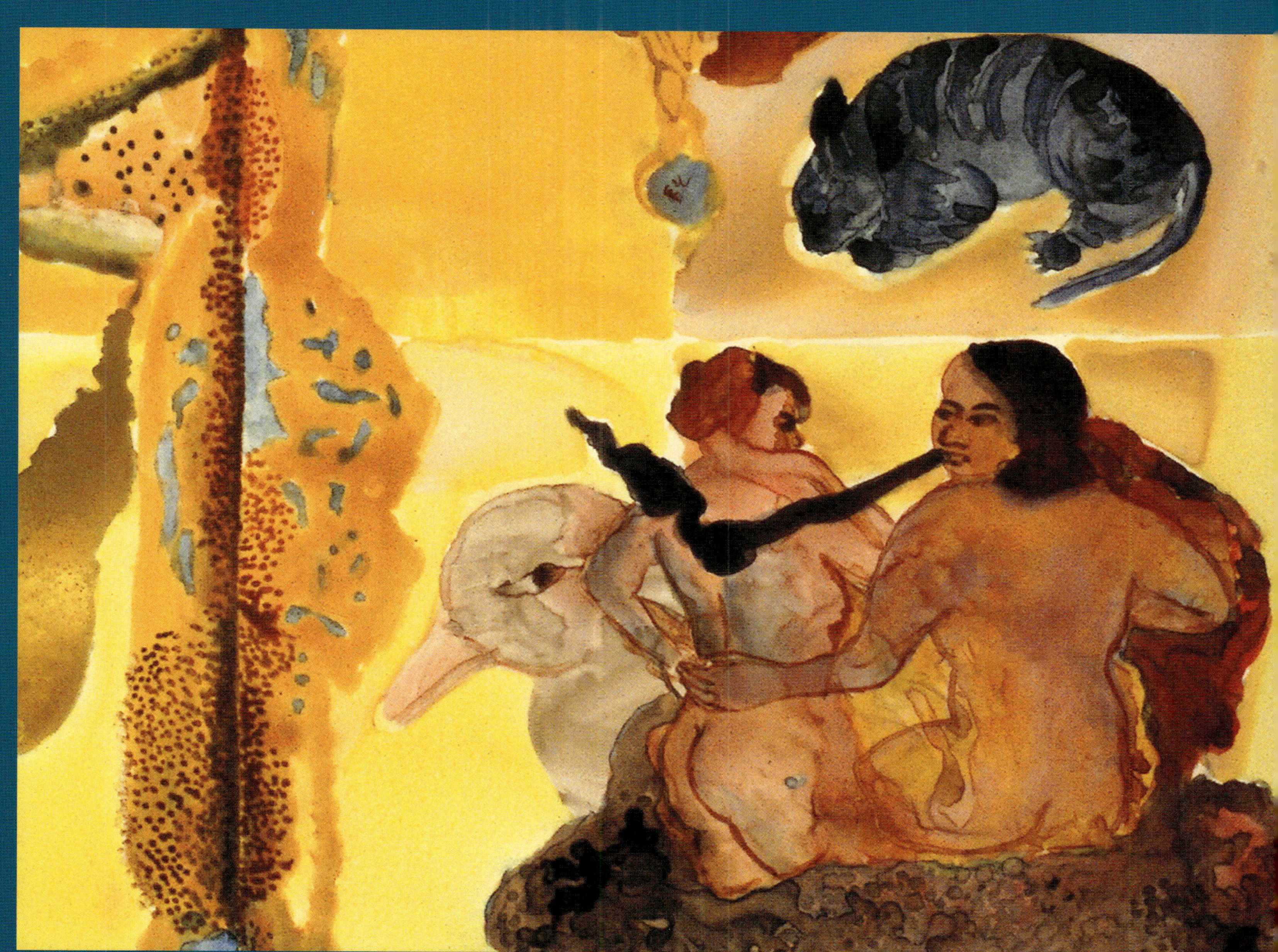

Nalini Malani. *Sita/Medea 2*, 2004. Detail, see page 102.

LOOKING BACKWARD
Interpreting Texts

Reena Saini Kallat

·

Sheba Chhachhi

·

Nalini Malani

·

Atul Dodiya

·

Jitish Kallat

Reena Saini Kallat

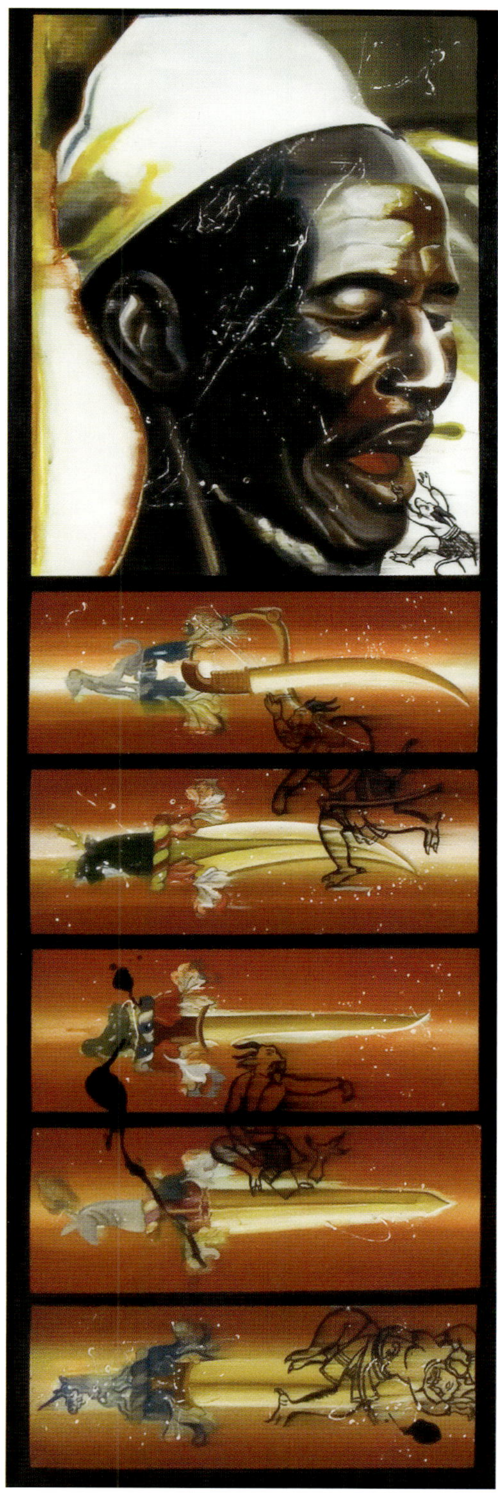

Reena Saini Kallat. *Sword Swallower, No. 2*, 2004.
Acrylic on paper; 78x28 in.
Collection of Mr. Adhiraj Singh, New Delhi.
Photography: Courtesy of Gallery Chemould and
the artist.

With the grafting of an everyman's (or -woman's) head and torso above a graphic-novel version of Indian mythology, Reena Saini Kallat insinuates the connective thread of cultural history into her series of *Sword Swallowers*. Their life-size, vertical format, with a naturally realized head at the top and a classic comic book depiction of gods or demons below—where the body should be—asks the viewer to consider that the mythological cultural essence of India is in the blood of every person; there is no escape, history has been swallowed with the sword. Sadly, violence is in our blood and embedded in the core of our being.

The artist wants us to consider the men-on-the-Mumbai-street (the heads are taken from printed news media) and what fundamentalism means to them. The Hindu Right in India is delivering sacred myths with the sword. A balancing act between traditional and contemporary narratives teeters along the edge of that blade.

The onyx skin of *Sword Swallower, No. 2* is in sharp contrast with his traditional white Muslim cap; his open mouth (in prayer, perhaps) reveals a tongue the same color as that of all humans. He appears to be warding off the onslaught of a mythological demon with his voice alone. Disregarding the visual boundaries of each cel, this same linearly depicted *asura* (demon) skates on the knife edges of a variety of traditional weapons. Ignoring also the talismanic power of their animal headed hilts, he lies defeated in the bottom panel.

Bisecting a medieval European heraldic panel, *asura*s dominate the three central panels of *Sword Swallower, No. 9*—one in active combat with Reena Kallat's mighty flamboyant sword, the other lying defeated with limbs akimbo. The young woman above gazes shyly, seeming unaware of the symbolic warfare that swirls below.

Sword Swallower, No. 10 is a child in white who bears the ultimate injury of the artist's narrative swordplay. The damaging blade is embedded in his core, replacing his sternum as support for the ribcage that protects his heart.

BS

Opposite page
Left:
Reena Saini Kallat. *Sword Swallower, No. 9*, 2004.
Acrylic on paper; 78x28 in.
Collection of John Lynch, New Delhi.
Photography: Courtesy of Gallery Chemould and the artist.

Right:
Reena Saini Kallat. *Sword Swallower, No. 10*, 2004.
Acrylic on paper; 78x28 in.
Collection of Amrita Jhaveri, Mumbai.
Photography: Courtesy of Gallery Chemould and the artist.

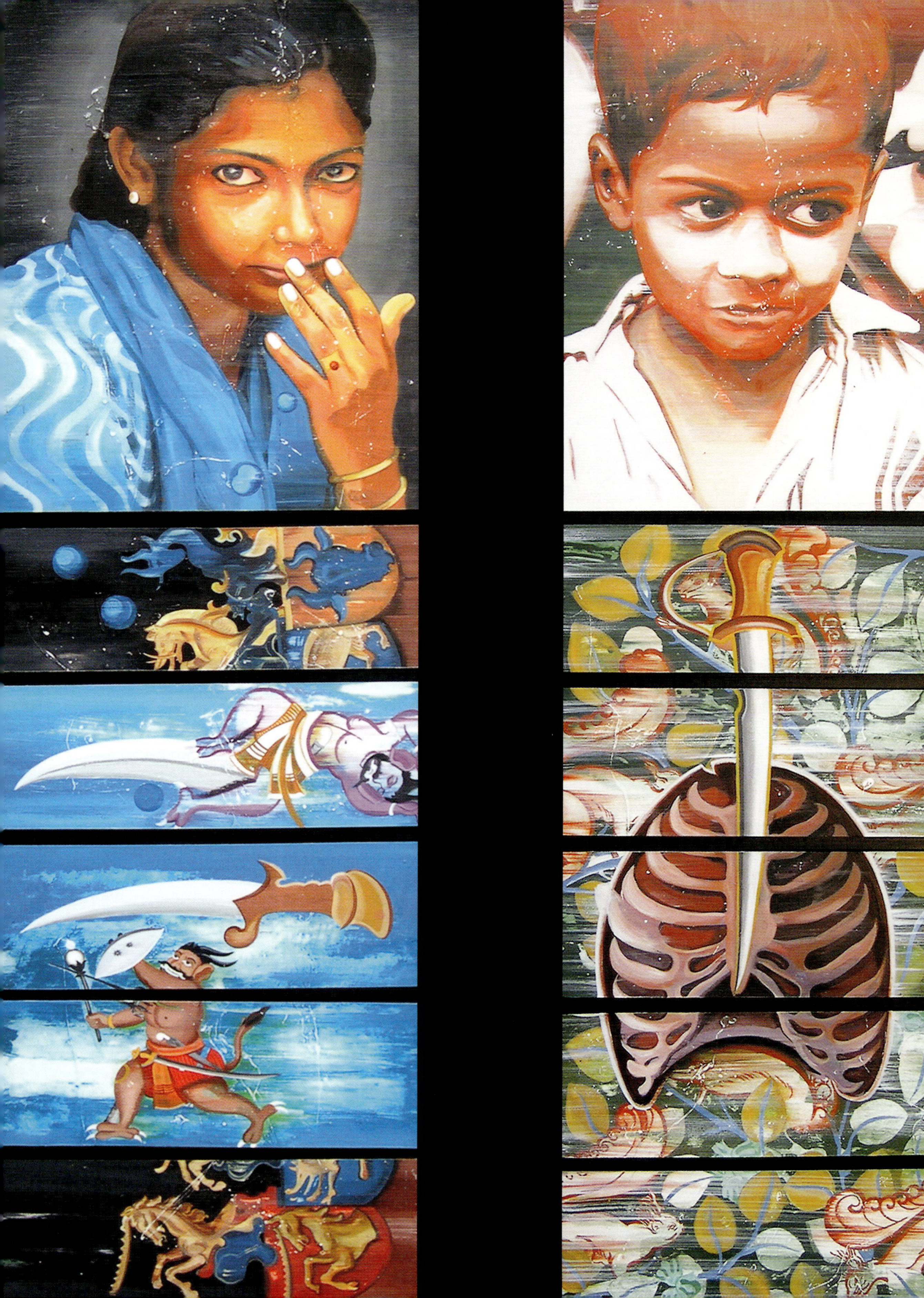

Sheba Chhachhi

Walking into the installation *Neelkanth: poison/nectar* is like taking a bird's-eye view over a mythical city in which hundreds of skyscraper towers are made of a shining reflecting metal. As one draws closer, one notices images of sense organs on the tops. Eyes, ears, mouths, fingertips, nostrils transform the cityscape into a massive living organism. At the four corners are translites with photographs of the daily residues of the city in the form of massive garbage landfills. These sepia-toned frozen moments—seductive, attractive even—are reminiscent of colonial landscape photography, but are, after all, the city's garbage. The birds and a lonely cow trying to find some food to survive in this debris remind us of the environmental responsibilities created by rapid Indian urban development in the process of globalization. To question this situation Chhachhi turns in this installation to an ancient—but extant—Indian myth, the story of Neelkanth (Blue Throat):

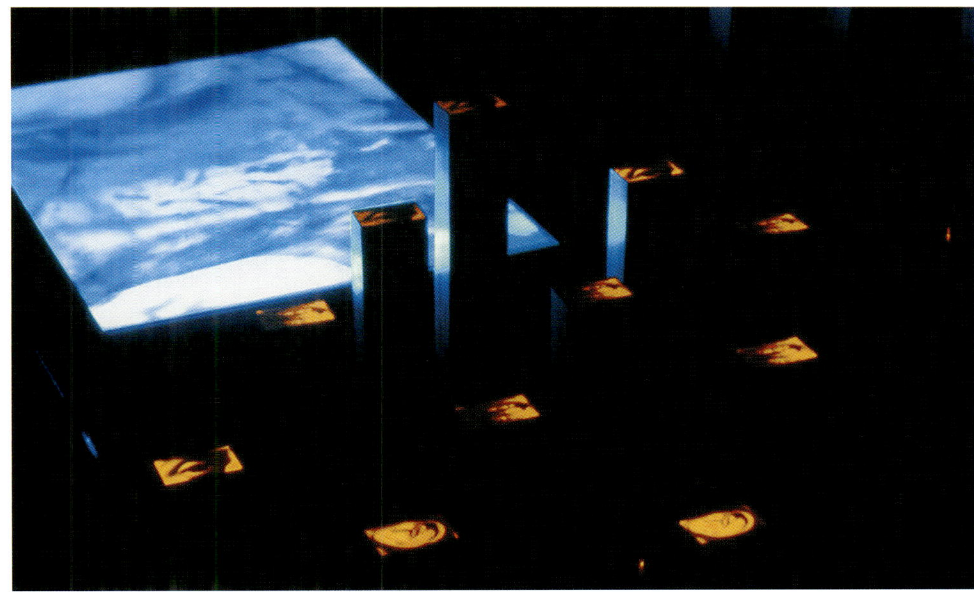

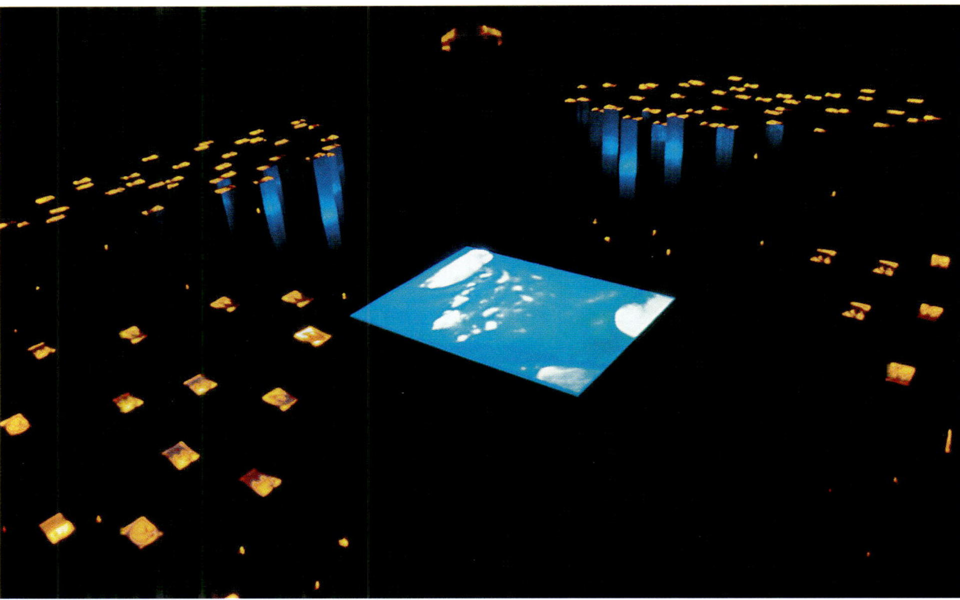

Pages 94–97:
Sheba Chhachhi. *Neelkanth (Blue Throat): poison/nectar*, 2002.
Installation with flat screen, 240 aluminum towers each with photograph and light, four translite boxes; 5.5 minute video loop; installation size variable.
Collection of the artist, New Delhi.
Photography: Courtesy of the artist.

For once, the legend tells us, the gods and the demons decided to cooperate.

Driven by greed and the desire for immortality, they began to churn the cosmic ocean, forcing it to yield *amrit* (nectar), the elixir of immortal life. The giant serpent Vasuki, king of the *naga*s (snakes) was the rope. The gods held Vasuki's tail, the demons his head. As the ocean heaved and spat, a terrible, burning mass of poison emerged. Blazing with venomous fumes, it threatened to destroy all of creation. The gods realized that in their greed for immortality they had generated Death. This poison was the concentration of all the greed and suffering of the universe. Horrified, the gods cried out for help.

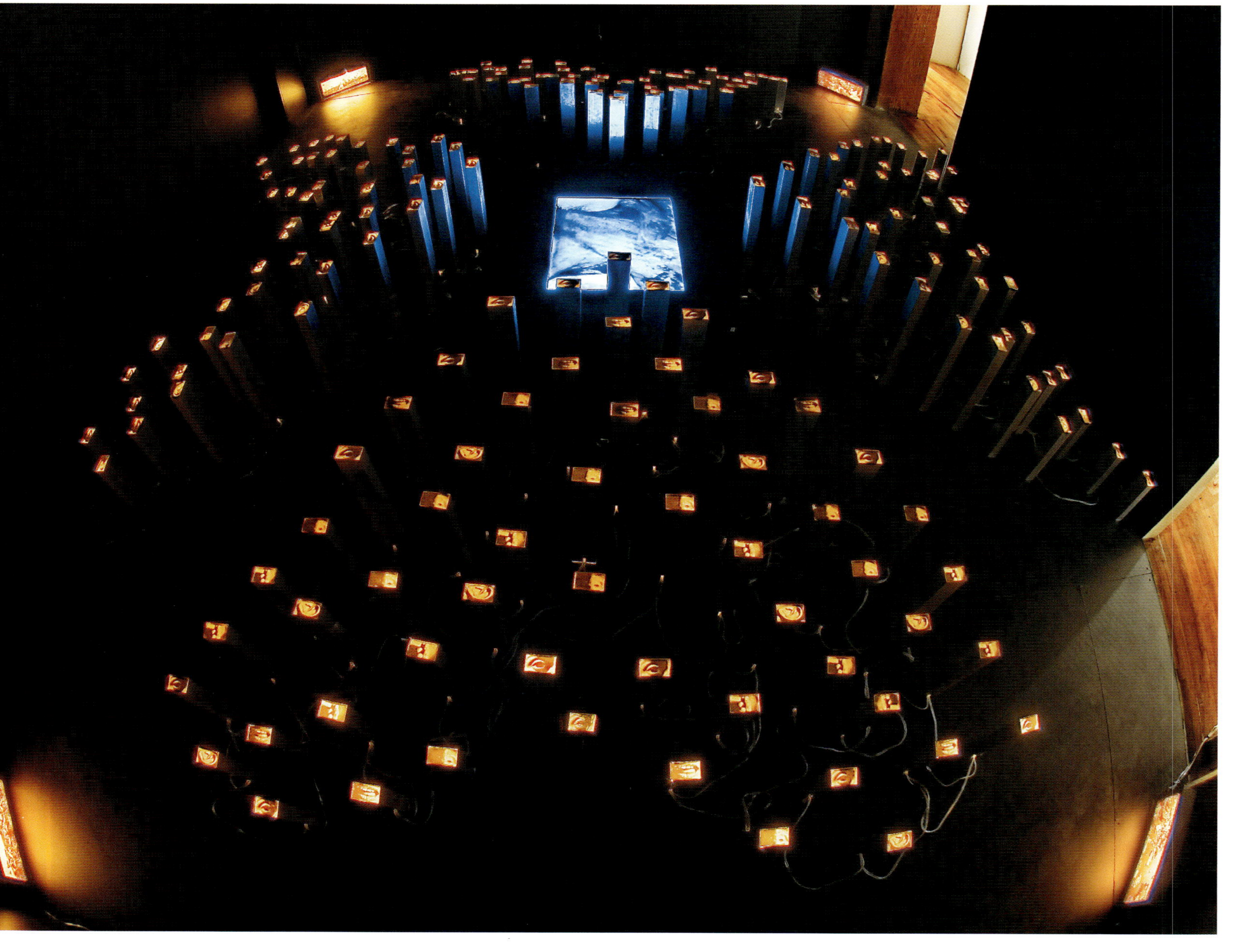

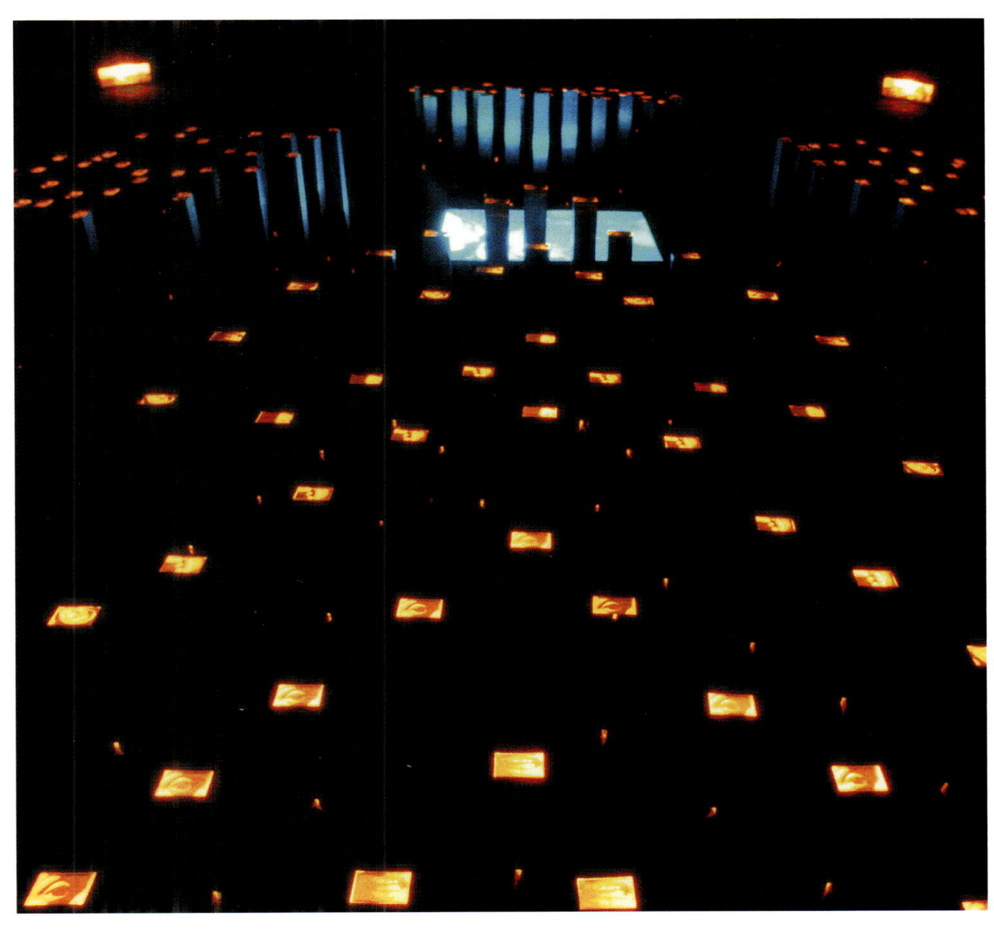

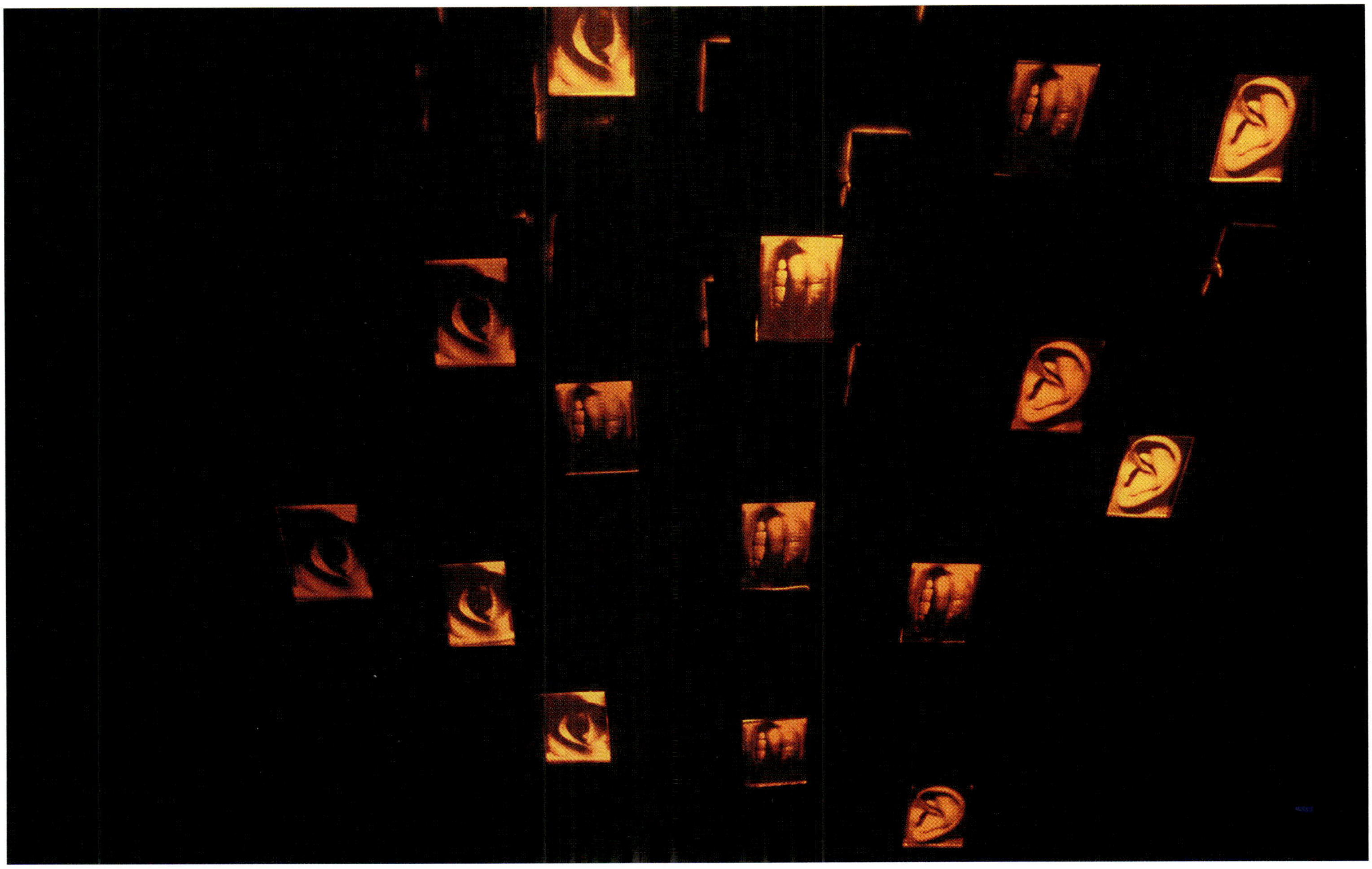

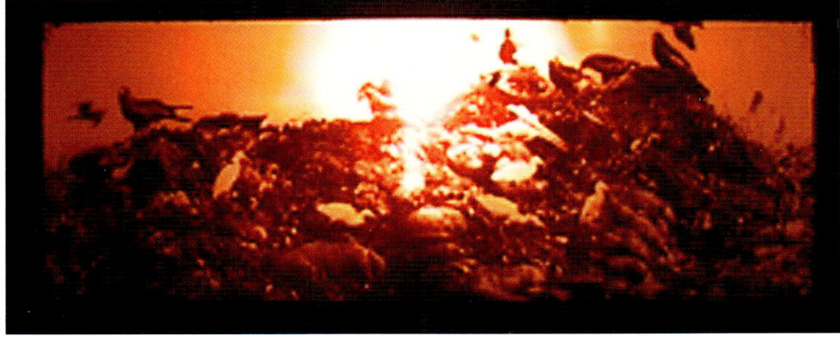 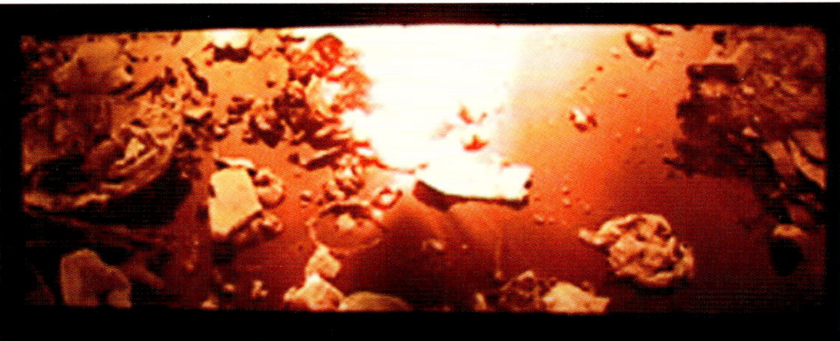

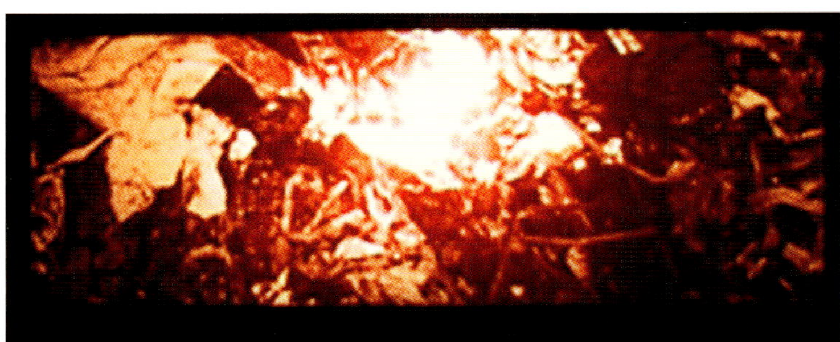 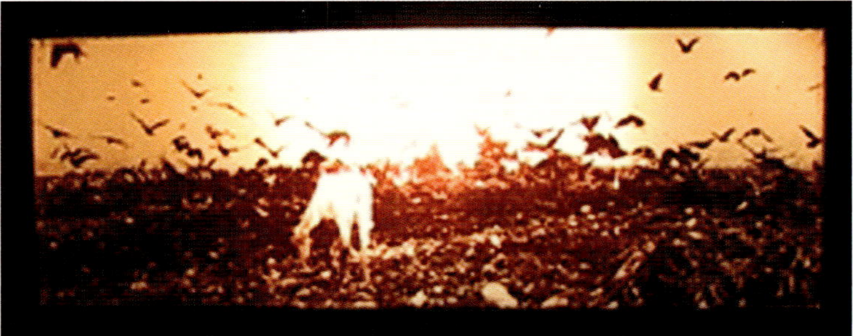

Shiva, aloof and watching, heard their confession. Moved by compassion, he opened his mouth and swallowed the flaming black mass that was going to destroy the world. He contained the terrible poison in the *vishuddhi chakra*, the center of purity, which lies in the throat—the center from which rises the power of speech, the Word. The black poison did not harm him, but left a dark blue stain.[1]

On the floor, in the center of the mandala-like installation, one encounters a blue video image of an enlarged human throat. Images of garbage similar to those in the corners appear, dissolve and change. The throat, both human and archetypal, tries heroically to swallow and ingest whatever comes to it. Despite brief moments of respite in which it seems that the waste is contained, the effort and discomfort are palpable. The video loop plays out an ongoing visceral struggle without end.

For Chhachhi, in the contemporary Indian city each of the five elements (earth, fire, water, air and ether), the five senses (smell, sight, taste, touch and hearing), and the power of the word itself are already poisoned. She asks herself, if in this fragile state, at this point of history, "Can the city be a mandala for the generation of knowledge from the mass of information that floods us? Can we, like the archetypal Neelkanth, find means of containment and transformation? Can we make nectar from poison?"

JP

---

1   This telling is the artist's reweaving of the myth of Neekanth from ancient texts—the *Mahabharata, Markandeya Purana, Skandha Purana*—and popular contemporary narrations.

Nalini Malani

Nalini Malani. *Stories Retold–Putana*, 2002.
Reverse painting, watercolor, acrylic and enamel
on Mylar; 60x40 in.
Shumita and Arani Bose Collection, New York.
Photography: Courtesy of Bose Pacia Gallery and
the artist.

Nalini Malani. *Ecstasy of Radha*, 2004.
Reverse painting, watercolor, acrylic and
enamel on Mylar; triptych, left and right panels
64x25.5 in, middle panel 64x40 in.
Shumita and Arani Bose Collection, New York.
Photography: Courtesy of Bose Pacia Gallery.

Nalini Malani responds with visual vehemence to the injustices of contemporary India. Her paintings and video installations are vehicles that channel her rage against colonization, against violence to women and against violence to the earth and the ultimate woman, *Bharat Mata*, Mother India. In her recent thematic exhibitions she has broadened her politics from local to global. She has appropriated female heroines from Western and Indian literature in *Stories Retold*, to demonstrate the depth of the problems she addresses.

Radha, paramour of the Hindu god Krishna, and symbol of *bhakti* (unconditional love of god) is depicted in a posture that recollects the ecstasy of St. Theresa in Catholic lore. Radha's route to that rapture, as represented by Malani, is as treacherous as a real-life game of Snakes and Ladders, where a wrong turn on the minefield of this grid (note the linear, cartoonish depictions of explosions along the paths) can prove tragic.

Putana is the demoness sent by Kansa to kill Krishna by suckling him with poisoned milk. Rather, he takes her nipple and literally sucks the life out of her.

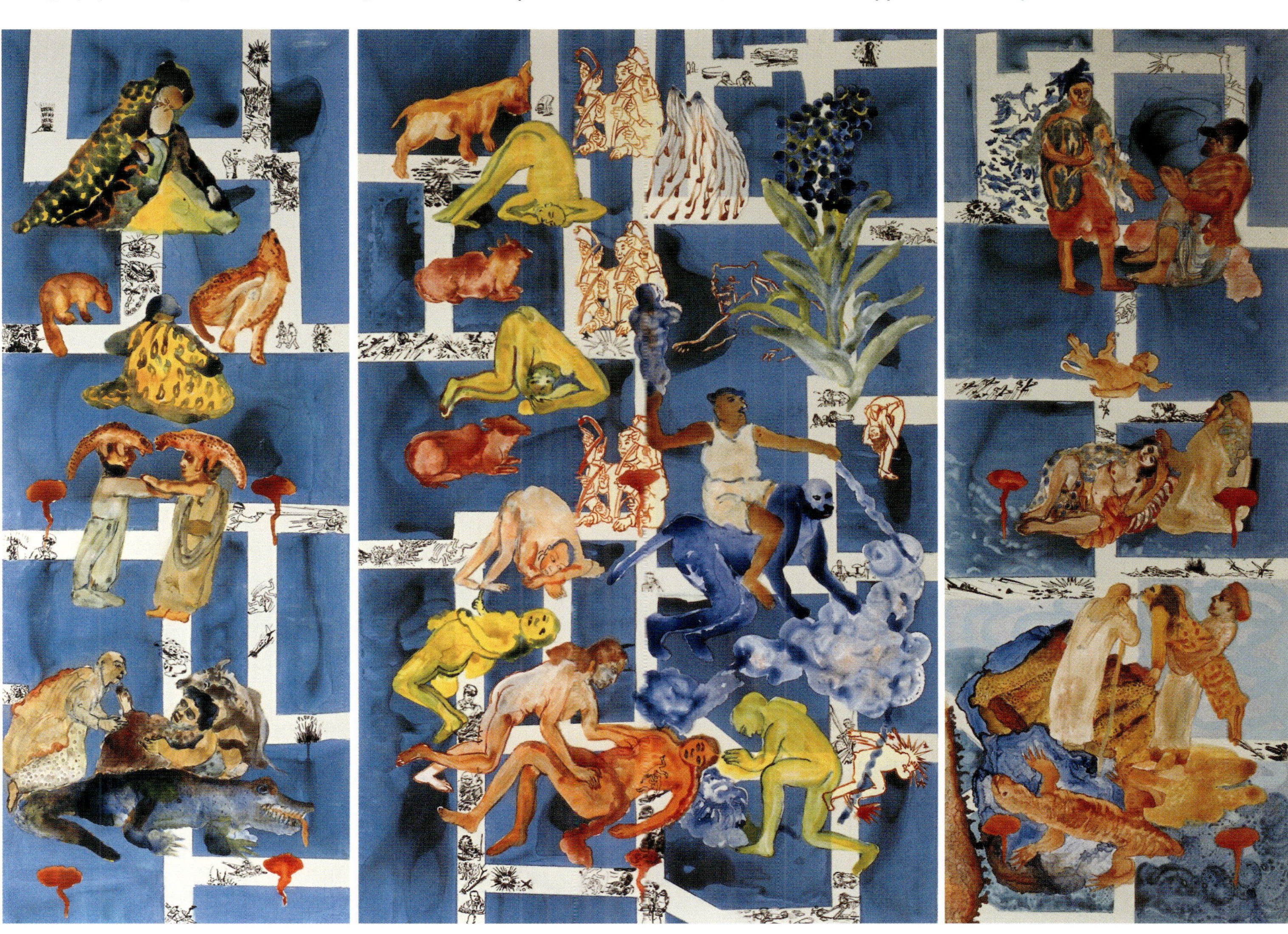

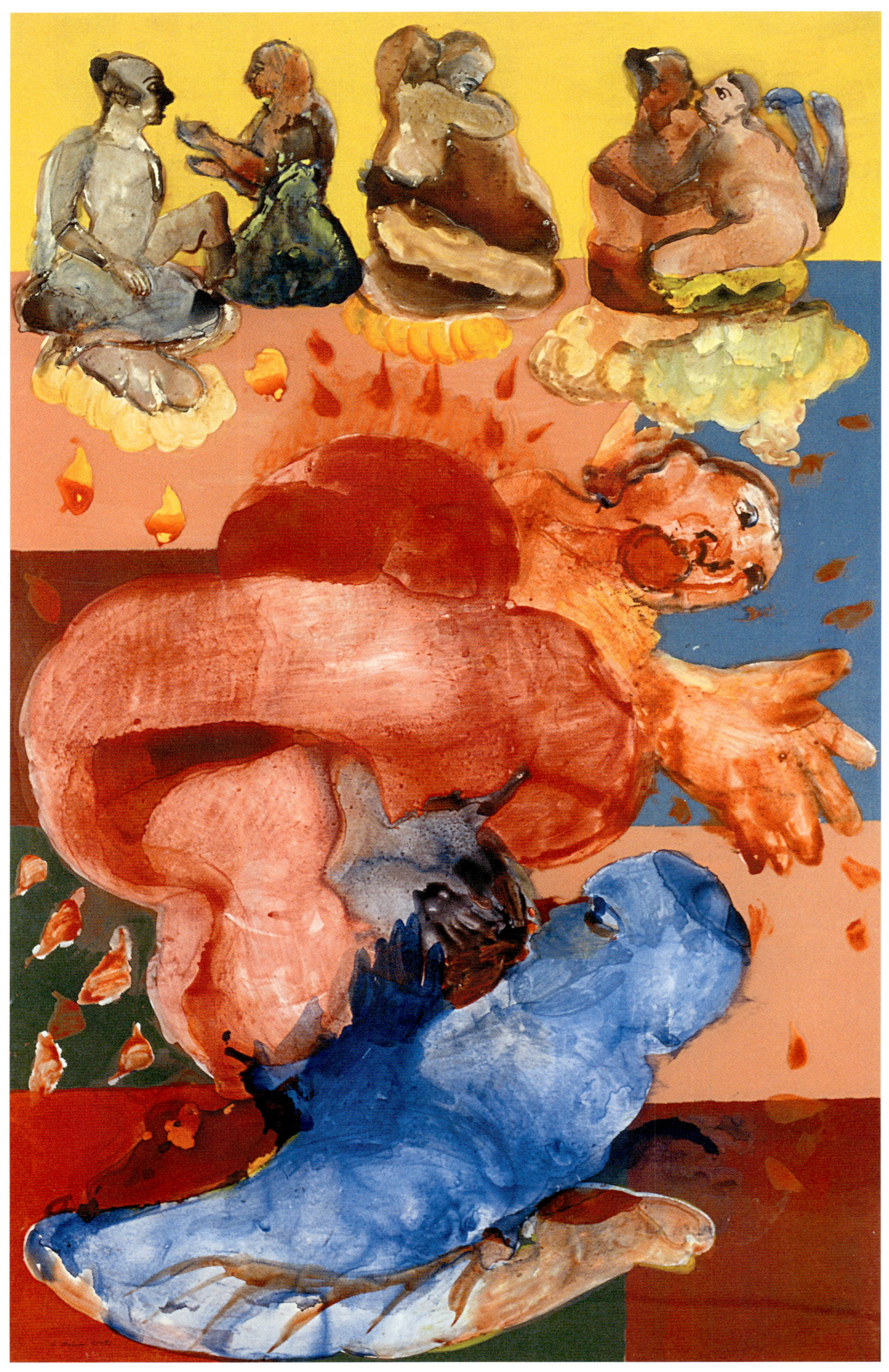

As presented in the *Bhagavata Purana*, this is read as a miraculously heroic act. But here Malani seems to have taken Putana's point of view, acknowledging that she was a pawn in a plan that backfired. Large with life and interestingly depicted in the shape of a map of India herself, Putana howls with the recognition that her vitality is being drained out of her by an adult-sized child/god—perhaps the artist's response to the Hindu Right's commandeering of India's spiritual heritage.

Malani has found a parallel to the story of Sita (the heroine of *Ramayana*) in the Greek tragedy *Medea*. Medea betrays her own people by enabling Jason's escape with the fabled Golden Fleece. Ultimately, Jason abandons Medea. On the eve of his wedding, Medea presents his new bride-to-be with a robe, poisoned to cause an excruciating death. Her terrible revenge continues with the murder of Jason's sons—Medea's own children. Even in this bare-bones retelling, we can see *Medea* as a narrative of colonial desire, collusion, betrayal and violence. Medea is betrayed by a lover who wants her only for her riches. Malani has transformed Medea's loss of her body and subsequent murder of her children into an allegory of the political and ecological rape of a nation.

The miraculously earth-born princess Sita forsakes her royal life as Rama's wife to follow him into exile, where she is abducted by Ravana, the ten-headed demon-king of Lanka. Soon after her rescue, Rama publicly humiliates Sita by doubting her chastity during her fourteen years of captivity. To prove her virtue, Sita undertakes a trial by fire and emerges unscathed, validating her purity. Years pass until Rama demands a second flame test. Sita refuses, calling as witness her mother, the Earth, who welcomes her back into the womb from which she was born.

Malani's conflation demonstrates obvious parallels between the iconic European and Indian heroines, exiled for their husbands' sakes and subsequently betrayed. They are potent tragic symbols of gender bias in both mythologies. Malani has portrayed them as sisters in pain and uses their stories to focus the rage of her response.

Sita/Medea 2 is formatted like a game board of squares. A closer look suggests an aerial view of a landscape dominated by a central furrow, from which the infant Sita was retrieved and to which she will return after her betrayal by Rama. Tangential stories are suggested in cel-like plots on either side of the furrow. In one, Sita is approached by Ravana, disguised as an old hermit to engage her trust before abducting her. It is only one of the many instances of broken faith that occur in the epic. Malani has depicted her two heroines as sisterly, twinned in their parallel tragedies; we see them embracing in the lower right. Both are treated as polluted pariahs. Medea gazes into the void, attempting to suckle a colorless (perhaps already murdered) child. Beneath her, a pockmarked (i.e., contaminated and thus marginalized) woman sits disconsolate. The life force of their ultimate tragedy bleeds through the boundaries of each individual cell.

For her 2005 series of paintings, *Living in Alicetime*, Malani has again conflated the notion of India with a Western literary figure—this time, Bombay (now Mumbai) with Lewis Carroll's Alice. In seeking to visualize the problems of an increasingly polluted urban center, Malani has found the perfect heroine in Alice,

Opposite page:
Nalini Malani. *Sita/Medea 2*, 2004.
Reverse painting, watercolor, acrylic and enamel on Mylar; 64x40.5 in.
Shumita and Arani Bose Collection, New York.
Photography: Courtesy of Bose Pacia Gallery and the artist.

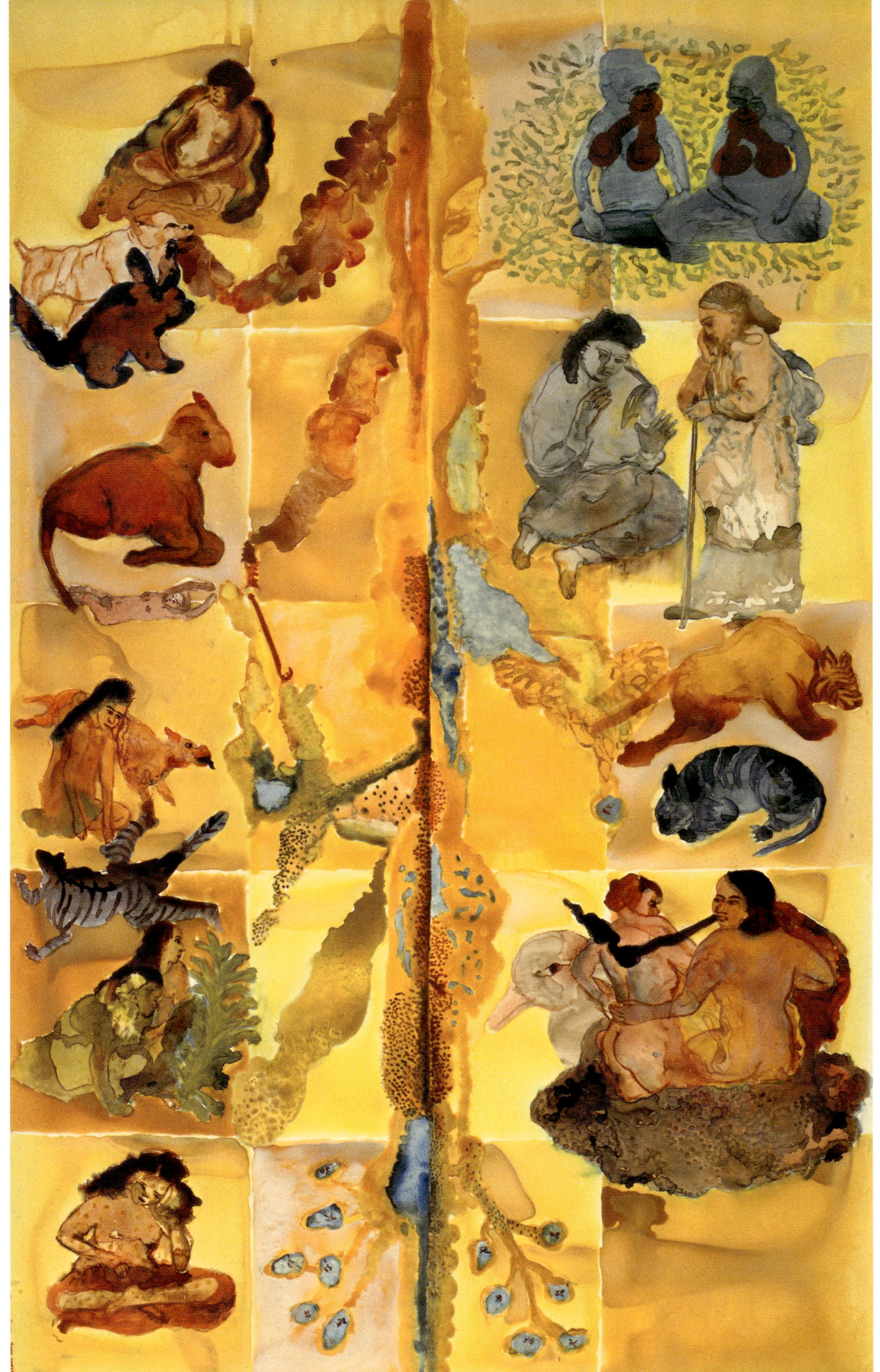

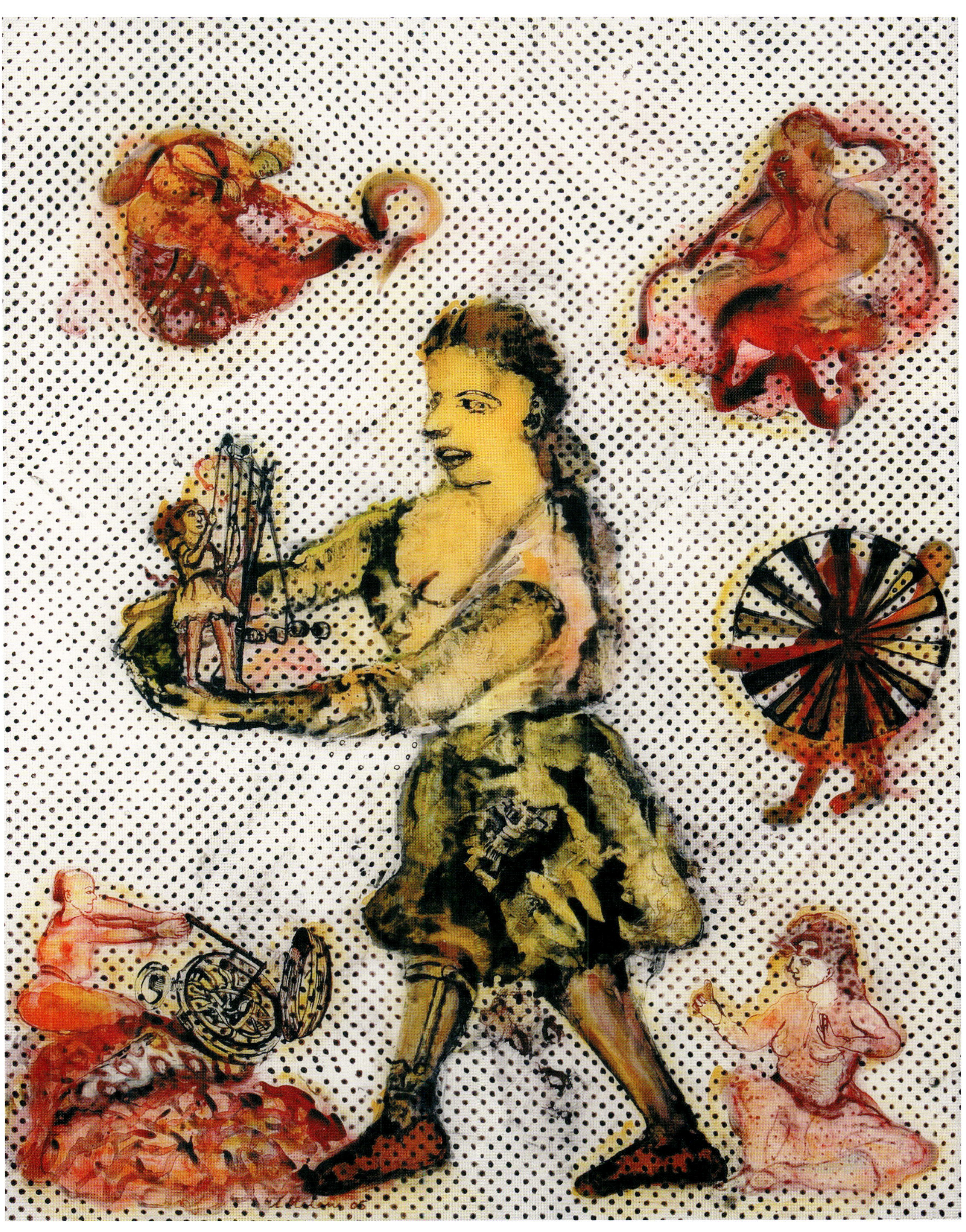

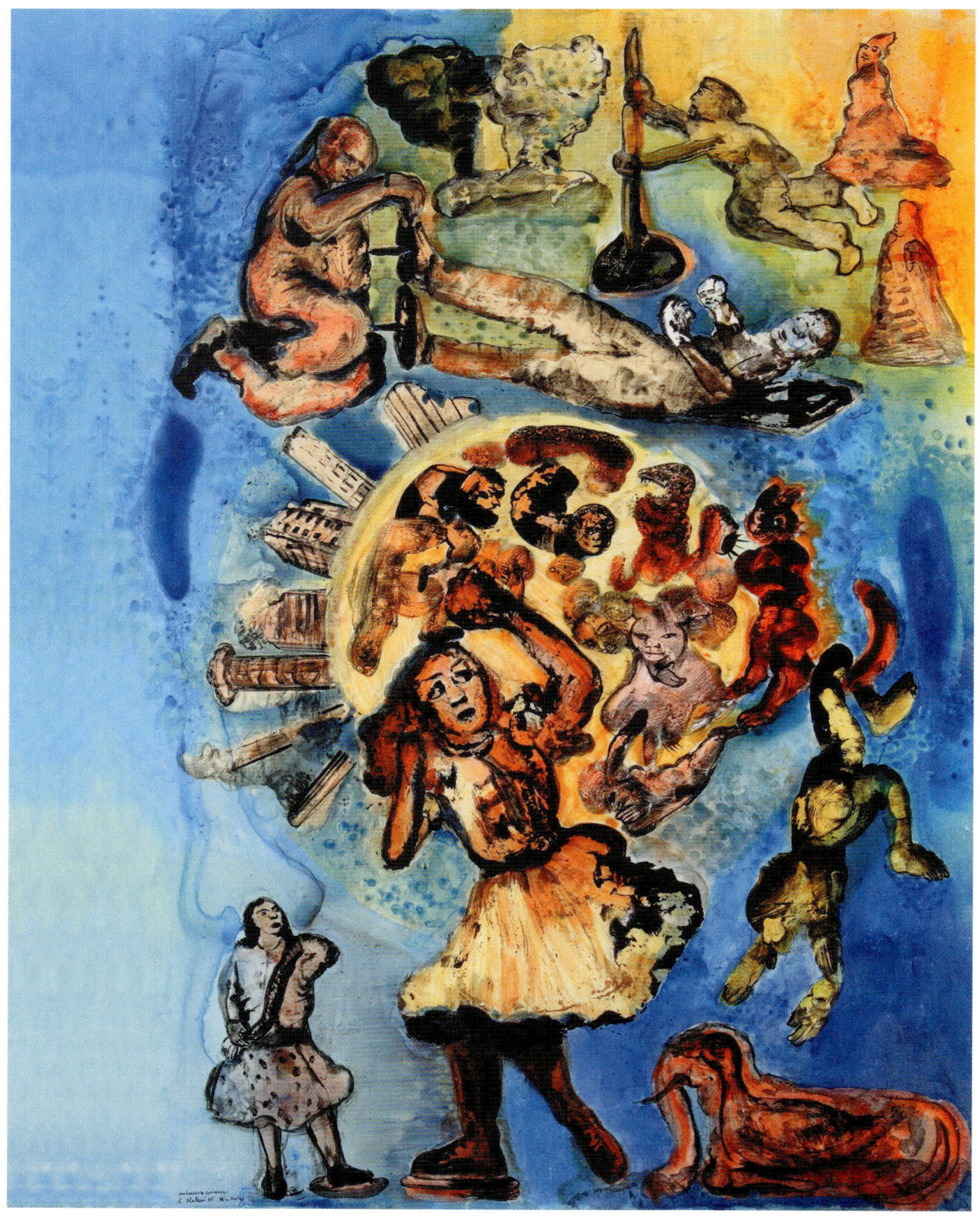

Nalini Malani. *Broken Alice I—Living in Alicetime*, 2005.
Reverse painting, watercolor and acrylic on acrylic sheet; 60x48 in.
Collection of Pallak Seth, New Delhi.
Photography: Courtesy of Sakshi Gallery.

Nalini Malani. *Curiouser and Curiouser/Alice in Mumbai—Living in Alicetime*, 2005.
Reverse painting, watercolor and acrylic on Mylar; 60x40 in.
Collection of Sujoy Bose and Sona Varma, Mumbai.
Photograph: Courtesy of Sakshi Gallery.

another adult-sized child. Plagued by illusion and delusion after her descent into the rabbit hole, she struggles to make sense of the chaos that whirls around her. Her perceptions are challenged. Nothing is quite what it seems. Alice, like other of Malani's appropriated female protagonists, has to renegotiate her understanding of her universe.

In *Curiouser and Curiouser*, the "rabbit hole" is Mumbai during the catastrophic deluge of 26 July, 2005, when an angry, monsoon-swollen Mithi River surged over sluices blocked by plastic and industrial debris, turning much of Mumbai into a roiling inland sea of putrid water. We can recognize the city by the landmark buildings along the Queen's Necklace and Chowpatty Beach. In the upper right, a figure is holding a *tanpura*, the stringed instrument used for the drone in Indian music. However, in this instance, its shape could be mistaken for a toilet plunger—and the futile attempts of its user in the face of a fetid onslaught. Malani's adept handling of a watery medium (reverse painting on Mylar) creates cloudy forms and slippery boundaries that enhance her narrative.

BS

Atul Dodiya

Like skulls in European Renaissance paintings, Atul Dodiya's gallows are *mementi mori*, demonstrating awareness of life's impermanence. Here, they are particularly cruel reminders of man's inhumanity. One's end may be hanging at the end of another's rope. Personally painful for Dodiya, a Gujarati, is the religious strife that plagues contemporary India in the early twenty-first century, the epicenter of which was the horrific rioting in Gujarat in 2002. "How can any sensitive person not respond to what is happening in Gujarat today? All my life, I have believed that

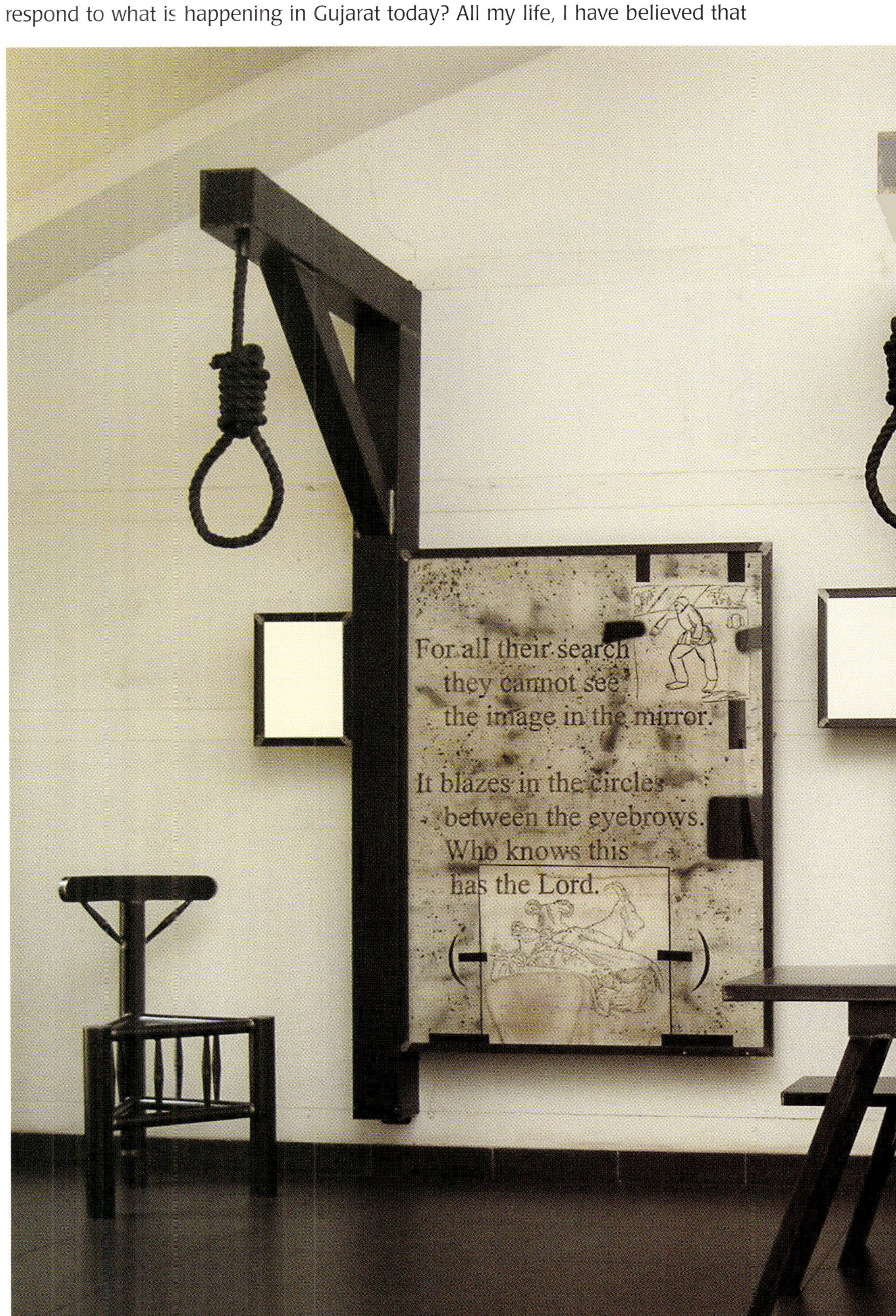

Atul Dodiya. *Devoured Darkness I*, 2006. Center, as part of original installation. Steel, fiberglass, mirror; watercolor and charcoal on paper; 114x60x36 in (overall installation dimensions). Shumita and Arani Bose Collection, New York. Photography: Courtesy of the artist.

India has a unique culture that enriches all of us and, therefore, communal riots sadden me."[1] However, he rises above the local to see the issues as global—the inhumanity of humans to each other is not limited by place.

Dodiya's installation series, *Devoured Darkness*, takes its name from a line in one of the poems of Allama Prabhu:

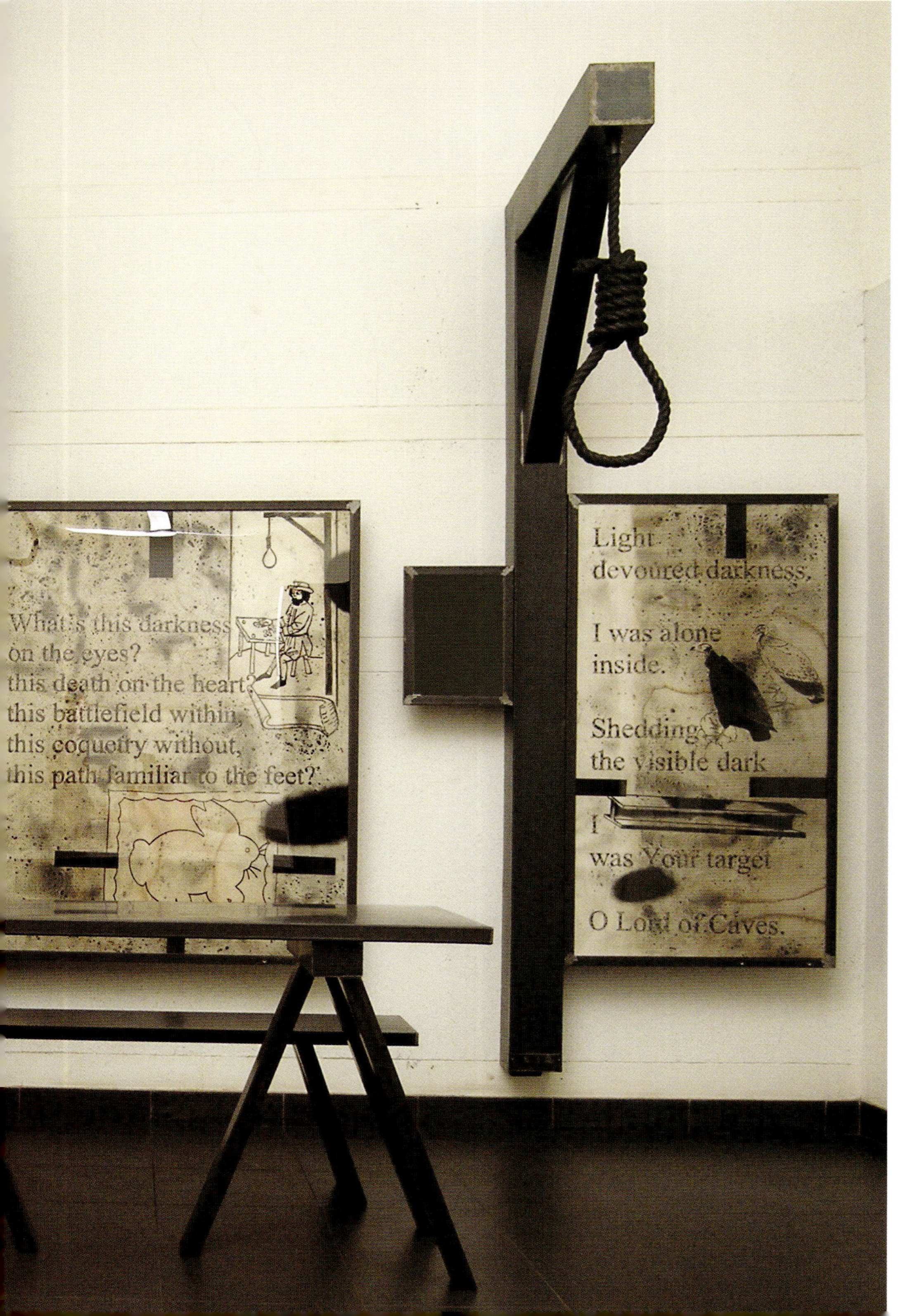

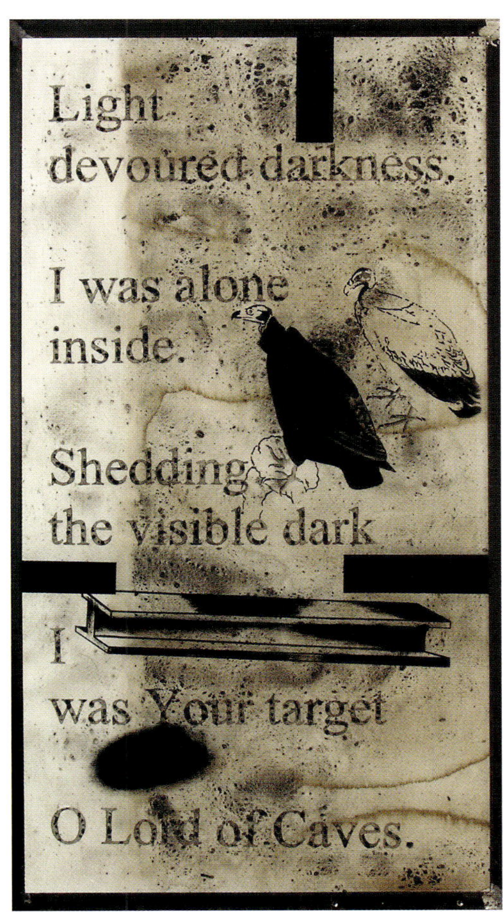

Atul Dodiya. *Devoured Darkness III*, 2006. Detail.
Steel, fiberglass, mirror; watercolor and charcoal
on paper; 114x60x36 in (overall installation
dimensions).
Collection of Bodhi Art, New Delhi.
Photography: Courtesy of the artist.

Opposite page:
Atul Dodiya. *Devoured Darkness V*, 2006.
Steel, fiberglass, mirror; watercolor and charcoal
on paper; 114x60x36 in (overall installation
dimensions).
Collection of Anurag Bhargava, New York.
Photography: Courtesy of the artist.

Light
devoured darkness.

I was alone
inside.

Shedding
the visible dark

I
was your target

O Lord of Caves.

Allama Prabhu (translated by A. K. Ramanujan)[2]

During the medieval period (around the tenth century), a "protestant" movement, Virasaivism, was fomented by poet-saints in South India. The foremost of them was Allama Prabhu. His unpretentious *bhakti* poems were radical (*bhakti* is a form of Hindu religious practice that focuses on unconditional love of god). They were anti-ritual, anti-temple, anti-priest. In sum, these *vacana*s (free verse lyrics) quietly stated that spiritual practice could be personal, direct and inclusive—available to all classes of people. As the translator A. K. Ramanujan has said, "…by mockery, invective, argument, poetry, loving kindness and sheer presence, Allama brought enlightenment to laymen, and release to the saints themselves."[3]

Dodiya has used the poems of Allama as counterpoint in his boldly realistic installation of gallows (now separately owned by private collectors). Each work includes a poem on one side of the gallow's pole, illustrated with the artist's adept handling of watercolor and the additions of collaged images. Dodiya is not a serendipitous artist. Preliminary work—drawings, deliberations over the placement of objects—assure that the viewer will see exactly what the artist wants him/her to see. Nothing is left to chance. Context is crucial. On the other side of each gallow's pole, he has installed a simple mirror, inviting the viewer to be as reflective as the poet in contemplating his life and death, and the spiritual practice that supports it.

In these works, Dodiya has syncretized the medieval protest against the hierarchical strictures that impede a devotee's path to god with his own protest against the violence that accompanies exclusionary religion and politics.

BS

1   Devina Dutt (interviewer), "Work in Progress: Atul Dodiya," *The Little Magazine*, 2002, http://www.littlemag.com/faith/atuldodiya.html.

2   A. K. Ramanujan, tr., *Speaking of Siva* (London: Penguin Books, 1973), 164.

3   Ramanujan, 147.

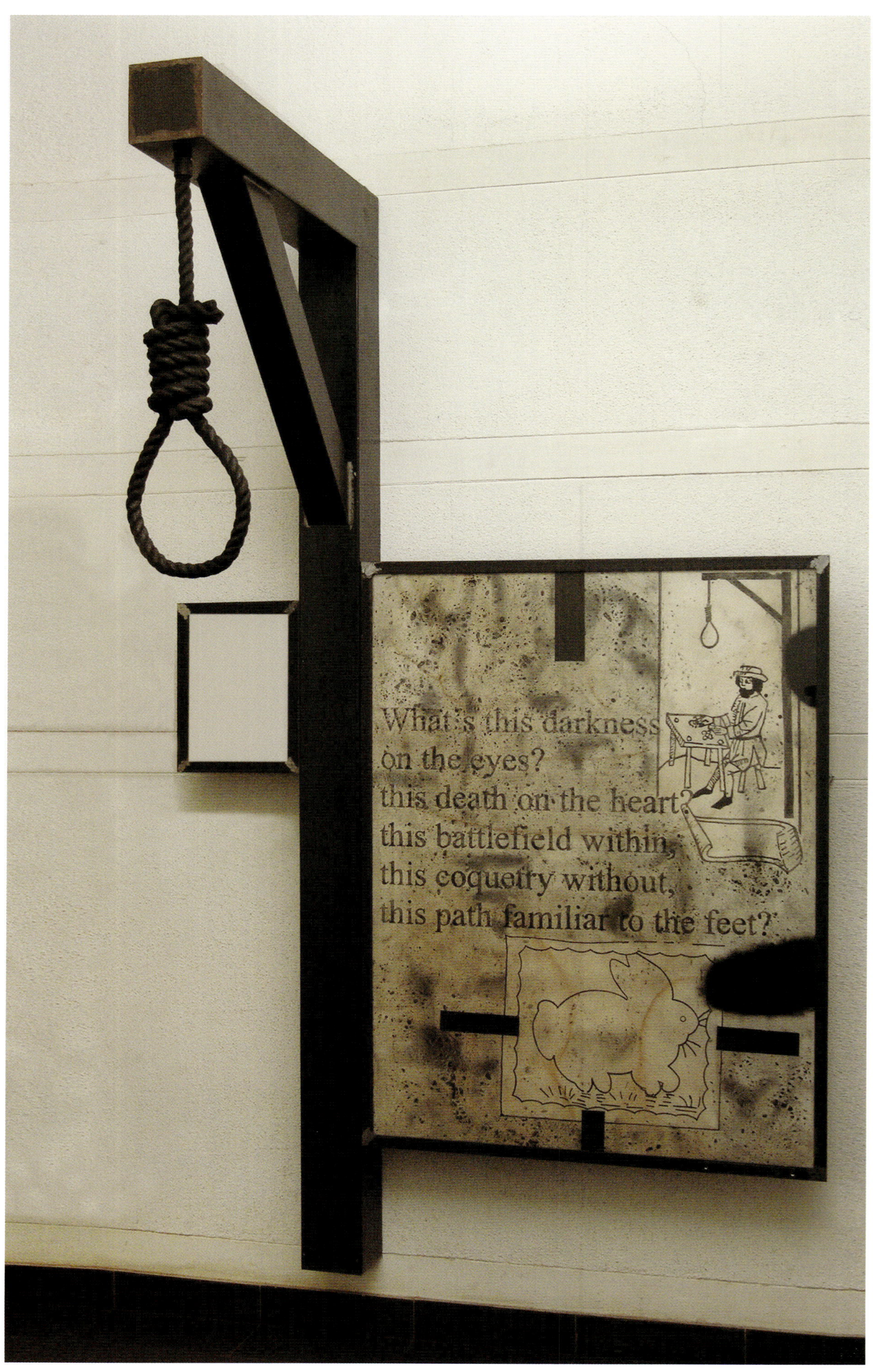
What's this darkness
on the eyes?
this death on the heart?
this battlefield within,
this coquetry without,
this path familiar to the feet?

Jitish Kallat

Around the anniversary of the September 11 attacks on the World Trade Center, Jitish Kallat was invited to make a work for exhibition in Chicago. More than a hundred years earlier, also on September 11, another young man from India had been invited to Chicago—Swami Vivekananda introduced Hindu religious philosophy at the Parliament of World Religions in 1893. His was the first proclamation of the universality of Hinduism outside India.[1]

The coincidence of dates struck Kallat, but it was the content of Vivekananda's speech—a celebration of individuality and an exhortation to embrace tolerance and acceptance—that proved to be Kallat's muse.

I am proud to belong to a religion which has taught the world both tolerance and universal acceptance . . . we accept all religions as true.

Swami Vivekananda.[2]

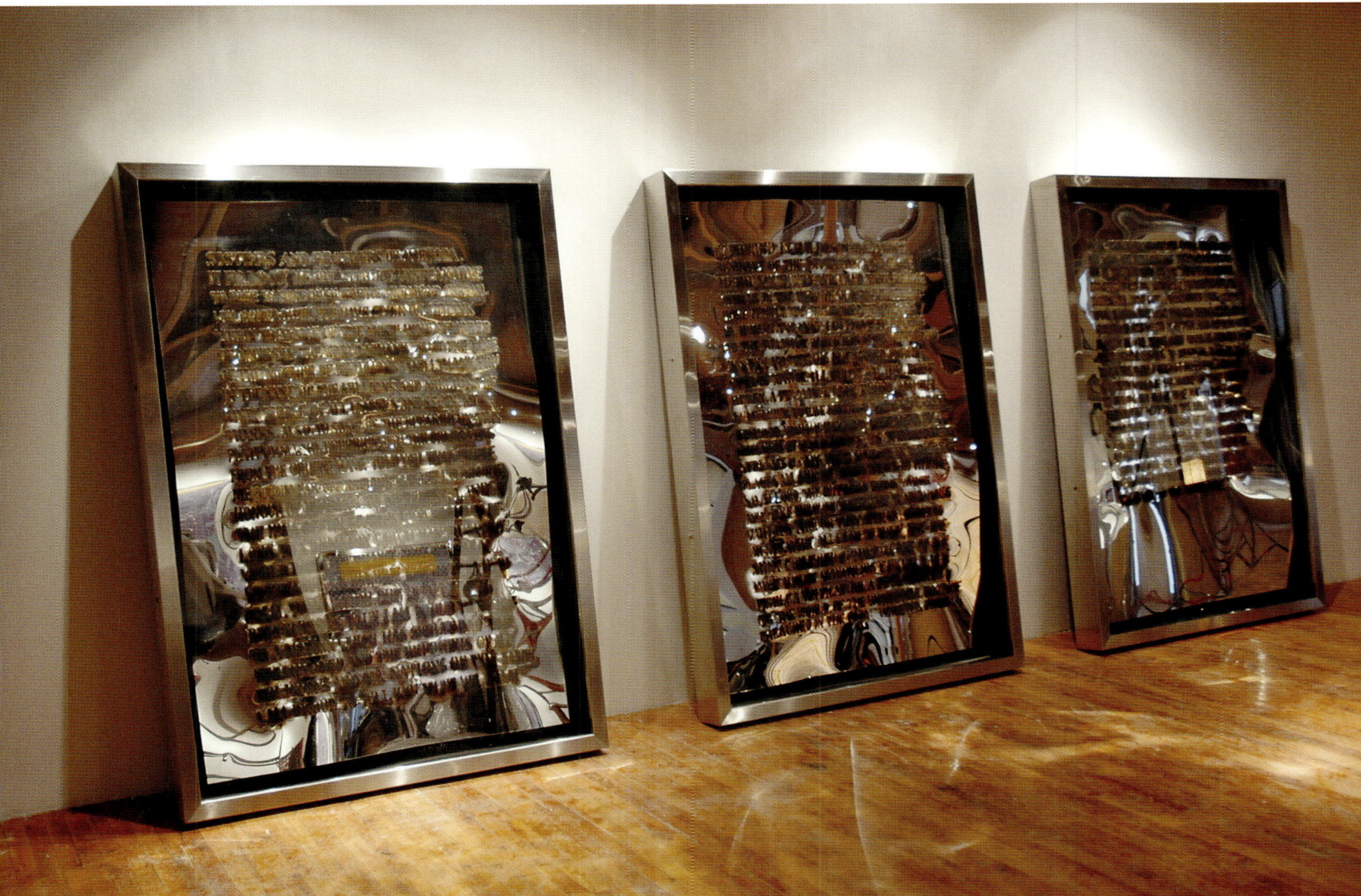

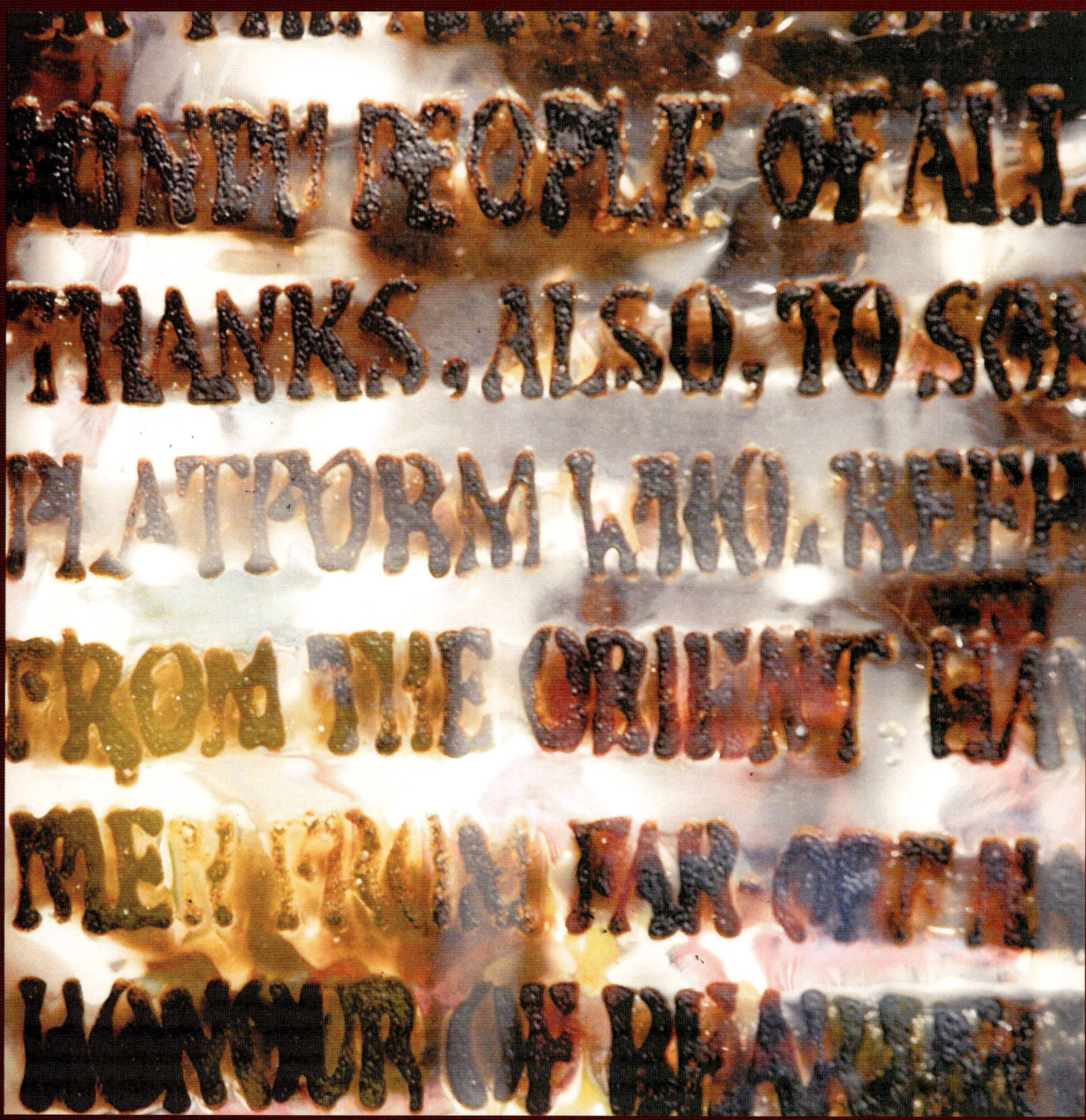
MONEY PEOPLE OF ALL
THANKS, ALSO, TO SO
PLATFORM WHO, KEPT
FROM THE ORIENT IN
MEN FROM FAR-OFF
HONOUR OF WEARERS

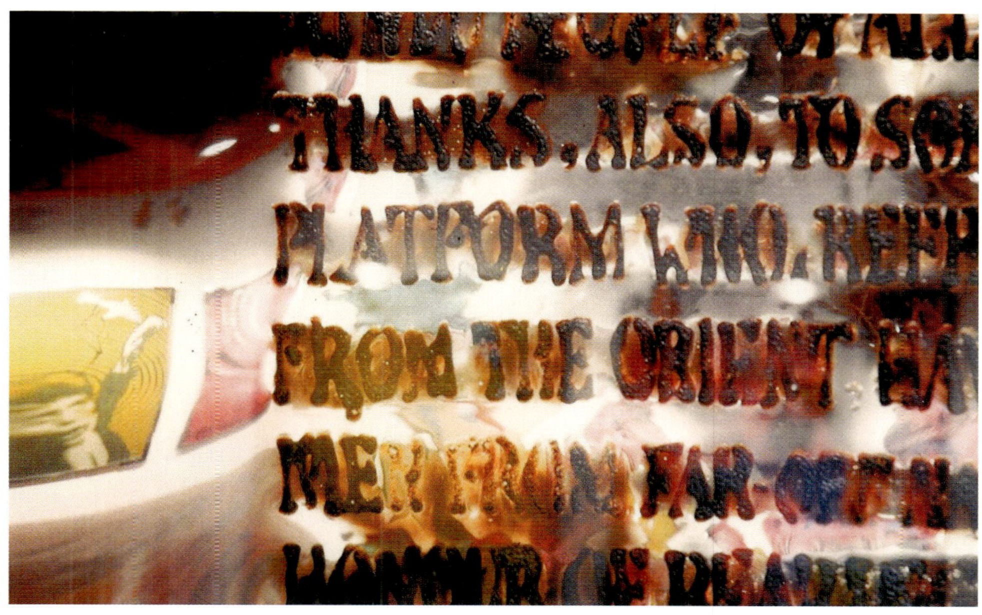

Visual manipulation of this historic text elicited a personal narrative from Kallat, one that reflects (an apt word here) upon the original groundbreaking message. Each letter is tediously inscribed with rubber adhesive on a triptych of acrylic mirrors. The completed text is then meticulously "cremated" (the artist's word of choice), letter by letter.[3] Through controlled unpredictability, the text is charred and the mirror melts. Using process as well as content to depict the duality of violence and tolerance, Kallat has employed an abrasive technique to re-deliver Vivekananda's message of peace.

Thus, as Kallat himself has said, "The reading of the text is at all times intersected by the [distorted] reflection of the self."[4] The "funhouse" mirrored surface forces the viewer to confront the duality of the absurd and the deeply serious. With his cremation of the mirrors, the artist has manipulated the very ground that supports the image, which in this case is language itself.

Kallat has titled the work *Detergent*, clearly implying cleansing, an idea that is enhanced by the flames of his process. Purification by fire—sacrifice or cremation—is a ritual tradition in India. Flames not only remove pollution but are vehicles of renewal. They evoke reincarnation. By burning the text, Kallat has given it new life. His is a timely plea for religious tolerance and acceptance.

BS

1   Vivekananda's address was delivered in what is now Fullerton Hall, at the Art Institute of Chicago. Ironically, the Parliament occurred during the Columbian Exposition that marked the 400th anniversary of Christopher Columbus's so-called "discovery" of America while trying to reach the so-called "Indies!"

2   "Implications of Swami Vivekananda's Speeches at The Parliament of Religions: Chicago 1893," http://www.geocities.com/neovedanta/a32a.html.

3   Anna Poplawska, "Art Exhibit Commemorates 9/11 and Swami Vivekananda's Historic Speech," www.yogachicago.com/nov04/artreview.html

4   Jitish Kallat, quoted by Julie Walsh, "September 11, 1893/September 11, 2001: 108 years later in America." (Chicago: Walsh Gallery [press release], 2004).

Jayashree Chakravarty

b. 1956, Khoai, Tripura

Received a B. F. A. in Painting from the Art School at Visva-Bharati University, Santiniketan, West Bengal (1978); and a Diploma in Painting from the Faculty of Fine Arts, M. S. University, Vadodara (1980).

Lives and works in Kolkata.

Jayashree Chakravarty has been developing her pictorial language since the 1980s. During her tenure as Resident Artist at the École d'Art in Aix-en-Provence, France (1992–95), her complex painting technique in ink, gouache, watercolor, and oil underwent a transformation when her characteristic overlapping forms and fluidly rendered images were enhanced by experimentation with materials—rice paper, cellophane, tissue. Layered surfaces continue to be a visual device in her work.

Sheba Chhachhi

b. 1958, Harare, Ethiopia

Educated at Delhi University and the National Institute of Design in Ahmedabad.

Lives and works in New Delhi.

In the 1980s, Sheba Chhachhi's work as documentary photographer focused on the Women's Movement in India, which in turn led to collaborations with women activists. In the 1990s, her work expanded into multimedia projects, often integrating photographic works into her larger installations. Her most recent work includes video, sound and light, along with physical objects. Chhachhi's works address transformation, marginality and the play between the mythic and social in the context of gender, representation, urban ecologies, violence and visual culture. Given her multi-faceted approach to art-making, she can be described as an installation artist, photographer, sculptor, and writer.

Anju Dodiya

b. 1964, Mumbai

Received a B. F. A. from the Sir J. J. School of Art, Mumbai (1986).

Lives and works in Mumbai.

Strong draughtsmanship is the key to Anju Dodiya's *oeuvre*. Each of her drawings and paintings includes a central female figure that resembles the artist, suggesting that it is Dodiya herself who is the protagonist of her powerful narrative images. Dodiya's signature paintings also rely upon her skill as a storyteller. She appropriates from literary, religious and mythological sources and incorporates themes of physical and psychological—external and internal—struggles into her personal iconography. In recent years, Dodiya has ventured from the two-dimensional surface, exchanging canvas or paper for an actual mattress as the ground for her lyrical narratives.

Atul Dodiya

b. 1959, Mumbai

Received a B. F. A. from the Sir J. J. School of Art, Mumbai (1982); and studied at the École des Beaux-Arts, Paris.

Lives and works in Mumbai.

History continues to be an influential factor in Atul Dodiya's artistic output. His 1999 series of watercolors on the life of Mahatma Gandhi brought him immediate recognition as a painter. Beyond Gandhi, many of Dodiya's projects have explored such diverse subjects as the *Ramayana*, old European maps of India, the poems of the medieval poet-saint Allama Prabhu, and recently, the life of his friend and mentor, Bhupen Khakhar. Drawing inspiration from graphic sources that include comic strips, popular religious iconography, advertising billboards, cinema culture, and both Western and Eastern art history, Dodiya extends the idea of the two-dimensional painted surface by incorporating found and readymade objects from urban life into the exhibition space.

Anita Dube

b. 1958, Lucknow

Received a B. A. from the University of Delhi; and an M. A. in Art Criticism from the Faculty of Fine Arts, M. S. University, Vadodara (1982).

Lives and works in New Delhi.

Anita Dube was initially trained in art history and criticism. She began making art later in life. Dube transforms existing materials—bones, artificial eyes, velvet, plastic and other industrial materials—into sculptural objects and installations that carry personal and cultural meaning. Recently, she has chosen the video camera as a new tool. To this medium, she brings a combination of humor and wit, as she herself would say, "to shake the nervous system out of its comfort zone."

Shilpa Gupta

b. 1976, Mumbai

Received a B. F. A. and an M. F. A. in Sculpture from the Sir J. J. School of Art, Mumbai (1997).

Lives and works in Mumbai.

Shilpa Gupta creates fake worlds that simulate the culture of her environment, while simultaneously standing this culture on its head. In these works she explores local issues that have global connections—be they cyber coolies, illegal organ trade or clashes of communities. Gupta often takes an existing visual vocabulary, gives it a twist and creates a new narrative experience for the visitor. Her presentations, whether online with *Sentiment-Express.com, Diamonds and You.com* or *blessed-bandwidth.net* or in galleries with *Kidney Supermarket* or *Blame,* look deliberately casual.

Subodh Gupta

b. 1964, Khagaul, Bihar

Received a B. F. A. in Painting from the College of Art and Craft, Patna (1990).

Lives and works in New Delhi.

Subodh Gupta continues to work in a range of media, including painting, sculpture, photography, video, installation and performance art. In recent exhibitions, Gupta has incorporated found objects and everyday materials—cow dung, milk pails, kitchen utensils, tiffin boxes, bicycles and scooters. along with Ambassador taxis, suitcases and airport trolleys. With such objects, he demonstrates the extreme contrast between rural and urban life in India today. When placed within the gallery space, these elements become a commentary on the complexities—and friction—that have accompanied India's rapidly globalized society.

N. S. Harsha

b. 1969, Mysore

Received a B. F. A. in Painting from the Chamarajendra Academy of Visual Arts (C. A. V. A.), Mysore (1992); and an M. F. A. in Painting from the Faculty of Fine Arts, M. S. University, Vadodara (1995).

Lives and works in Mysore.

N. S. Harsha's intricate paintings depict subject matter that covers the spectrum of Indian life, always infused with wit and a sense of irony. He is influenced by his own life experiences as well as popular street and commercial art, handicrafts, folk art, and children's storybook images. His work maintains an element of the theatrical and his canvases are typically figurative and

narrative in nature. They respond to a wide range of issues, including the current state of the art market, national cultural institutions, and politics. Since 1999, Harsha has worked on collaborative installations with the public—gallery visitors, school children, passers-by—to explore notions of the relationship of the individual to the greater population.

Tushar Joag

b. 1966, Mumbai

Received a B. F. A. in sculpture from the Sir J. J. School of Art, Mumbai (1988); and an M. F. A. from the Faculty of Fine Arts, M. S. University, Vadodara (1989).

Lives and works in Mumbai.

Over the years, Tushar Joag's art practice has been divided between his personal works and his political and cultural group projects. In 1998 he co-founded Open Circle, an initiative for the organization and development of an interactive platform for artists in Mumbai. His latest projects in this area are his contributions to the World Social Forum in India, Brazil and Nairobi. In his own video and sculpture installations Joag shows a similar deep concern with the rapidly changing urban environment. Sometimes he disguises himself in projects like *Unicell* where he satirizes the Mumbai Public Works Department.

Ranbir Kaleka

b. 1953, Patiala, Punjab

Received training at the College of Art, Chandigarh, and the Royal College of Art, London.

Lives and works in New Delhi.

Ranbir Kaleka's years of training and expertise as a painter provide the core of artistic strength in his more recent new-media endeavors. His video work began in 1998–99 with *Man Threading a Needle.* Since then, it has evolved into works that integrate painting with video by using multiple slowly moving projections. His innovative and engaging approach to video art enables Kaleka to craft richly layered narratives.

Jitish Kallat

b. 1974, Mumbai

Received a B. F. A. from the Sir J. J. School of Art, Mumbai (1996).

Lives and works in Mumbai.

Jitish Kallat's large-scale two-dimensional works incorporate photography, painting, text and collage, as well as bold experimentation with technique an figuration. Beyond painting, he has worked with the re-presentation of text that both

requests and requires participation from the viewer. As demonstrated by both *Death of Distance* and *Detergent*, Kallat uses his art production to create an ongoing critique of urban problems, social injustice and contemporary politics—Indian *and* global.

Reena Saini Kallat

b. 1973, New Delhi

Received a B. F. A. in Painting from the Sir J. J. School of Art, Mumbai (1996).

Lives and works in Mumbai.

Reena Saini Kallat uses diverse techniques—painting, sculptural installations and photography—to examine issues of identity, self, nationalism, fragmentation and isolation. Her narrative sources include mythology and history, combined with images of people on the street, to deliver sharp social and political commentary. As a young girl, Kallat spent eight years studying *Bharatnatyam* (classical Indian dance). Meticulous craftsmanship, with particular attention to the depiction of gesture, may be a reflection of her early training.

Nalini Malani

b. 1946, Karachi, Pakistan

Received a B. F. A. from the Sir J. J. School of Art, Mumbai (1969); and a French Government Scholarship for Fine Arts, Paris (1970–72).

Lives and works in Mumbai.

Nalini Malani has been working in painting, drawing, and mixed media since the 1960s. In the past decade, she has gained international recognition for her multimedia video installations. In all media, Malani is known for the political nature of her work, which incorporates subject matter from diverse sources, such as ancient Greek and Hindu mythology and European literature and drama. Malani's work aims to identify universal truths related to the human condition. Both an artist and an activist, Malani draws inspiration from the voices of the marginalized and the stories of the subaltern.

Pushpamala N.

b. 1956, Bangalore

Received a B. F. A. and an M. F. A. in Sculpture from the Faculty of Fine Arts, M. S. University, Vadodara (1985).

Lives and works in Bangalore.

Pushpamala N. was trained as a sculptor and started later in life to forge alternate ways of viewing, using performance photography. She has been fascinated by the power of the photograph as an ethnographic tool for documentation, which has led her to deconstruct cultural myths and traditional images of women. Drawing inspiration from art history, advertisements, religious iconography and cinema, each photograph is infused with tongue-in-cheek humor. This quality is also found in her recent video works. Black and white footage recalls recent history that is distanced and treated as rediscovered past.

Tejal Shah

b. 1979, Bhilai

Received a B. A. in Photography from Royal Melbourne Institute of Technology (2000) and was a Visiting Artist at the School of the Art Institute of Chicago (1999–2000).

Lives and works in Mumbai.

In just half a decade, Tejal Shah has proven to be a provocative artist. In a passionate and engaged manner, she deals with specific issues such as gender and politics. She uses performance-based video or staged photography. Important works in these areas are her photo-tableau series *Hijra Fantasies,* her single-channel video works *Stinging Kiss* and *I Love My India*, and her recent two-channel video installation *What Are You?* Her desire for active social intervention recently led her to initiate an ongoing series of city-based site-specific performances called *Encounters with Varsha Nair.*

Gulammohammed Sheikh

b. 1937, Surendranagar, Gujarat

Received an M. F. A. from the Faculty of Fine Arts, M. S. University, Vadodara (1961); and an M. A. from the Royal College of Art, London (1966). Professor of Art History (1960–63, 1967–81) and Professor of Painting (1982–93), Faculty of Fine Arts, M. S. University, Vadodara.

Lives and works in Vadodara.

In the mid-1960s, during his studies at the Royal College of Art in London, Gulammohammed Sheikh traveled widely within Europe. His experience of the early Renaissance masters during this formative time profoundly impacted the craftsmanship and style of his painting. In 1963, Sheikh was one of twelve young artists who founded Group 1890, an artists' collective whose mission was to revolutionize that which they perceived as no longer relevant modernism. Sheikh is also a distinguished Gujarati poet. His paintings and painted books manifest a parallel poetic complexity and lyricism. His interest in process and dialog lends a dynamic quality to his ongoing projects such as *Book of Journeys*.

Valay Shende

b. 1980, Nagpur

Received a B. F. A. and an M. F. A. in Sculpture from the Sir J. J. School of Art, Mumbai (2004).

Lives and works in Mumbai.

Valay Shende belongs to the youngest generation of bold and politically engaged artists of Mumbai. His first international recognition came with his single-channel video work *Scrolls* (2002) while he was still a student. His most recent work innovatively combines video with large-scale mixed media sculpture, by using found footage that Shende re-edits. These ingeniously crafted objects incorporate a range of materials including cast fiberglass, barbed wire, welded coins and multinational logos.

Arpita Singh

b. 1937, West Bengal

Educated at the School of Art, Delhi and received a Diploma from Polytechnic Delhi (1954–59).

Lives and works in New Delhi.

Arpita Singh began her career as a designer for the Weavers' Service Centre during the mid-1960s. During the succeeding decades, pattern and color as they relate to textiles have remained elements in the composition of Singh's paintings. She experimented with abstraction during the 1970s, but by the 1980s her signature style of repeated familiar forms—flags, cars, teapots, vases, guns—was well established. Singh has described her subject matter as the "secret world" of women, often reflected in her depictions of contemporary family life and the experiences of women of all generations. A preoccupation with violence has produced a new collection of "everyday" objects that repeat in the patterns of Singh's paintings—men in uniform, motorcycles, airplanes, more guns.

Vivan Sundaram

b. 1943, Shimla

Received a B. F. A. from the Faculty of Fine Arts, M. S. University, Vadodara (1965); and a post-Diploma from the Slade School of Fine Art, London (1968).

Lives and works in New Delhi.

Vivan Sundaram works in media ranging from painting and drawing to sculpture, photography and video. His artistic practice is a vehicle for reinterpreting history—both political and personal. Sundaram has been an activist since his student days and began creating politically charged installation art in the 1990s. Recently, he has been working with video and photography, digitally manipulating images from his family photo archives.

Vasudha Thozhur

b. 1956, Mysore

Received a Diploma in Painting from the College of Arts and Crafts, Chennai (1979); and post-Diploma from the Croydon School of Art and Design, U. K.

Lives and works in Vadodara.

Vasudha Thozhur's autobiographical canvases present intimate stories from the artist's world. Her craft demonstrates academic training in traditional depictions of the human figure. Using her own figure and others appropriated from popular media, Thozhur tells her story by incorporating bits of text and some mere hints of calligraphy. In multiple-panel paintings, she creates mysteriously narrative tableaux. Each presents the viewer with the option to either interpret her symbols or simply admire the artist's painterly skill.

Hema Hirani Upadhyay

b. 1969, Vadodara

Received a B. F. A. and an M. F. A. in Painting and Printmaking from the Sir J. J. School of Art, Mumbai (1995, 1997).

Lives and works in Mumbai.

Hema Hirani Upadhyay uses photography and painting to explore concepts of *home* and related issues of migration, isolation, dislocation and alienation. Multiple mini-Hemas are often collaged onto the surface of her paintings. She is introspective, seeing and representing herself as both individual and every-person, understanding the outside world by looking inward. Upadhyay has often collaborated on many installation projects with her husband, painter Chintan Upadhyay. For *New Narratives* she has produced a site-specific installation by collaborating with her mother, Bina Hirani.

Selected Bibliography

Adajania, Nancy and Susan S. Bean. *Nalini Malani: Living in Alicetime*. Mumbai: Sakshi Gallery, Synergy Art Foundation Ltd., 2005.

Adajania, Nancy, Gieve Patel and Ranjit Hoskote. *Anju Dodiya*. New York: Bose Pacia, 2006.

Adajania, Nancy. "Tasting the Acid Kiss." *Anju Dodiya: The Cloud Hunt*. New Delhi: Vadehra Art Gallery, 2005.

——. "Waiting for an Image: Anju Dodiya's End-of-the-Century Tales." *Anju Dodiya*. Mumbai: Max Mueller Bhavan and New Delhi: Vadehra Art Gallery, 1999.

——. *Black Flute (and Other Stories)*. Mumbai: Gallery Chemould, 2004 and New Delhi: Nature Morte, 2004/2005.

Ananth, Deepak *et al. Indian Summer: La jeune scène artistique indienne*. Paris: École Nationale Supérieure des Beaux-Arts, 2005.

Ananth, Deepak. "Subodh Gupta." *ArtAsiaPacific* 48 (Spring 2006): 60–65.

Brooks, Peter. *Reading for the Plot: Design and Intention in Narrative*. New York: Vintage Books, 1985.

Carroll, Allison *et al. Fire and Life*. Melbourne, Australia: Asialink, 1996.

Chandrasekhar, Indira and Peter C. Seel (eds.). *body.city: siting contemporary culture in India*. Delhi: Tulika Books and Berlin: The House of World Cultures, 2003.

Chea Gab, Yun *et al. Hungry God–Indian Contemporary Art*. Beijing: Arario, 2007.

Chitre, Dilip. "Anju Dodiya: Enigmatic Variations." *Anju Dodiya: Recent Paintings*. Mumbai: Gallery Chemould, 2001.

Dalmia, Yashodhara. *Amrita Sher-Gil: A Life*. New Delhi: Penguin Books, 2006.

Das, Soumitra. "Memories, Maps and Music." *Route Map of Experience*. New Delhi: Vadehra Art Gallery and Kolkata: Galerie 88, 2003.

Devenport, Rhana and Chaitanya Sambrani. *Nalani Malani: Stories Retold*. New York: Bose Pacia, 2004.

Dysart, Dinah and Hannah Fink (eds.). *Asian Women Artists*. Roseville East, NSW, Australia: Craftsman House, 1996.

Gangar, Amrit and Johan Pijnappel. *Art in India–A mighty river of the unique and the universal*. Tokyo: Artlt, 2007.

Harsha, N. S. and Naomi Siderfin. "E-mail conversation with N. S. Harsha and Naomi Siderfin." *Drawing Space: Contemporary Indian Drawings; Sheila Gowda, N. S. Harsha, Nasreen Mohamedi*. London: inIVA (Institute of International Visual Arts), 2000, 74–85.

Hoskote, Ranjit. "Reaching for the Oxygen." *Jitish Kallat: First Information Report*. New York: Bose Pacia, 2002.

——. "The Poetics of Testimony: Reflections on Atul Dodiya's Antler Anthology." *Atul Dodiya: Antler Anthology*. Mumbai: Chemould Publications and Arts, 2004.

——. *Jitish Kallat: Chicago/Mumbai*. Chicago: Walsh Gallery and Mumbai: Gallery Chemould, 2004/2005.

——. *The Artist Lives and Works in Baroda/Bombay/Calcutta/ Mysore/Rotterdam/Trivandrum*. Mumbai: Galerie Mirchandani + Steinruecke and Berlin: The House of World Cultures, 2005.

"Implications of Swami Vivekananda's Speeches at the Parliament of Religions: Chicago 1893." http://www.geocities.com/neovedanta/a32a.html

Jhaveri, Amrita. *A Guide to 101 Modern and Contemporary Indian Artists*. Mumbai: India Book House, 2005.

Juncosa, Enrique and Thomas McEvilley. *Nalini Malani*. Dublin: Irish Museum of Modern Art, 2007.

Kallat, Jitish. *Skin: Reena Saini Kallat*. Mumbai: Gallery Chemould and New Delhi: Vis-à-Vis Art Inc., 2000.

Kapoor, Kamala and Amita Desai (eds.). *Nalini Malani: Medeaprojekt*. Mumbai: Max Mueller Bhavan, 1997.

Kapur, Geeta. *When Was Modernism: Essays on Contemporary Cultural Practice in India*. New Delhi: Tulika Books, 2000.

Keserii, Katlin. *Vivan Sundaram: The Sher-Gil Archive, an Installation*. Budapest: Dorottya Gallery, 1995.

Le Guin, Ursula. "Some Thoughts on Narrative." *Dancing at the Edge of the World: Thoughts on Words, Women, Places*. New York: Grove Press, 1980.

Monnet, Livia and Johan Pijnappel. *Tejal Shah: What Are You?* Mumbai: Galerie Mirchandani + Steinruecke, 2006.

Nagy, Peter and Johan Pijnappel. *icon: India Contemporary*. Montalvo, CA: Lucas Artists Programs, 2005.

Nagy, Peter *et al. Subodh Gupta*. New Delhi: Nature Morte and Mumbai: Sakshi Gallery, 2006.

——. *Anita Dube–Illegal*. New York: Bose Pacia, 2005.

——. "Jayashree Chakravarty: Painting to the nth Degree." *Jayashree Chakravarty: Memory Record*. Mumbai: Gallery Chemould and Kolkata: Galerie 88, 2004.

——. "The Liquidity of Imagery (or Slipping Between the Cracks)." *Hard Copy: Jitish Kallat/Reena Saini Kallat*. Kolkata: Galerie 88, 2003.

——. "Thoughts Ricochet (on the Works of Jayashree Chakravarty)." *Exhibition of Recent Works by Jayashree Chakravarty*. New Delhi: Vadehra Art Gallery, March 2000.

Pijnappel, Johan and Pooja Sood. *Video Art in India*. New Delhi: Apeejay, 2002.

Pijnappel, Johan. *Indian Video Art–History in Motion*. Fukuoka: Fukuoka Asian Art Museum, 2004.

——. *CC: Crossing Currents–Video Art and Cultural Identity*. New Delhi: RNE, 2006.

——. *Indian Video Art: Partitions of Memory*, in Brad Butler and Karen Mirza (eds.) *Cinema of Prayoga, Indian Experimental Film & Video 1913–2006*. London: now.w.here, 2006.

Poshyananda, Apinan *et al. Contemporary Art in Asia: Traditions/Tensions*. New York: Asia Society and Roseville, Australia: G+B Arts International, 1996.

Ramanujan, A. K. (trans.). *Speaking of Siva*. London: Penguin Books, 1973.

Sambrani, Chaitanya. *Edge of Desire: Recent Art in India*. New York: Asia Society and Perth: Art Gallery of Western Australia, 2005.

Sen, Geeti. *Image and Imagination: Five Contemporary Artists in India*. Ahmedabad: Mapin Publishing Pvt. Ltd., 1996.

Sengupta, Shuddhabrata *et al. Shilpa Gupta*. New York: Bose Pacia, 2006.

Sheikh, Gulammohammed. *Contemporary Art in Baroda*. New Delhi: Tulika Books, 1997.

Sheikh, Nilima, Peter Nagy and Deepak Ananth. *Arpita Singh: Memory Jars*. New York: Bose Pacia, 2003.

Sundaram, Vivan. *Retake of Amrita: Digital photomontages based on photographs by Umrao Sher-Gil (1870–1954) and photographs from the Sher-Gil family archive*. New Delhi: Tulika Books, 2001.

Tuli, Neville. *Indian Contemporary Painting*. Ahmedabad: Mapin Publishing Pvt. Ltd., 1997.

Wörgötter, Michael. "Casting Anchors in the Digital Flood of Images." *Ranbir Kaleka: Crossings*. New York: Bose Pacia, 2005.

Acknowledgments from Gregory Knight

We wish to sincerely thank all the artists, lenders and our numerous other collaborators who have actively helped make this exhibition a reality. The list would be too long if we tried to individually thank everyone who lent us advice and assistance as we organized this exhibition over several years. Every person along the way has been extremely gracious and generous with their experience and expertise, and we sincerely thank them collectively. Foremost, however, we wish to extend our unconditional thanks to the artists represented in this exhibition and catalog. Each is highly creative in his or her own right, and together they represent an exciting aspect of the global contemporary art world that seems to have few borders now. My personal gratitude is reserved for Betty Seid, the brains behind this adventurous undertaking, as well as to Johan Pijnappel, who later joined our team to make it as current as the work of Indian artists is today.

Like life itself, each new major exhibition is a journey; this special journey is ongoing, now only mid-stream with its premiere in Chicago. As it continues to tour the United States and gains even broader recognition through this publication, we look forward to its cumulative contributions to a greater global recognition of these artists outside of India.

And finally, we are deeply grateful to our corporate sponsor, The Boeing Company, for its leading place in underwriting this initiative. Additionally, our gratitude goes to the Boston Foundation for its generous support. Also, we greatly appreciate gifts from Barbara and David Kipper of the Kipper Family Foundation, the Pritzker Foundation, Gaylord India Restaurant, Champagne Ruinart, Abt Electronics, Rohini Dey, Barbara Ruben, and Pooja and Peter Vukosavich of Studio V. Design.

Chicago, April 2007

Acknowledgments from Betty Seid

This exhibition could not have been possible without the collaboration of the Chicago Cultural Center. Gregory Knight, Deputy Commissioner/ Visual Arts, immediately understood my vision, and has supported *New Narratives* from its inception. Thanks, Dude. More thanks go to Jaclyn Grahl Valentine Judge, Greg Lunceford, Debra Pruden and Sofia Zutautas of the Chicago Department of Cultural Affairs. They have been essential in bringing this exhibition to fruition. Johan Pijnappel has my gratitude for bringing his expertise in new media and video art to enhance our concept of a truly twenty-first-century show. We are indebted to all the artists, collectors, and gallerists who have assisted us in countless ways. Thanks to all for welcoming our requests to borrow their precious works of art. Special recognition is due to our exhibition assistant, Megha Ralapati, not only for her superb organizational skills, but also for her remarkable diplomacy, calm demeanor, and boundless good nature. And finally, my loving appreciation goes to Richard Seid, for his patient understanding, assistance and encouragement throughout this endeavor.

Chicago, April 2007

Lender List

Vinita and Arun Agarwal
Ruchira Agarwal
Radhika and Rajan Anandan
Anurag Bhargava
Bhayana Family Collection
Bodhi Art
Shumita and Arani Bose
Sujoy Bose and Sona Varma
Jayashree Chakravarty
Gallery Chemould
Anita Dube
Thomas Erben
Shilpa Gupta
Subodh Gupta
Amrita Jhaveri
Sangita Jindal
Tushar Joag
Prshant Lahoti
John Lynch
Nalini Malani
Pushpamala N.
Pallak Seth
Gulammohammed Sheikh
Valay Shende
Adhiraj Singh
Vasudha Thozhur
Neville Tuli
Hema Hirani Upadhyay
Walsh Gallery
and
Private collections

Exhibition Advisory Committee

Rajinder Badwal
Maneet Chauhan
Rohini Dey
Madhuvanti Ghose
Kavi Gupta
Rhona Hoffman
Barbara Levy Kipper
Lewis Manilow
Ralph Nicholas
Barbara Rossi
Barbara Ruben
Niranjan Shah
Smita Shah
Pooja Vukosavich
Julie Walsh